## Praise for *Dementi...*

*Dementia and the Church: Memory, Care, and Inclusion* is a treasure chest of insight, inspiration, and guidance for churches that seek to practice "informed compassion" for people affected by dementia. With sensitivity birthed from painful personal experience and knowledge gleaned from extensive research, Dr. Cail has provided a much-needed resource for faith communities and their leaders.

—Bishop Kenneth L. Carder, Ruth W. and A. Morris Williams Professor Emeritus, Duke Divinity School, and author of *Ministry with the Forgotten: Dementia through a Spiritual Lens*

Having been involved with ministry to dementia patients as a deacon and chaplain for over thirty years, I am so glad to have this book available. I teach pastoral care ministers and chaplains to the sick, and I wish this book had been available when I started many years ago. Dr. Mary McDaniel Cail's book is a touching and yet very practical approach to understanding dementia and Alzheimer's disease. It provides insight for those who are involved and are ministers to these wonderful and precious people. Having had my own family members go through these times in their lives, I have learned to value those who know how to minister to people in this time of their lives.

—Deacon Jack Conrad, director of spiritual care, CHRISTUS St. Vincent Regional Medical Center, Santa Fe, New Mexico

This is a deeply helpful and much-needed book, filled with powerful stories, important information, abundant resources, pastoral wisdom, and practical steps that all of us can take. It offers both an unflinchingly realistic account of what it is like to live with dementia and a hopeful way forward for pastors, individual church members, and congregations as we seek to do better at walking alongside people with dementia and those who care for them. I will be recommending it widely in my dementia ministry with churches and using it as a textbook in my seminary course on ministering to those living with dementia.

—Rev. Dr. Suzanne McDonald, professor of systematic and historical theology, Western Theological Seminary

Dementia is a complicated journey. It is one that we often fear as we anticipate it and wonder who will care for us and love us as we move into it. The church is a space of love within which Christians live out the beautiful truth that *nothing* can separate us from the love of God. In order to make the belief believable, we need a community who can live out that love and help us to live into it as we move on in our dementia journey. In this thoughtful, moving, and deeply practical book, Mary McDaniel Cail offers us maps, ways of thinking, and practical guides for the journey that can help us as individuals and communities to enable love, lament, and joy as we walk with one another along difficult roads. This is an important book that offers new and exciting possibilities for creating communities where everyone truly belongs.

—Rev. Dr. John Swinton, professor in practical theology and pastoral care, King's College, University of Aberdeen; Fellow, British Academy and Royal Society of Edinburgh; author of *Dementia: Living in the Memories of God*

Church congregations are aging. The aging process brings with it unique opportunities and some very specific challenges for churches. The opportunities are endless and include wisdom, a lived history, amazing stories, and an endless desire to help. One of the challenges of aging for both the congregation and the pastors and deacons who serve in congregations is the illness of dementia. Mary McDaniel Cail has not only given us a glimpse and a firsthand account of dementia in its main forms, but she has also presented us with a blueprint and model for what she refers to as "informed compassion." This book gently guides the reader through the caring process for caregivers and for those who receive the care. This book is very practical in that it offers the definition of dementia, as well as the realities of those living with dementia and of those who care for someone with dementia. She guides the reader through the process of creating a caring ministry, including educating the congregation and preparing leaders and volunteers to carry out this important work. She provides vocabulary, programs, and activities that work. She even includes a comprehensive bibliography for additional study.

As someone who was a caregiver for a parent and a spouse, I highly recommend this book to all congregations, pastors, deacons, and anyone else caring for someone with dementia. This book is well on its way to becoming a seminal piece of literature for caring ministries.

—Deacon Dr. Cecelia Travick-Jackson, retired associate professor, California Lutheran University; Assistant to the Bishop for Senior Adult Ministry, Southwest California Synod (ELCA); and deacon for senior ministry, Mount Cross Lutheran Church, Camarillo, California

There's no subtle way to put it: *Dementia and the Church* should be assigned reading for seminarians, clergypersons, pastoral care professionals, and counselors the world over. In it, Dr. Mary McDaniel Cail sheds desperately needed light on the crucible of cognitive decline and how best to care pastorally for those who live with it—which my decades in Christian ministry have shown me is many more people than we realize. This beautifully written, impressively well-researched, and deeply compassionate book is a gift to the church and all those who seek to embody the grace of God to sufferers.

—David Zahl, Director of Mockingbird Ministries and author of *Low Anthropology*

# Dementia and the Church

# Dem entia

## *and the* Church

MEMORY, CARE,
AND
INCLUSION

## Mary McDaniel Cail

FORTRESS PRESS
MINNEAPOLIS

DEMENTIA AND THE CHURCH
Memory, Care, and Inclusion

Scripture quotations, unless otherwise indicated, are from the New Revised Standard
Version Bible, copyright © 1989 National Council of the Churches of Christ in the
United States of America. Used by permission. All rights reserved worldwide.

Library of Congress Control Number: 2023934146 (print)

Cover design and illustration: Brad Norr Design

Print ISBN: 978-1-5064-8239-2
eBook ISBN: 978-1-5064-8240-8

To my father, Jack P. McDaniel, M.D.

# Contents

# Introduction

With the Lord one day is like a thousand years, and a thousand years are like one day.

—2 Peter 3:8

I confess that for three decades, I was an inveterate church visitor, hardly ever missing a Sunday. I visited some churches a handful of times, some for years—Baptist, Catholic, Episcopalian, Methodist, Moravian, nondenominational, Presbyterian, Unitarian. I don't remember all of them. I supported these churches, at least the ones I attended regularly, and I served in their soup kitchens, Sunday schools, nurseries, altar guilds, missions, prayer groups, and committees. (They never wanted me in choir, but once I was invited to join the bell ringers, to hold the smallest, least audible bell.)

I didn't join a church until I was in my early sixties. I had been going to an old Episcopalian church with Tiffany stained-glass windows dating back a hundred years, that spread the story of the gospel around the nave like pages taken from a book. This would have kept me there for a while, just to watch those windows emerge in the sunlight on Sunday mornings. I joined, though, because I felt welcome; I felt at home, and I thought almost anyone would. The rector learned my name. I was one of hundreds of people to him, streaming in and out of four services. I joined because, even though I hadn't joined, the clergy took care of me through the deaths of both of my parents. They prayed for me. They visited me at the hospital. They allowed me to bury my mother's ashes in their memorial garden.

This book is about becoming a welcoming church to people with dementia and their caregivers and loved ones. My father died with vascular dementia and Parkinson's disease. His thinking and behavior were erratic. Sometimes he said things that were remarkably perceptive, but more frequently, toward the end, he fell into episodes of despondent weeping and silence when he couldn't seem to make sense of anything. He lost control of his body, reduced to almost an infantile state, in which he labored just to keep breathing. My father was a fighter.

During the church visiting years, I went through hard times, some of them unspeakable. I'm using this word, *unspeakable*, imprecisely. I mean by it that I cannot speak about them because they feel too deeply rooted, still, in pain; it's easier to say nothing. After the passage of time, I can talk about my late husband, a quiet, brilliant man who graduated first in his class in medical school. He took his own life a few months after undergoing surgery for a brain tumor. I found him in his office, hanging from a dog leash. A year before, during Christmas, I had miscarried our only pregnancy after five years of infertility treatment—sixty months, with hardly a break. My brother, born in the same calendar year as I was, dropped dead of an undiagnosed heart condition while he was raking leaves, at the age of fifty. I was going to a community church at the time. I sat in the same pew, week after week, with tears I could not control slipping down my cheeks. I know about grief.

The grief of dementia is different. It hurts in a different way to witness a loved one lose his mind, or her mind, in fragments, until you've become a stranger and they have, too, in many respects. Dementia is hard. It provokes a gamut of behaviors between people, from withdrawal to aggression and disinhibition. My father, who never failed to write a note to me without inscribing it with the acronym, SWAK (sealed with a kiss), could be menacing on nights when he struggled with sundowners, making violent, outlandish threats. I knew this arose from his brain dysfunction. It hurt nonetheless. He would find himself on other nights and tell me, as was characteristic of him, that I was the best little girl he ever had. A church's approach, whether through programs, ministries, or services, must be based on the understanding that one person at a certain stage may have very different needs and reactions from another and that people with dementia can be unpredictable. This book will give you an awareness of what the condition may bring about and how the church can help.

It's tempting, when you're with someone who has lost all ability to reason, who repeats himself over and over again or becomes agitated when he is separated from his caregiver, to see childishness. It's reasonable, when you are at the bedside of a person barely able to swallow and unable to speak, to think of a return to infancy. But the Bible, as we know, is liberally sprinkled with references to our blindness, meaning our human proclivity to miss the main point of things. What we take in through our senses is unavoidably filtered by our understanding of what it means to us, usually in terms of either pleasure or problems. In an older person fumbling within a fog of dementia to interact with his or her surroundings, we cannot help but see dysfunction. We cannot help but imagine the impossibility of simple tasks—making a sandwich, zipping a jacket, sorting the mail—and feel overwhelmed by the idea of what each day must hold in terms of sheer frustration. We must also keep in mind, though, the achievements, griefs, hardships, and successes that distinguish a long life. It's our job to see a fraction of what God sees—through, with, and beyond the dementia. I wish the people who easily dismissed my father as a wasted old man slumped in a wheelchair could have seen him crouched in surgical scrubs, receiving with gloved, bloodied hands one of the ten thousand babies he brought into the world.

Churches strive to be inclusive, and as such, they attract a diversity of people, most of whom fit into groups around which ministries are organized: children, youth, singles, seniors, and so on. The word *dementia*, logically the choice for a ministry with this group, is stigmatizing, even if it modifies *friends* or *family* (referring of course to the church family). It shouldn't be, but it is. You don't need to look beyond a thesaurus to see why. It's a bit tricky to identify such a ministry with a descriptive term people will quickly recognize, while avoiding an unwelcome label. As a starting point, let me suggest the word *memory*, as in "memory ministry"—without the addition of the word *loss*. Dementia in all of its forms affects memory, a fact with which most are familiar. A church's outreach to people living with dementia will necessarily rekindle long-term memories of worship by employing the stories, hymns, and rituals that become engraved in our collective minds through frequent repetition. We can all share in this experience. Such a ministry should also seek to instill, at least in the minds of others, the memory of what these people accomplished in the past and a true sense of what they can offer to us in their present lives, so they are seen holistically by those around them. My father may have been frail and uncommunicative at the end; he was still a physician, and he deserved to be called "doctor," not the belittling terms of endearment people used when he was no longer able to defend himself.

Old age makes us vulnerable, and in a culture that exalts youth, the elderly are easily nudged to the fringes, particularly when their minds are less sharp and words come less quickly. Too often, they are not protected in hospitals and nursing facilities, the very places we must, under common circumstances, entrust with their care. If I am ever able to reconcile my sadness and anger over the neglect my father suffered at the close of his life, no matter my fight to prevent it, it will be by God's mercy alone. I kicked against the goads. I contended as never before with feelings of hate. I was a solitary person, it seemed, struggling against a system set up to push him further and further into impairment and pain.

During this terrible time for my father and me, one of the ministers of that Episcopalian church, the final stop in my long church pilgrimage, showed up, to my surprise, at the hospital where Dad was slowly dying, and we sat outside the room, among muted wall coverings and furnishings meant, no doubt, to encourage calmness in people. I was a torrent of stress, sadness, anger, and helplessness beneath a veneer of exhausted control. In this man's steady presence, words surged from me as though they had burst from a dam. He didn't interrupt; he didn't talk about God, or salvation, or love, or faith, or courage. He simply listened, and back in my father's room, he prayed a tender, reverent prayer for us. It was comforting, strengthening, quieting. *I will quiet you*, God seemed to say in those minutes of his prayer, *with my love* (Zephaniah 3:17).

My work, my life's work, since those years occluded by grief, has been to advance what I call "informed compassion." We feel compassion when we are confronted by another's despair, but compassion alone does not give us an understanding of what to say and do to help someone whose life has been upended. Despair is dangerous, isolated despair even more so, and isolation can happen in the company even of people who care deeply, if those people are unaware or inadvertently insensitive. Informed compassion means taking the time to learn enough that you understand in broad brushstrokes what a difficult grief, loss, or diagnosis signifies. In this case, it means bringing the church as a whole to a point of understanding, so parishioners do not feel awkward, and programs and services are well tailored to the needs dementia engenders. It's about knowing how to accept, how to pray, how to relieve, and how to comfort—in these ways, showing to those who must live with the difficulties of dementia the soul-quieting God who says to each of us, *Can a mother forget the baby at her breast and have no compassion on the child she has borne? Though she may forget, I will never forget you. See, I have engraved you on the palms of my hands* (Isaiah 49:15–16, NIV).

# CHAPTER 1

# Dementia

Bill sat across from me at a table in a fellowship hall with high ceilings and picture windows. Soft light filtered in through a haze of summer clouds. The room, part of a dementia center at a church, smelled like fresh paint and new furnishings. I would have guessed Bill's age to be mid-sixties maybe, not approaching eighty. His hair, still full and brown, was stylishly cut, his face lined but not sagging. His shirt was neatly tucked and clean despite his participation earlier that day in a baking activity during which seven people clustered around a kitchen counter and made strawberry shortcake from scratch. He folded his arms and looked at me with interest.

"How can I help you?" he asked.

"I'm writing a book about a church program," I said, "and I'm talking to people about it." He nodded. "Your wife tells me you were a fire chief most of your life." He nodded again, and his face brightened. "I'll bet you saw some big fires."

"Yes, I did," he replied.

"That sounds dangerous."

"Well, it was," he said and gave it a moment of thought. "Once I almost got trapped in a fire. I was going around a room, hand over hand against the wall." He pantomimed advancing his hands one over the other, palms flat. "That's what we did, when we couldn't see the way out. We'd feel for a doorway. And I found a doorway. I was thinking that was the exit, only it wasn't. It was a closet, so I was feeling my way around in this closet. I got disoriented. Eventually, long story short, I figured out where the exit door was and got out."

"Were you scared? I would have been."

"It was exciting. The job was always exciting." Bill shook his head slightly, caught in a wave of nostalgia. "Another time, we were the first engine at a big house fire. I got to the house first, and I ran in and ran up a flight of stairs. I opened the door to a room, and there were two kids in there alone. I managed to get them out. So it was a pretty exciting job."

"He won awards for rescuing people," Mary, his wife, prompted. "Remember the river?"

"That time," Bill said readily, "it was after a big storm, and we were at the river, and it was high, rushing really fast. It was heading toward a thirty-foot waterfall, not as far away as here to the door." He pointed across the room. "There was a boy holding onto a rock, like a little island in the middle with the water rushing all around him. I got one of my men, and we got in the boat to go get him. The current was strong, pulling us right into that waterfall. You could hear it roaring, and we had to fight to keep the boat steady." He held his hands out to show that the waves were almost as high as the boat's gunwales. "But, long story short, we got him. We got him into the boat, and we got back, but it was hard to get the boat back. We almost didn't make it." The boy and his father had been further up the river, Mary explained, when the engine of their boat failed, and it capsized. The father was swept away and drowned before the rescue crew arrived.

Just before Covid lockdowns were imposed in 2020, Bill was diagnosed with a mixed form of dementia caused by Alzheimer's disease (AD) and vascular changes in the executive system of his brain, which involves the ability to coordinate, organize, reason, problem solve, and plan. Although the term *dementia* is sometimes used as a clinical diagnosis,[*][1] it actually refers to a group of symptoms characteristic of many diseases and conditions, more than fifty, that impair brain function. Occasionally dementia is reversible, if due to remediable circumstances such as thyroid disorders, depression, alcohol use, medication effects, or certain vitamin deficiencies. Most often, however, dementia is progressive and fatal. Bill's diagnosis consists of the two most common types, AD and vascular dementia (or major vascular cognitive impairment). Loss of executive function is a classic symptom, also,

---

* *A note to the reader*: This book contains three types of endnotes. Superscript in regular type indicates source citations; bold type indicates Biblical references; italic type indicates endnotes with additional comments, information, or further reading.

of frontotemporal lobe dementia, a third main type. Along with a newly recognized form of dementia similar to AD, limbic-predominant age-related TDP-43 encephalopathy (identified by the acronym LATE), and Lewy body dementia, these five types comprise most dementia cases.

Mary says the church has been essential in reducing the isolation that defines not only dementia but old age in general. "At our age, our friends are beginning to die off," she observes, "and some of the ones that are left don't know how to react to dementia. I think reaching out to seniors is one of the most important things a church can do." Their church, with its engaging respite program, music cafes, and senior luncheons, gives the couple a much-needed social outlet. This book discusses many ways churches can open doors to people living with dementia, like Bill and Mary. Their needs are specific to its challenges and can vary broadly according to the diagnosis, to the stage, and to the inherent differences between people. To better understand, we'll look in this chapter at dementia's main forms. Let me begin, though, with a clarification about the term "living with dementia."

Although the English language contains 171,156 words (or it did in 2020), there is not one good, non-stigmatizing word for people with dementia. Some writers resort to use of the acronym PWD. This is a function of efficiency, not compassion; constantly repeating the phrase makes for cumbersome writing. There are times, given the appropriate audience, when clarity is the main goal and terms should be direct, whether diplomatic or not. I use descriptive words in this book that I would not use in church communications: The word "patient," meaning for our purposes a person diagnosed in a medical setting with some type of dementia, may be efficient (for us) but conveys a connotation of weakness and exclusion that should generally be avoided. Inspiring a certain cultural climate within a church is a different intention, in which absolute clarity is second to inclusion and compassion.

The phrase "living with dementia" is in widespread use as a more empathetic way to refer to people "with" dementia, or who "suffer from" dementia. And I think it can be applied to caregivers, as well, in the church setting. Caregivers live with dementia in the sense that their lives eventually become dictated by its demands. To live with something implies a certain strength; it means that you've come to terms with an unavoidable difficulty or are trying to, as best you can. I suggest "living with dementia" as an umbrella term, when possible—but without becoming too rigid or fussy about it.[2]

## ALZHEIMER'S DISEASE AND LATE DEMENTIA

Alzheimer's disease (AD) is named for the German psychiatrist and neuro-anatomist, Alois Alzheimer, who first reported the disease in 1907 by identi-fying its two main pathologies, amyloid plaques and neurofibrillary tangles. Five years earlier, Alzheimer had encountered a patient who baffled him: At the relatively young age of fifty-one, Auguste Deter was unable to recall her own name or address. Beset by "a general imbecility," she suffered from periods of agitation and anxiety when she shrieked accusations and feared that she was in imminent danger of harm, even from her physicians.[3] Her neurological symptoms had emerged rapidly, over a period of months. She remained institutionalized until she died of sepsis from an infected bedsore. Alzheimer examined her brain microscopically and found tangled filaments in about a third of the neurons in her cerebral cortex. His sketches of the affected nerve cells resemble jumbled headphone wires from an old cellphone. He also discovered scattered clumps of "a pathological metabolic product" that looked to him like birdseed. Her brain was atrophied, as might have been expected in a much older person.[4]

Although there are other abnormalities in AD, the two cellular charac-teristics Alzheimer described must both be present to indicate the disease. Until recently, an affirmative diagnosis could only be made by microscopic examination of brain tissue, which would normally be performed only during an autopsy.[5] With today's many advanced imaging techniques and measures, particularly of irregularities in cerebrospinal fluid, the disease can be confirmed with confidence in most patients.

Alzheimer's unfolds in stages, which will be discussed in greater detail in chapters 5 and 6, in a series of learning activities that can be used to educate the congregation about dementia. But do take a few minutes now to study the sequential self-portraits of artist William Utermohlen,[6] diagnosed with AD at age sixty-one, for a compelling, graphic example of these stages. The last portrait is little more than a blob resembling a head—with an unmistak-able expression that nonetheless poignantly conveys Utermohlen's dignity, suffering, loss, and talent.

Although in Utermohlen's case, the disease advanced rapidly, it can also be quite lengthy, with some people living twenty years after the onset of symptoms. We now know that Alzheimer's has a preclinical or asymptomatic stage, which may last for an additional two decades, perhaps longer, when the cellular changes of AD are occurring in the brain, but the disease is not yet advanced enough to produce symptoms. The implications of this fact are obvious: If 5 percent of people (one in twenty) have symptomatic AD at the age of sixty-five,[7] 5 percent have preclinical AD in their mid-forties and are unaware of it. The risk of AD increases exponentially with age. More than 30 percent of people age eighty-five and older have Alzheimer's disease, indicating, alarmingly, that one in three people by age sixty-five may be well into the preclinical phase of the disease. No small wonder that the word "staggering" is frequently used when reporting the statistics. By 2050, it is estimated that 152 million people worldwide will have dementia; 106.8 million of these people will have Alzheimer's, even more if cases of mixed dementia are counted.[8]

Understanding where the disease starts and initially spreads in the brain gives insight into its initial symptoms. A 2013 study at Columbia University Medical Center demonstrated that the disease begins specifically in the lateral entorhinal cortex,[9] located in the brain's temporal lobe and frequently described as the "gateway" to the hippocampus, a structure with a critical role in memory and learning.[10] The disease spreads to the parietal cortex, which is involved in the interpretation of sensory input, spatial relationships and navigation, as well as the ability to plan and carry out a sequence of nonhabitual actions, learn new material, and use language effectively.[11]

I interviewed a therapist who told me his first noticeable symptom was a strange, occasional tendency to lose his sense of direction when driving back and forth to his office of over twenty years. These episodes only lasted a few seconds, and he ignored them at first, feeling relieved when his spatial maps suddenly snapped back into place. Kris Bakwoski, a nationally recognized Alzheimer's advocate for the past two decades was diagnosed at the relatively young age of forty-six and has worked relentlessly since then to help people understand the disease. On a personal note, over the years I've received, to my great pleasure, a collection of her intricate handmade cards. As a part of her advocacy, she chronicles her experiences in a blog I recommend for its candor, optimism, and brave acceptance of her condition. In one of her first entries, November of 2004, she describes her early difficulties with language:

> This hasn't been a real good week for me. And, the bad thing is that when I have a bad time, it is very difficult for me to find the right words to tell somebody about it. Usually my husband picks up on it and helps me along but he hasn't

been doing that lately—I think he is just missing the cues. But, I can't tell him about it because I can't find the right words to express myself. Never having had a problem with expressing myself before, this makes it even more difficult to deal with. I guess it goes back to the "aloneness" of Alzheimer's—you feel so alone because you can't communicate effectively.[12]

As her early symptoms became evident, Kris recounts her frustration at feeling marginalized, as though she is on the outskirts of her friends' lives, unable to participate in their activities the way she could before the disease emerged and sensing that, as a result, she may not be as welcome.[13]

Alzheimer's disease presents researchers grappling for a cure with a bedeviling problem: Its main pathologies, the steady accumulation in the brain of beta amyloid,[14] an abnormal protein, and the spread[15] of neurofibrillary tangles within neurons, occur simultaneously, and the science behind each process is almost indescribably complex. And to add a preventable layer of difficulty, research efforts are not necessarily transparent or collaborative.[16] Most of the newsworthy research in pursuit of a cure has been aimed at reducing or stabilizing the formation of amyloid plaques, although past failures in clinical trials of drugs like bapineuzumab ("bapi") seem to suggest that decreasing amyloid load does not automatically result in improved cognition, at least not once the disease has progressed beyond a certain point. One new drug now available, aducanumab, does stabilize or slow early AD in some patients by combating plaques, but at a prohibitive price for most. Treatments are limited to a handful of medications that increase the bioavailability of certain chemical messengers (primarily the neurotransmitter acetylcholine) involved in memory retention. These medications have no impact on the disease process, meaning that they do not reduce plaques or tangles. They make it possible for a limited number of patients—those who respond and can tolerate the side effects—to remain somewhat more capable for a limited period of time. In other words, there is no cure and, at present, no cure on the horizon. It's unlikely that we'll see a breakthrough akin to the recent experimental cancer drug that made tumors literally vanish.[17] I think the most reasonable hope lies in early detection and the potential ability to slow the disease by intervening before it even becomes symptomatic, thus enabling people to live with it.

Limbic-predominant age-related TDP-43 encephalopathy (LATE dementia) is worth mentioning because of its similarity to Alzheimer's disease, despite a different cellular pathology, and apparent prevalence:

It is suspected that up to half of the population over the age of eighty, the main population it affects, have this form of dementia in their brains, and in about 25 percent, it is sufficiently advanced to produce symptoms that mimic those of AD.[18] Like Alzheimer's, LATE degrades the hippocampus, causing profound memory loss. As LATE progresses it strips the ability to carry out even the most basic self-care skills, necessitating a similar level of caregiving. When the two are comorbid, which would have to be frequently true, statistically speaking, symptoms of agitation and aggression are heightened, and the dementia advances more rapidly.[19] Due to the fact TDP-43 encephalopathy was identified relatively recently, its diagnosis, treatment, and impact on the "oldest old," a steadily increasing group within the world, are not yet well understood. Scientists readily identify the need for urgent research in this area.[20]

## (SEVERE) VASCULAR COGNITIVE IMPAIRMENT

Vascular cognitive impairment (VCI), referred to as vascular dementia (VaD) in its most acute form, results from damage to blood vessels in the brain, including the deeper microvascular networks which are crucial for transmitting information. It accounts for up to 20 percent of dementia cases. Vascular lesions can be caused by strokes, some so tiny they can only be recognized microscopically, and other conditions that affect the brain's supply of blood and oxygen. For example, Bill suffered throughout adult life from obstructive sleep apnea, which has been linked to both vascular dementia[21] and Alzheimer's disease.[22]

Unlike AD, vascular dementia can happen quickly, following a "cerebrovascular accident," a medical term for stroke, or it can unfold more gradually. Memory impairment may or may not be present. The lesions frequently impact executive function, which results in poor judgment and the inability to carry out plans, solve problems, and interpret information. While vascular dementia can resemble AD, the symptoms vary considerably, depending on which parts of the brain are affected. As I've said, my father died with vascular dementia, but he had times of lucidity when he could think and reason, right up until his death. His inconsistent cognitive strengths did not change the fact that he was significantly impaired by the vascular changes in his brain, which were accruing in stepwise, not continual, fashion. Alzheimer's presents with a persistent, gradual decline, leading to complete disability and death; in certain cases, vascular dementia may stabilize for long periods of time.

Vascular dementia can sometimes be treated, when due to modifiable risk factors, like hypertension, diabetes, and obesity. However, overwhelming clinical data indicates that it is commonly comorbid with AD and other forms of dementia, interacting synergistically,[23] a circumstance that is devastating in its destructiveness and complexity. Bill's AD at this point is evidenced mainly in episodic memory loss. Mary says that while he remembers the church respite program, arising cheerfully on the four mornings a week that he attends, and getting himself ready, he cannot recall, when she picks him up in the afternoon, anything he has done during the day. Vascular dementia, on the other hand, has already wreaked havoc on his executive function, leaving him in need of continual supervision to ensure his safety. One morning following a bad storm, she went to the grocery store and left him cleaning up the sticks and branches in the yard. She returned home and gasped in alarm. He was in the middle of the speedy thoroughfare that fronts their house, sweeping the debris to one side. She says that although he can operate their riding lawn mower, she cannot allow him to do the chore because he runs the mower out into this busy street to make the turns more easily. Her objections spur his anger, and he testily explains, as though to someone rather dull, why it makes perfect sense for him to do it his way. "I've had to pick my battles," she says. "If he's not doing anything where he might hurt himself or someone else, I let him do it."

Bill has lost the ability to use his shed full of carpentry tools, and his understanding of how to solve simple problems with household gadgets seems absent, too. Mary awoke one night to a strange, dull thudding noise and went to investigate. She found Bill standing in front of an overflowing toilet, jabbing at the bowl with a pole (not a plunger) as water rushed out. This situation resulted in the need, as the catastrophe unfolded in full, for a ten-thousand dollar repair to fix the bathroom, patch and paint the ceiling, and install new carpet downstairs. "He could put in a whole bathroom before his dementia," she said. "I didn't know whether to laugh or cry."

"Well, I know what I would have done," I replied.

Mary seemed resigned, relating these events to me with laudable patience and control. Her resolve faltered only once while we talked, as she contemplated the eventual need to have Bill placed in a facility. Her eyes filled with tears and her voice broke when she used the word "abandoned" to describe how he might feel. Although their marriage has been challenging, her commitment to him and love for him were clearly evident. But she must deal with the confluence within his brain of two forms of dementia, both of them disabling and one inevitably progressive and lethal. She will not always be able to care for him.

## FRONTOTEMPORAL DEMENTIA

Frontotemporal dementia (FTD) is caused, like Alzheimer's, by misfolded proteins. These proteins aggregate and cause neuronal toxicity as a consequence of complex disease mechanisms that are not well understood. Forty percent of FTD cases result from tangled tau, which is one of the main pathologies of Alzheimer's disease.[24] However, in contrast to AD and vascular dementia, FTD has a younger onset, typically between the ages of forty and sixty. Ten percent of dementia cases among people younger than sixty-five are a result of frontotemporal lobe dementia, according to a review of prevalence studies conducted over a twenty-seven-year period.[25]

Frontotemporal dementia, as the name implies, affects the frontal lobe, a paired structure directly behind the forehead—which is involved in executive function, emotional control, and motor skills—and the temporal lobe, also a paired structure (right and left) near the temples, which controls speech, memory, language, and the integration of sensory input. Both are strongly linked to personality. A research study conducted at University College London assessed personality change in a group of patients with FTD using the Big Five Inventory, a test that measures traits according to a five-factor model frequently applied in personality research.[26] When taken as a group, participants showed a significant decrease over time in agreeableness, conscientiousness, extraversion, and openness. Predictably, neuroticism, the overtly problematic component, had increased.[27]

Physicians first learned the vital functions of the frontal lobe in 1848, when a young railroad foreman named Phineas Gage suffered a horrific accident. Gage's frontal lobe was completely destroyed in an explosion that sent a thirteen-pound iron rod hurtling through his face and out the back of his skull. Gage had been using the rod to tamp gunpowder into a hole, producing a spark that ignited the powder. Remarkably, he survived but not as the same man. He became "grossly" profane and disengaged from other people. No longer even-tempered, energetic, and popular, he was fitful, irreverent, and "pertinaciously obstinate, capricious, and vacillating" about his plans, according to the physician, John Martyn Harlow, who documented his case, stating unpretentiously, "I dressed him. God healed him."[28] For the rest of his life, Gage, blind in his right eye from the accident, carried the tamping iron around with him as a talisman.

Frontotemporal lobe dementia has two main variants, behavioral and language, with the latter further divided into several subtypes. To be diagnosed, the behavioral variant must cause at least several of the following characteristics, any one of which would be socially problematic: a decline in executive functioning (without memory loss of recent events), disinhibition and inappropriate behavior, apathy, unresponsiveness to the needs of others, repetitive or ritualistic behavior and speech, and a change in dietary habits along with hyperorality, which is a weird compulsion to examine objects using the mouth.[29] People with the semantic subtype of language variant FTD struggle to name familiar objects, write coherently, and recognize words. The nonfluent subtype results in impaired and hesitant speech, sometimes with an inability to assemble grammatically correct sentences, and difficulty understanding complex word constructions.[30] A third type, the logopenic variant (from *logos* and *penia*, meaning "lack of words" in Greek), causes slow and simple speech that is nonetheless accurate, pseudoword reading (breaking words into separate nonsense sounds: "dif, fer, ent" for *different*), problems understanding spoken language, word-finding difficulty, and deficits in phonological working memory, which enables processing sounds into words.[31] A group of researchers at the Cognitive Neurology and Alzheimer's Research Center in Chicago provide the following example of an email written by a patient with language variant FTD: "I will come my house in your car and drive my car into Chicago. . . . You will back get your car and my car park in my driveway. Love, Mom."[32]

Frontotemporal dementia, like Alzheimer's disease, has no cure. Treatments are limited to symptomatic relief intended to minimize problematic behaviors such as impulsivity, depression, apathy, and disinhibition.[33] Researchers from the Department of Psychiatry at Case Western Reserve University suggest certain environmental adjustments to help people with frontotemporal dementia. These include limiting interaction to small groups, minimizing noise and other distractions, exercise, and the use of simple activities, games, and familiar hobbies.[34] The goal is to create a soothing environment for people who are struggling in frustration to interpret the continual barrage of sensory information most of us take in and process automatically. These recommendations would apply to most people with any form of dementia.

## DEMENTIA WITH LEWY BODIES

After the beloved actor Robin Williams died,[35] his autopsy revealed abnormal structures within the cytoplasm of neurons throughout his brain and brain stem. "As you may know," his wife Susan Schneider Williams writes in an essay intended to help neurologists better understand dementia with Lewy bodies and its constellation of symptoms, "my husband Robin Williams had the little-known but deadly Lewy body disease. He died from suicide in 2014 at the end of an intense, confusing, and relatively swift persecution at the hand of this disease's symptoms and pathology. He was not alone in his traumatic experience with this neurologic disease. As you may know, almost 1.5 million nationwide are suffering similarly right now."[36]

Dementia with Lewy bodies (DLB),[37] as in Alzheimer's disease, LATE, and frontotemporal dementia, is a reaction to misfolded proteins that aggregate in the brain; in the case of DLB the culprit is alpha-synuclein, which creates toxic, insoluble "bodies" or inclusions within the cytoplasm of neurons that spread throughout the brain. Based on examination of brain tissue at autopsy, it is estimated that 50 to 60 percent of people with clinical AD may also have significant alpha-synuclein pathology in their brains. The proteins implicated in AD and DLB do not coexist independently. They interact within the brain to produce a rapidly advancing, complex dementia with more aggressive symptoms.[38] According to some sources, DLB, not vascular cognitive impairment, is the second leading cause of dementia among the elderly.

People with Lewy body dementia may initially experience short-term memory loss as a symptom, but not always. Early cognitive symptoms, in similarity to frontotemporal lobe dementia but not AD, can be limited to inattentiveness and problems in executive functioning or with visual-spatial processing. These symptoms usually arise gradually, after age fifty-five, more often in men than women.[39] Williams struggled to memorize the lines of the last movie he filmed and with a hodgepodge of other symptoms, seemingly unrelated but all—both curiously and commonly—associated with Lewy body dementia: varied gastrointestinal problems due, most likely, to lesions in his autonomic nervous system,[40] insomnia, loss of his sense of smell,[41] depression, and a transient tremor in one hand.[42] A panic attack blamed on the anxiety of his strange new difficulties prompted a physician to take the unfortunate step of prescribing an antipsychotic, which, evidencing another main symptom of DLB, quickly made things much worse.[43] Lewy body dementia causes extreme sensitivity to neuroleptics, and the use of these medications can in some patients result in irreversible damage and even death.[44]

While Williams never mentioned hallucinations,[45] most people with Lewy body dementia, up to 80 percent, do experience such visual disturbances, providing valuable diagnostic information. This is particularly true when they occur early on, as this may steer physicians toward a more correct idea of what could be happening. Williams was first suspected of having diverticulitis, not dementia; he was later diagnosed inaccurately with Parkinson's disease. Hallucinations are often of small animals and children and, as such, are nonthreatening. Early on in DLB, individuals seem to recognize that they are hallucinating. However, there have been tragic exceptions: Researchers at East Tennessee State University report an awful case, in which a retired marine in later stage DLB, experiencing its characteristic sleep problems, began to hallucinate early one morning that terrorists were approaching his house. He armed himself with a loaded handgun and managed, as the situation escalated to the point of crisis, to shoot his wife and himself. His wife survived.[46]

The course of DLB is faster than Alzheimer's, with a median time of survival after symptoms begin of only about four years. While it may be true that its shorter duration is a mercy, bear in mind that people with DLB and their caregivers are often not provided with accurate information about the disease's symptoms or what to expect,[47] and those relatively few years can be fraught with bizarre, unpredictable difficulties. The title of Susan Williams's, *The Terrorist Inside My Husband's Brain*, is telling. "Robin was losing his mind and he was aware of it," Williams writes, trying to convey her husband's heartbreaking experience. "Can you imagine the pain he felt as he experienced himself disintegrating? And not from something he would ever know the name of, or understand? Neither he, nor anyone could stop it—no amount of intelligence or love could hold it back." Even when the diagnosis of DLB has been properly given and people are seeking help in all the right places, the right help may not be forthcoming, perhaps because this dementia causes such a wide range of dysfunctions involving multiple bodily systems. One of the professionals involved in Williams's case said it was as though he had cancer in every organ in his body.[48] Melissa Armstrong, a neurologist at the University of Florida and her colleagues report that DLB caregivers feel confused, conflicted, and misinformed as they struggle to make crucial decisions and act as advocates for their loved ones. Many who participated in the research told, for example, of having been given hospice "comfort packs" containing haloperidol, an antipsychotic. It caused one caregiver's relative to almost bite off his own tongue.[49]

There is no cure for DLB, and medical treatment is limited, for the most part, to careful pharmacological management of the symptoms, physical and speech therapy, and certain types of brain stimulation.[50] One important nonmedical intervention is caregiver support. Others include counseling, sensory activities, exercise, and music to relieve stress and elevate mood.[51]

## CONCLUSION

Later in this book, I caution ministers and other lay leaders who may be planning a memory ministry to consider holding back the more disturbing facts when educating the congregation about dementia, to encourage the kind of enthusiasm and active participation an effective dementia program needs. People living with dementia, like gentle, resourceful Mary and her heroic Bill, have much to offer the parishioners who befriend and help them. It's hardly a one-way street. But dementia is terrible in the true sense of the word, and people coping with it must have at least a few others in their lives who understand and can frankly commiserate with its challenges. Mary said her minister asked her one Sunday morning how she was doing with Bill. Mary brushed away his question, replying in good humor, "Ask me no questions, and I'll tell you no lies!"

Later the minister called her. "You're having a hard time, aren't you?" he said. This act of connection meant a lot to Mary. It meant she wasn't alone; someone could see that she was struggling and cared enough to follow through.

As the afternoon we spent together drew to a close, I asked Mary how her faith has helped her through a life that from childhood has never been easy. She worked hard throughout her marriage, scraping and saving to ensure that her own children had a kinder, better start in life. In a soft voice she said simply, "I find myself talking to God a lot. I don't have answers. . . . God makes things come when you most need them. This [church respite] program has been a godsend."

Mary thought about the question for another minute and then told me a story from her work as a trauma nurse in a rural hospital. One afternoon a little boy was carried into the emergency room by his father, the family's other children trailing alongside. Both of the child's legs had been severed in a brush hog accident, and they were dangling from his body by nothing more than bits of calf muscle tissue. The child's face, Mary said, was as white as blank paper. "I remember looking at that child," she said, "and automatically, from somewhere, I just knew what to do." Mary instantly took over for a more experienced nurse and quickly, efficiently stabilized him. When the doctor arrived after finishing another case, their eyes met, she said, and wordlessly they began working together to try to splint the child's terribly mangled legs. He was flown by helicopter to a larger medical center, and as they watched the aircraft dip and turn away, they feared he would die.

Many months later, a woman approached Mary as she walked across a park. "Weren't you the nurse who worked on my son?" she asked. "The boy who was in the brush hog accident?"

"Yes, I was. I remember," Mary replied in surprise and caught her breath, thinking to herself that he probably had not survived. The mother, however, pointed to nearby monkey bars.

"That's him," she said, indicating a boy who was jumping and running like any normal eight year old, with no sign of having ever been injured.

"No doubt in my mind that it was God," Mary said to me. "I had never done anything like that. Someone who's not a believer wouldn't understand. It wasn't something I did. But God is, God is . . . " She hesitated, searching for words. "God carries us through a lot. It will be an interesting journey," she said, referring to her future with Bill and his inevitable decline. "I just know that if God shuts one door, another one will open someplace."

## CHAPTER 2

# Living with Dementia—What We Fear

Literature on the church's role in the worldwide crisis of dementia and the spiritual needs of people living with the condition often focuses on God's constancy, the enduring soul, and the lifelong need of all people for social connection. The brain, regardless of its unparalleled importance in our earthly existence, is an organ, and it can fail; the soul cannot. Many stories have been shared by ministers and lay leaders about the ability to meaningfully connect with people, even in late-stage dementia. The Lord's Prayer and familiar verses, stories, rituals, and hymns can remain in memory when the ability to dress and eat without help are gone. These facts underpin the church's ministry for people living with dementia and infuse it with meaning and joy.

One of this book's goals, however, is to provide understanding not only of the inexpressible benefits of such a ministry, both to its recipients and providers, but also of the inexpressible difficulties of the condition. To have informed compassion, you must have a realistic sense of what this hardship is and what specific griefs it causes. It may not be important for the congregation as a whole to be confronted by the truly distressing ordeals of dementia, but it is for ministers and others who will work to construct the programs of such a ministry and seek to deeply comfort those living with it.

To this end, chapter 2 looks at four main fears among people living with dementia: fear of adverse changes on every front of life; fear of inadequate resources to meet the demands of a long, incurable, incapacitating condition; fear of a blighted future; and fear of loneliness and isolation. But although I've tried to group these fears for purposes of organization, you will see that they cannot be easily teased apart—I could almost have interchanged the headings. Dementia fears are pervasive and interrelated. A single ambitious study identifies myriad themes and emotions: having a life that seems hidden and misunderstood; ideations of suicide and homicide; and feeling lonely, ambiguous, exhausted, confused, hopeless, depressed, angry, guilty, grief-stricken, abandoned, unsupported by friends, and detached.[1] In its complexity, dementia defies discrete categories of fear and loss, and the four fears that follow unavoidably overlap.

### *We fear the changes dementia will bring.*

We all fear the wrong kind of change, despite the noble declaration that we do not, though earth itself is shaken, waters rage, and mountains fall into the heart of the sea.[2] There will be a phone call, a knock on the door, an unexpected conversation or revelation, a life-threatening diagnosis, and we'll plunge in an instant into an altered world, one in which there is terrible loss or the anticipation of it. Life may go on, but not as we've known it. Fear is an instinctive response to any serious threat. For most of us, it isn't controllable. It sweeps like a wave over our sense of stability and security. And there are few threats in all of human experience more daunting than a disease that leads to brain atrophy, with its implication that nothing in life will remain unscathed.

Dr. Richard Taylor, who was, until his death, an Alzheimer's advocate and internationally known speaker[3] told me, as he has many others, "My wife and I cried nonstop for two weeks when I was diagnosed. We cried until there were no tears left." Richard held both my hands in his while we talked. He stared intensely at my face, as though willing himself to remember me but realizing he'd forget before I had even left the conference room where we met. There was good reason for his tears. Dementia means, without exception, that the patterns of life will be pulled apart and reorganized around disability and the attempt to minimize problems, which escalate on an almost daily basis.

In my initial work on Alzheimer's, I shadowed a book publisher, Bert Brown,* and his wife, Willa, a physician so accomplished that she had once

---

\* I interviewed Bert and Willa Brown and others in this chapter for my first book, *Alzheimer's a Crash Course for Friends and Relatives.* You can find their stories there, too. If requested, I change the names of people I interview in my work and the identifying details of their lives, but Bert wanted his and Willa's full names used, as a last legacy to her life, which was spent in the service of public health.

been long-listed as a candidate for surgeon general. When we met years later, she had moderately severe dementia. Bert offered essentially to be a living documentary for me. I could sit with them, he said, whenever I wanted and watch for hours at a time. Their house was among a row of old Victorians edged by sidewalks, where Willa shuffled along on twice-daily walks with Bert, occasionally stopping to puzzle over house numbers and street signs. Large packages of incontinence pads leaned in a stack against the kitchen wall. The refrigerator was crammed with pots of cooked rice and oatmeal. A sign posted on the back door instructed all visitors to wash their hands before entering, the additional trouble of a viral infection being almost unthinkable. Homemade gates confined Willa to two rooms for most of the day. She seemed relieved to have her world thus restricted, puttering around as though in a continual mode of discovery.

This was all a stark change from the life they had shared before Willa's diagnosis. They'd had the kind of relationship that most of us experience only in the first stages of romance. Bert sang love songs to Willa; she read to him. He watched her sail and swim; they danced; they had breakfast in bed. But over a relatively short time, she lost the ability even to speak her own name, and everything that had filled their lives with pleasure stopped. Willa had been a capable pianist. In the mid-stage of dementia, she occasionally brushed her fingers over the keys of an old upright piano, but Bert couldn't persuade her to play a scale. She had been a keen table tennis player. Having lost the ability to understand all but the most rudimentary games, she batted awkwardly at a huge inflated beach ball, marshaling, it seemed, all of her remaining intellect to send it bouncing correctly in Bert's direction. He sang a little song when they played, helping her keep track of the back-and-forth rhythm.

Dementia robs the simplest tasks of meaning and purpose. Cathryn, like Bert, a caregiver for many years, remembers finding her husband, Neal, bleeding in the bathroom one morning when he was still living at home with her. Cathryn and I were sitting together, talking, in a room so tidy it almost looked staged. She had recently placed Neal in a nursing home, finally unable to care for him, and had put considerable effort, apparently, into removing the evidences of her caregiving. She was flipping through the pages of a diary she had kept throughout his illness, recalling incidents that happened over the past several years. Listening to her stories was like seeing images of an earthquake. Neal was formerly an executive whose work involved traveling the world, negotiating with corporations and governments, but he had regressed to a state in which he was amused by the large puzzles and coloring books in his nursing home recreation room. Everything had been lost. "He was trying to shave," Cathryn said, "looking in the mirror at his face bleeding, holding the razor in his hand, completely bewildered."

Try for a few moments to imagine the fear of knowing that you will lose the memory of how to feed and dress yourself or that you may not recognize your own spouse and children, and that these changes will occur while your friends are still gardening, reading, and helping to care for grandchildren—or are young enough still to be working. Think of facing such comprehensive losses and realizing that the best possible outcome will be to have your anxiety meld into a sense of peace and acceptance, an ability truly to enjoy life in the present moment and to look ahead with faith. How could you keep from fearing these changes?

Some caregivers do become adept at finding the positives. "He never complimented me before," Laura, the wife of an army officer, said with a rueful smile. Her husband had been known throughout adulthood for his arrogance and irascibility. We were sharing a sofa in a room with heavy drapes pulled against late afternoon sun, and she fingered the edges of an afghan. "I had my hair cut in a different style once. He never even noticed. Now he'll look at me and say, 'Well, don't you look pretty today!'" But these moments come at great cost. She fears her husband when he becomes enraged. She feels unsafe driving with him. Their world—once whirling with social activities, museums, musical and theatrical events, and board meetings—has closed down. She remains at home most of the time, with the doors to the outside locked shut by concealed bolts, installed to prevent her husband from wandering.

A person whose mind is breaking down (and is aware of it[4]) can hardly keep from fearing the hard questions: How will I not become a burden if I cannot even button my own shirt or find my way around the house? Will my family and friends stop loving me when I'm no longer myself? How will I be able to live with the frustration of not being able to read, follow the plot of a television show, or figure out how to make myself a sandwich? How will I ask for help, even from God? And that timeworn dilemma applied to innumerable human conditions, how can a God of love allow this suffering? How can I not fear when my earth is so profoundly shaken?

Dementia can bring about unpredictable changes in a loved one's disposition, not just the struggle to think and function in a world made unfamiliar, causing the structures of a predictable relationship to collapse. "It means, that over the course of years, you are going to lose the person you knew," Bert told me once. "In my case, my best friend, partner, lover, entertainer, my helpmate. Willa was brilliant. She's not aware of it anymore, of how she used to be. She can't hold a thought for very long. I don't have companionship with her. She has it with me, to the extent that she can understand companionship. I don't have it with her."

There are ample books and stories, *The 36-Hour Day*, for example, that fuel the fear of losing time. Caregiving can turn into the incessant duty to tend every need, every hour, of a person who has become a stranger. Willa thrashed and kicked at Bert when he changed her incontinence pads, an aid she required multiple times in a day. *How will I do this, day after day, month after month, year after year?* family caregivers ask themselves. How will I handle my own grief and somehow remain loving and cheerful? What will become of my work, my interests, my friends? She is my mother; he's my life partner. Is it wrong for me to feel this resentful? How can I pray for help and comfort when I'm so angry at the unfairness of it and at the disease itself? How can I not fear when *my* mountains, unseen to most, have been torn from the ground and fallen into the sea?

### We fear the lack of adequate resources—physical, emotional, and financial.

Karen Garner's[5] husband, Jim, was diagnosed with younger-onset Alzheimer's in his mid-forties. Barely on the cusp of middle age, he was forced to retire from work as a contractor, which meant the family unexpectedly lost its main breadwinner. Karen remembers her panic when they finally obtained a reason for Jim's intermittent confusion and the erratic behavior that earlier had driven the unsuspecting couple into a failed bout of marriage counseling. She felt abandoned by a medical system that left her with an accurate label for his condition after a two-year slog through the necessary evaluations, but provided not a word of advice about how to cope with it. She had no idea how she would pay a mountain of steadily accumulating bills while simultaneously acting as primary caregiver for Jim and parent of two children under the age of ten. It seemed impossible.

Karen's situation was somewhat unusual. Younger- or early-onset Alzheimer's, meaning the disease becomes symptomatic before age sixty-five, accounts for only a small percentage of cases. Her situation was not, however, unusual in the extraordinary stamina it required of her or the strain it put on the family finances. Families with a member in a more advanced stage of dementia must either provide or pay for care.[6] There is no safe way to leave a person with dementia alone, once the condition significantly impacts judgment and self-care.

"When my father was taking care of my mother by himself," Sarah began, her voice breaking as she struggled with grief. She held a wet rumpled tissue in her hand and dabbed at her face with it. Her mother was diagnosed in her early sixties with Alzheimer's, and Sarah took care of her from time to time, to relieve her father. "It was so physically overwhelming and so emotionally overwhelming that he had no reserve. He was consumed; his whole life collapsed. I remember when I was taking care of her, I was sitting on the floor, crying, because I couldn't get her to do what I needed her to do. You're so helpless. And everyone around you is giving suggestions: 'You should do this! You should do that!' It's as though they're thinking, 'If it were me (and not you), I'd be doing it the right way, and it would be fine.'" It has helped, she admits, having her mother in a nursing home. Sarah's father was eventually prescribed antidepressants. These medications made him able to move beyond the sense of purposelessness that overcame him as the disease went on and on, and his wife was reduced to sitting motionless in a chair, her face fixed and grim, or sleeping throughout the day.

The decision to place a loved one in a care facility is often driven by the family caregiver's failing health or mental stress. For most, the choice is wrenching. The responsibility of care, while no longer as absorbing of time and energy, does not end with the change, and new concerns may emerge: guilt, disapproval from family members who do not fully understand caregiving (having not done it themselves), and realistic worry that the loved one may be returned home if he becomes combative in this unfamiliar setting. Many facilities are unwilling to deal with physical aggression.

While Sarah's family had the resources to place her mother outside the home when it became apparent that her father was slipping into serious depression, for many families, this choice does not exist. They cannot afford it. The cost of inpatient nursing care, unless supplemented by private insurance or Medicaid assistance, available only to those with virtually no assets, exceeds the average family's yearly income.[7] Care at home is the only viable option, whether it compromises the caregiver's well-being or not. Dementia consumes time and resources, and the Bible has ample language to apply should the unpoetic facts not speak persuasively enough for themselves: "My dwelling, like a shepherd's tent, is struck down and borne away from me," Hezekiah laments, couching the material challenges of mortal illness in language as apt now as it was almost three thousand years ago. "Like a shepherd's tent my house has been pulled down and taken from me. Like a weaver I have rolled up my life" (Isaiah 38:12, NABRE).

Agency or private caregivers may provide relief, but this depends on financial strength and other considerations. At a minimum cost in most places of twenty-five dollars per hour, more at night and over weekends, the cost for a week of care is about $4,200. How many of us can afford such a price for long, if at all?

And how many of us want to trust a steady stream of strangers in and out of the house, some reliable—a few, at least in my experience, who act as if they've been granted access to a free store? My mother's heirloom linens and Christmas ornaments, collected over a lifetime, were stolen. These are not big losses in the scheme of things, but they hurt like splinters embedded in my willingness, now, to trust people I don't know. Dishonest people, not just hired caregivers with house keys, took advantage of my father, defrauding him of more than a hundred thousand dollars and stealing even the wheels from his car. He put his hands over his face, and his shoulders shook when he saw it, held up by blocks at a car dealership he had trusted to fix it. We donated the car to a charity willing to haul it away with no tires, too overwhelmed with other problems to fight with the service manager. We live in a fallen world, and it's never more apparent than when you are trying to keep an elderly person whose mind is failing from falling victim to crime and neglect. Unless you are present and in control at all times, it can happen no matter how diligently you try to prevent it.

Dementia plays out at great cost, both tangible and intangible. We find wisdom and comfort in Jesus's admonishments to think of sparrows, sold for a few coins but known and counted by God, and flowers, made beautiful for the benefit of a single season,[8] but when triggered by realistic circumstances, worry is difficult to tamp down. Money is finite, and so is strength. If a caregiver contracts an illness, or suffers an injury, or becomes clinically depressed—if his or her strength fails in some way—and there is not a viable backup plan, what will happen? And how can this possibility not spur worry, even in the most faith-filled among us?

I've been in the situation of feeling trapped by the lack of resources available to me in trying to provide for my father's care. A few months before his death, he was hospitalized to determine whether a physical reason beyond his dementia could account for his increasingly unpredictable behavior and periods of inconsolable wailing. This move, made at the recommendation of a physician, accomplished one thing: It prevented his return home, ever again.

In the confines of the hospital bed, without access to physical therapy or the freedom to move his legs, he quickly became physically disabled, and his powerlessness to do anything other than yell in frustration compounded, of course, the agitation that led to his admission in the first place. Notes taken by a dismissive psychiatrist, on the basis of a bedside visit, and reports from night nurses, who witnessed the worst of his outbursts, barred him from most facilities at any price, at least the ones with less than abysmal ratings, and home care was no longer an option: The hospital social worker, smiling tightly, had imposed the requirement—should she permit his release to my care—of securing two private, round-the-clock aides capable of operating a mechanical body lift. The cost of this arrangement was more than one thousand dollars per day. I remember gripping my cell phone, spelling out the urgent details to a financial advisor. She listened for a while and then said quietly, "You can't do that. You simply cannot." I felt as though I was trapped in a cubical of locked doors. I desperately needed to have this Red Sea part, and I made one mistake after another, trying in true desperation to do the right thing. I know what it is to be a person of faith and still feel thwarted at every turn by the realities of dementia. There are no easy answers.

### We fear missing our dreams and plans for retirement—a future that seems hopeless.

Unlike Moses, with eyes undimmed and vigor unabated until his death at age 120,[9] we ordinary humans realize that reaching the end of life with musculature intact means dying young. The expectation of cognitive strength to the end is a different matter, however. The brain, although changed in the process of normal aging, is engineered to last for well over a hundred years, not to fail decades before shoulders become stooped and hands curl with arthritis. All of us hope for some leisure time during retirement, which we can enjoy in relative comfort before being confined to a recliner. We may no longer be able to hike as far or as energetically as we did in middle age, but we expect to be capable of driving a car and locating the trailhead.[10]

With dementia, plans for the more enjoyable years of retirement, deliciously formed during the nose-to-the-grindstone years, are derailed. "I must say it's a dirty trick," Laura, the caregiver we met earlier, sighed, her face tight. "I thought we'd settle down, that I'd finally have time for myself." She began to speak in a clipped, sarcastic manner. "But nope. It's not going to be like that. It's a time when you learn what you're *not* going to do."

Early retirement was forced on Bert and Willa by her emerging dementia. In her late fifties, she was fired abruptly from her job as the director of a health care system due to her slipping job performance. She missed meetings, failed to act on memos, forgot to make phone calls. Willa's experience begs the question of how employers, who can see slipping job performance and may suspect dementia, can handle it with compassion. While there is no easy way to confront a person with such an alarming suspicion, the Bible does offer guidance: be gentle,[11] and speak the truth in love.[12] In the spirit of bearing one another's burdens, see if there is a way, possibly, that accommodations can be made for a while to avoid the stress of precipitous change.[13] Willa suffered a heart attack the evening she was fired.

Her symptoms worsened in the stress of this sudden change, so Bert quickly became a caregiver, and his professional work came to a halt. "It used to be that I couldn't wait until the end of the day. I wanted to get home to talk ideas over with her." He spoke quietly while Willa wandered around the house, randomly picking up objects and turning them over in her hands. "We enjoyed crazy things no one else would like. On Saturday mornings, we'd make love and then lie in bed reading law textbooks and discussing the Constitution." He laughed lightly at the memory.

Bert talked to Willa, back then, in a simplistic, sing-song voice: "Willa, would you like some ice cream? See the ice cream? We're going to have some now. Would you like to bounce the ball? Here, let's bounce the ball. That's right, Willa! Back and forth, back and forth. Very good! Do you remember when we had a pool, Willa? You loved that pool." Willa most often responded with a long, uncomprehending stare or by repeating expressionlessly, "Uh huh, uh huh, uh huh."

I couldn't fathom how he'd keep it up as I watched him with her, maintaining the same indomitable cheerfulness for hours on end. At sixty-five,

Bert was still relatively young then and healthy and so was Willa, as far as physical strength goes. Their lives were likely to go on unchanged for a long period. "Willa is so important to me," Bert said, as though stating the color of his eyes or some other fixed attribute, "that to take care of her is to take care of myself."

Willa declined over the next several years and was confined to her bed, too thin and frail to walk, vocalizing, when she made any sound at all, repeated single consonants (duh, duh, duh, ta, ta, ta). She died quietly, still loved as fervently by Bert as ever. In one of those sad, ironic twists that is both understandable and unthinkable, Bert died not long after Willa. He had met someone special, also a former caregiver. Looking ahead to a future that seemed full of new possibilities, new love, he faced a sudden diagnosis of advanced colon cancer. "Caregivers don't care for themselves," he told me, without a hint of the despair I might have felt under these circumstances. "We don't have time. I never had time to go to a doctor when I was taking care of Willa. I didn't have a colonoscopy." When I called to check on him for the last time, his friend answered the phone. "He's in hospice now," she told me. "They think it will be a couple of weeks, maybe."

Bert's life with Willa, despite the complex motivations of his love for her, was tedious. He couldn't have been criticized, had his feelings waned. For many caregivers, a loosening of affectionate ties, as a loved one sinks further into the distant world of dementia, is painful but inevitable. They have to let go—in the interest of sanity—and adopt an emotionally detached commitment to see it through as best they can. But this is still an extraordinary show of love, arguably the agape love the Bible encourages us to have toward others. It's not easy to remain steadfast when the cost to your own life is so great, and there is little reward other than the sense of having done what is right and necessary.

Michael, retired from a successful business, cared at home for his wife, Elaine, who was diagnosed with Alzheimer's in her mid-sixties. Within a few years, she was speaking in monological jargon, a stream of words with proper voice inflection and pronunciation but absolutely no meaning: "I've missed you at home. I was thinking about that if you had been in a rush one day, and someone found like to say, 'Well, I don't know what you found out about it, but anyway, I was just thinking.' And then there was this, like, whatever it was—that one that they just did."

"There's lots of communication going on here," Michael explained to me late one morning. We sat in his sunroom with Elaine, who was capably going through the motions of having a guest over. She sat poised, looking at me with interest, occasionally interjecting a remark: "Just getting over to the meltorations! And sure enough, I can't remember for sure."

"None of it makes any sense," he continued, "which is very lonely. The simplest questions, this morning, 'Do you want a waffle? Yes, or no?' She can't answer it. I don't expect answers, and it brings me further inward. Weekends are the worst. When you leave here," he said, gesturing at the door. "What are we going to do? Twelve o'clock. One o'clock. She'll just follow me around the house, sometimes talking, sometimes not." Michael, an avid golfer and a member of several civic groups, was in the initial years of his retirement, living in an active community with a club and opportunities for social engagement, but until he placed Elaine in a dementia care facility, his time was consumed entirely by caregiving.

As I spoke with him, I was stirred by the realization that a life with many outward blessings—his career success and robust health, longstanding friendships, his church, his children—held little pleasure. In addition to doing everything for Elaine (brushing her teeth and hair, dressing her, bathing her), he did all of the household cooking and cleaning himself, more often than not while trying to keep her from undoing his efforts: He'd make the bed, and she would unmake it. He'd clear the table after dinner, and if he wasn't watching her, she would carry dishes back into the dining room, setting them randomly around on the table and sideboard. She would open a salt shaker and pour the salt out, or take a stack of paper napkins from a drawer and scatter them about. He'd mop the floor, and she would walk on it while it was slick and wet, regardless of his protestations.

"I'm trying to think how this is for you," I said. "I'd be ready to explode after a while."

"Try five years."

"I was thinking more like after a day or two."

He laughed. "I don't know whether it will be better or worse when she goes into residential care. In a way, I'm anxious for her to go, so I'll have a little freedom. But I just don't know." I met Michael for lunch shortly before Elaine finally went to live in a facility. He was at the end of his rope, it seemed, exhausted even with her incessant cheerfulness.

Caregivers are counseled to separate the disease from the person with the disease. Similarly, as Christians, we're told to hate sin and love the sinner as a way of conceptualizing our inherent worth as children of God, regardless of our many shortcomings and failures. But it's hard for a person to cope every minute of every day with a spouse, parent, or partner whose brain no longer works, when the long relational history continually underscores the magnitude of the loss. Michael found himself unable to feel love for Elaine while hating the disease. She was no longer the woman he had known, not in the ways most important to him. She couldn't remember his name or the children they raised together. He knew it wasn't her fault, but she was fundamentally changed. His story—unlike Bert's and others I've heard from caregivers who do remain in love, so to speak, through dementia's ravages— legitimizes the fear among people suffering from the affliction that they will no longer be held in the same affection as before. Was Michael less virtuous for his resentment and discontent than Bert, for his unflagging devotion? I don't think so. Michael was a different person with a different reaction to the loss of his dreams for how later life would unfold and to his loss, irrevocably, of Elaine's love. That she was unable to control the withdrawal of her love was beside the point; it was an awful loss.

### *We fear being lonely and isolated.*

Dementia is isolating. Even when family and friends stay close, dementia erodes the bedrock of relationships—the ability to formulate complex thoughts and keep track of past discussions, to make and remember plans, to recip- rocate, to control anger and frustration. It makes daily life unpredictable. It reduces initiative. Social gatherings become tiring and confusing. "I feel like I'm no longer a part of things," an attorney in the early stage of Alzheimer's told me. "My wife and children talk about me when I'm in the same room, like I can't hear them, or it doesn't matter if I do. I want to tell them how I feel about it. Everything is different. They treat me differently. I'm afraid it will cause an argument, and I can't argue anymore."

As dementia intensifies, social life fades for both the caregiver and the loved one. Situations that once inspired feelings of connection and pleasure, like dinner parties and club memberships, confirm, instead, the reality of increasing dysfunction. Faces are no longer familiar, conversations are difficult to follow, questions are hard to answer. "He was a very serious church person," Anne said, talking about her husband. Anne was barely on the cusp of old age and still had the keen eye of a school teacher used to keeping rambunctious children on a tight rein. We were at a library close to her house, and as she went on, I realized our meeting must have been a great inconvenience, given the man's incessant need for her. Plagued by a form of mixed dementias, he had lost all vestiges of his former life as a researcher. "He was always active in church. It was important to him his whole life. When you have somebody with dementia in your life, all of a sudden, something is gone—disappeared. All of a sudden, one day I wake up and think, 'You know, he doesn't do that anymore. He doesn't want to go to church anymore.' All those little things. I don't pick up on it because someone doesn't announce it to me, 'Anne, take note of this! Your husband isn't interested in that connection of church or religion.' It just sort of disappears." Anne no longer goes to supper club, concerts, or the gym. "Your world shuts down," she said. "It's about going to doctors for all of the problems. To get him there, to get him home, to get to the pharmacy and then to solve all of the medication reactions he has. It seems to take every waking hour. Those places become your social life."

During the worst of the pandemic, we stayed at home, kept from our usual routines by the need to isolate. We shouted through doubled face masks and stepped back from friends and strangers alike. Think how much more challenging sheltering in place would have been, had it lasted for many years instead of months. It's hard enough to be confined at home for a long, long time with a person who makes you laugh, sympathizes with your moods, remembers a shared past with you, and can help clean the kitchen. Imagine, instead, a loved one whose face is as familiar to you as your own—your "family unit" of partner, parent, or sibling—having no idea who you are or what a kitchen is. Needing help with buttons, zippers, laces, brushes, spoons. Pushing your hands away uncomprehendingly when you try to give it. Reacting in fright or surprise to her own reflection in a mirror. This is what the harder years of dementia are like. They don't happen, I don't think, during the early stage, when cognitive strengths remain, despite the grief of emerging difficulties, or after communication and movement have ceased for the most part, despite the crisis impending death may cause. The hardest years are when nothing makes sense, and close relationships are either lost or redefined around extreme limitations and extreme needs.

Herman, a retired administrator who had managed huge budgets and overseen programs affecting thousands of people, found himself utterly confounded almost on a daily basis by his petite wife in the middle stage of Alzheimer's. She would sprawl on the floor seemingly unable to get up. He couldn't lift her or leave her lying there for hours on end. Their children didn't live nearby. Should he call the rescue squad again? Ask a friend for help? He constantly battled worry, unable to keep from ruminating about the inevitable problems the next weeks and years would bring. "I used to pride myself on being able to think." We were in the tiny apartment he shared with his wife in an upscale retirement community that offered daily activities for people with dementia. "I can't think clearly about what to do, and I need to think ahead," he said, rubbing his forehead with his hand, as though trying with the gesture to make the faculty more likely.

Herman had accepted his loss of Lenora in the role of wife and partner. She made no bones about her lack of recognition of him. "He's not my husband," she said flatly, to anyone who referred to him as such within earshot. Her dismissiveness caused more than the occasional sting. Perceiving him as a stranger, Lenora reacted with resistance to his attempts to control her, which made his life with her a series of conflicts. Desperate for a change, he once mapped out an ambitious trip involving a two-day drive. As is frequently the case when plans involve a person with advanced Alzheimer's, nothing about the departure went smoothly. They didn't leave in the afternoon, as he intended, but set out in late evening under a bank of ominous clouds. He ended up driving for hours in the pitch dark, with a steady rainstorm pummeling the car. When they finally arrived at the hotel, and he had dragged their suitcases to the room, he collapsed on the bed in exhaustion.

Lenora eyed him primly. "You know," she said, hesitating as though it pained her to deliver the bad news, "you're a nice man, but I'm not that kind of girl." Herman, with old-world decency, spent the night in a chair.

We smile over Herman's predicament, the sadness of lost intimacy notwithstanding. Some are less able than him to accept what is no longer within the realm of possibility. I talked with a man, relatively young, who found a lady-friend when his wife no longer recognized him, much to the dismay of his grown children.

"You're just like every other man," his daughter had accused hotly, "only interested in sex!"

"Honey, you don't know how goddam right you are!" he fired back. Recalling the confrontation, he glared at me for a moment, perhaps trying to gauge from my expression where my sympathies might fall in this sort of debate. I quietly held his gaze, and he looked down sadly after a moment. "It's not the sex, not the act of it. It's the companionship. She looks at you; she talks to you," he conceded, his eyes filling with sudden tears. We can feel equally pulled to each side—to the side of a daughter struggling with the heartrending evidence of her mother's uncountable losses and maybe with her own sense of right and wrong, and to the side of a man who simply wanted to feel loved again.

## CONCLUSION

These fears—of change, of inadequacy on multiple fronts, of a grim future, of loneliness and loss—are not inclusive or universally experienced. Every person living with dementia is different, but if you are aware that dementia threatens not only memories, rational thought, communication, self-control, and the stability of personality but also, in most cases, relationships, financial security, living arrangements, and any hope of a restful, stable retirement, then you understand the scope of its devastating effects.

As Christians, we lean on our faith to help us face the worst circumstances of life and assign meaning, if we can, to our suffering. We identify with a living God who suffered unspeakably when confined within a human body. In the next chapter we'll look at ways of offering compassionate counseling to people coping with dementia. As I have said, there are no easy answers; sometimes there are no answers at all. Comfort, though, is almost always within reach.

## CONCLUSION

## CHAPTER 3

# Comfort Through Pastoral Counseling: A Model

A 2018 Pew Research Center study examined the question of why Americans do and don't attend church. Not surprisingly, most attend to become closer to God. The fourth most important reason in the list, however, was to find comfort in trouble and sorrow.[1] The intention of this book is to help churches become a refuge of comfort and support for people who live with dementia. As we learned in the previous chapter, dementia causes a unique kind of grief and stress: It lasts for years and requires continual, often unpredictable adjustments to a steady decline in intelligence and sometimes dramatic changes in personality. If death or divorce or financial failure are like a tornado, dementia is more like a relentless storm in which the rising waters wash everything away over time. Our comfort must be ongoing and based on the understanding that with dementia, unlike other forms of grief, life will not gradually swing back into place (albeit a new place) after a period of sadness and heightened need. With dementia, grief and stress go on and on, and the church must steadily offer different kinds of support.

Counseling is one of the most important means of comfort because the counseling process, unlike other interactions in the church setting, allows for in-depth emotional expression, which has been shown to reduce even chronic physical pain[2] and certainly to help with the stresses of dementia.[3] Feeling understood heightens the sense of well-being and social connection and reduces emotional tension, which is not surprising: The changes in brain activity brought about by feeling understood (as well as misunderstood) can actually be witnessed through functional magnetic resonance imaging.[4] Loosely speaking, we may consider counseling to have occurred during a meaningful chat at coffee hour or for a few minutes before or after a worship service, and such encounters can be therapeutic. For those with more advanced dementia, such a brief encounter may be the only form of counseling possible. But for our purposes in this chapter, counseling mainly refers to a private, scheduled interview with a minister, a professional counselor employed by the church, or a trained lay person (such as a Stephen Minister) and a parishioner who would benefit from the opportunity to talk at greater length.

When providing counseling, it is, of course, crucial that clergy members and lay counselors stay within boundaries of training and competence. Compassionate listening, spiritual and biblical guidance, and facilitating referrals are generally well within these lines. Unless the care provider is properly licensed and trained, psychotherapy and other advanced interventions in which the intention is to treat mental health issues, behavioral disorders, and serious emotional problems are not and require referral. The attempt to give this kind of help can lead to a charge of negligence in the event of harm or injury that can be subsequently linked to the counseling process.[5] Law professor Constance Fain recommends that churches formulate specific counseling policies and use a signed agreement in which counselees acknowledge the difference between mental health and spiritual counseling and between ministers or other church officials and professional counselors.[6] It's regrettable that we must carefully review insurance policies, become familiar with applicable laws, and exercise other cautions to avoid the repercussion of legal action in response to our sincere if imperfect efforts to relieve suffering, but such is our litigious world.

People most often seek counseling when they find themselves overwhelmed by life. They're struggling with relationships, with grief, with hard circumstances, with unwanted change, loss, failure: The list goes on and on. The list of what they need, however, is fairly short, unless there is dysfunction or trauma. They need to be understood and helped to understand; they need to feel comfort, hope, and relief; they need to see things in a way that engages strength and enables choices. This is true whether they are living with dementia or not.

As Christians we can interpret every aspect of our lives, over the entire course of life, as a means of moving either toward or away from God, based on our understanding of what it entails to remain in conscious relationship with

God. This is quite a different lens through which to view human motivation than has been used in developing the practices of modern psychology.[7] There is one method, however—client-centered counseling[8]—that can serve as an introduction to the material in this chapter. Although secular, it is lodged theoretically in Christian themes of non-judgmentalism and empathy and has been linked, somewhat surprisingly, to improvements in the complex problems of agitation, psychiatric symptoms, and depression in dementia patients.[9] Cecil Patterson, a ministry-minded sociologist and prolific author of books on psychotherapy,[10] sums up the core value of connection in client-centered counseling: "The best way to help a client, whether only for an hour or a hundred hours, is to provide the highest level of a therapeutic relationship of which the therapist is capable."[11] In other words, walk in love.[12]

Anyone who has taken an entry-level course in counseling is familiar with Carl Rogers and his method of engaging people, no matter what problems they bring to the table, with authenticity, interest, and compassion. Beneficial change, Rogers tells us, occurs when a person is brought into a relationship in which the goal is understanding and complete acceptance, and within this relationship, they are able to help themselves.[13] We're so familiar with Rogerian counseling that it almost seems like a cliché to speak of unconditional positive regard and its use in creating a safe psychological space where counseling clients can essentially make themselves better. In the next chapter, we'll consider the painful reality among people living with dementia of stigmatization by the larger culture and the problem of being misunderstood by friends and relatives, as much as by strangers. Dementia can seem like a foreign country with harsh living conditions and unsympathetic neighbors. In contrast, a place in which there is freedom to spill a very overburdened heart without fear of judgment, unwanted advice, awkwardness, disapproval, or the sudden appearance of a cell phone and the assurance, instead, of positive regard (a term remarkably similar to agape love) and active, compassionate listening can feel more like a transcendent sanctuary than an ordinary room supplied with comfortable chairs and tissues.

Drawing on my own experience with grief, I've developed a model of pastoral care that I call "sacred holding." It expands on the principles of client-centered counseling to help parishioners cope not only with dementia but other conditions of loss and distress. The model has four components: initiation, compassionate listening, witness, and prayer. As you will see, the events that led me to formulate this approach happened mainly before my experiences with dementia. But I am hoping that what I've learned in my life about helping others through grief can benefit almost anyone who faces it, for almost any reason.

Let's look first at how sacred holding differs from client-centered counseling with regard to the counselor's role and its view of suffering. Ministers operate from the perspective that the therapeutic—or healing—relationship involves more than a meaningful interaction between two people, one of whom is trained to help the other by providing a unique relationship of compassionate acceptance. A healing relationship at heart is about God and the understandings of God we gain through studying the Bible, praying, reading, contemplation, and other means of "soul" learning. We are not alone. We're in the presence of a God who is at once unfathomable and intimate: a fire that can burn without consuming. God, not an expert with a degree in one of the helping professions, is at the center of this relationship. Apart from God, people are not able truly to help themselves—whether they are aware of God's presence in their lives or not. This *necessary* reliance on God in sacred holding is the most fundamental difference between the approaches.

In sacred holding, we need to metaphorically remove our sandals to enter into a helping relationship with a person in some kind of trouble. In ancient times, sandals or shoes symbolized the power gained by the possession of such things as land, offspring, and authority, or displays of wartime bravery, so removing one or both shoes was an indication of respect.[14] Priests were not permitted to enter temples with their shoes on. Stepping on a defeated enemy expressed to him physically the new reality of his subjugation, hence God's promise in Psalm 110 to make David's enemies a footstool under his feet. When another person entrusts us with their deeper feelings, they become liable both to our reaction and to the shift in power that occurs when divulgences are entirely one-sided. It's hard enough to be self-revealing to a therapist with whom there is slim chance of contact outside the counseling office, but it's even harder to risk such exposure with a revered minister regularly met in church settings. For the care provider to figuratively slip off the shoes honors this trust with humility in which we understand our place: Only God can search the heart and test the mind.[15] We can speak only from a place of compassion.

This form of counseling differs from secular counseling in its orientation, as well, to suffering. Psychotherapists as objective witnesses generally try to discern how a client's values (religious or otherwise) impact her adjustment to the circumstances of her life. They wonder, in other words, are religious beliefs associated with themes of guilt, peace, punishment, and so on, and to what extent do these beliefs need to be explored and challenged to bring the client to a point of increased mental health? In the church, we recognize that questions of faith are at the very core of suffering.

Many of us are beset by what I call the "thrashing" questions: Why didn't God answer my prayers? Why do I have a fatal disease when God could have prevented it? Why doesn't God help me with the despair I feel? If God is with me, then why do I feel so scared and miserable? I thought I was doing God's will, as much as I can understand it. Why am I now trapped in this relationship with someone who no longer recognizes me—or facing any circumstance that makes life bad and unhappy and from which there is no conceivable escape? Who is this difficult, abstruse God who claims with baffling simplicity to be my father? Sometimes, like Richard Taylor of the previous chapter, we cannot help but cry until there are no more tears. But at the end of all that crying, we need to feel, instead of empty and depleted, that we are held in love by the God who counts our tears[16] and who uses his people to do some of the holding.[17]

We imagine an awful responsibility as Christians to have answers that might credibly interpret the worst of events, even the certainty of a slow and complete destruction of one's own brain by disease. We're torn between our ideal disposition as the simple trusting children to whom heaven belongs[18] and the inescapable reality that we are adults who fear that our framework of beliefs may crash under the pressure of inexplicable suffering. It's hard to accept that we suffer for reasons known only to God.[19]

Despite our desire to have answers and the fact that we have at our disposal a Bible that supplies them, the act of sacred holding permits only a gentle steering of the counseling boat, done with some real sense of the ocean's depth. As counselors, we represent a perfect God of infinite love but also a God we cannot fathom. If directly confronted by this unfathomable God, we could manage, like Job, the absolute paragon of suffering, only to confess our ignorance and despise ourselves.[20]

Far removed as most of us are from Job's contrition in dust and ashes, we may be seduced instead into overconfidence. I once told a minister (of sorts) that I felt abandoned by God. He raised his eyebrows in reproach and said in an indulgent, grandfatherly tone, as though speaking to a child in the throes of a piddling tantrum, "Now, now then. God did not abandon you." He paused for effect and looked me in the eye. "You," he said, wagging an accusatory finger, "abandoned God." The fact this person spoke the truth did not mean he spoke in love or with any understanding of the events that had compelled me to ask for his help. People who come to a church for counseling need to leave feeling that they've been figuratively held, that they've been heard, and that they are loved. We are each on a singular journey and must be met where we are—not snatched up, given a shake, and pressured to accept ideas that compete badly with our despair. When at wit's end, my late husband and I met with a minister who listened to us carefully but then summed things up as though attesting to a fact about which we had until that very moment been woefully ignorant: "God is not a Coke machine" she said, regretfully. "You don't put in a quarter and get out what you want." I know this minister was trying to help, wholeheartedly, it seemed, but we were being buried beneath a load of incomprehensible catastrophes, and everywhere we turned for help, a door slammed in our faces. As ministers, or counselors, or friends, we must (I use this word *must* deliberately) resist the temptation to sweep pain beneath easy ideas, even if we pluck them from the Bible, or worse, misguided humor. We do not comprehend as God does the level of suffering some people feel. Two weeks after that meeting, I found my husband in his office at the hospital, his body swaying lifelessly, his face a pale contorted mask in street-light streaming through a window. He had been dead, I later learned, for no more than a few minutes. He was still warm when I put my arms around him in an attempt to lift his body from the weight of the leash. That minister was the first person I called from the hospital. She sat with me, lovingly, for most of the night, and this is all we are asked to do: help carry each other's burdens for a while. We do not have the power to explain suffering or take it away.

While our sacred holding model may differ from secular counseling with regard to suffering, a second important issue, confidentiality, is handled in much the same way in both. Trust is essential in any meaningful relationship, and sacred holding does not differ from client-centered or any other counseling approach in its commitment to confidentiality. Ministers who counsel or advise parishioners on personal matters or who are privy to personal information by other means are bound, if not by ethics alone, then by legal obligation in most cases, to act within commonly accepted codes of confidentiality and privacy. Churches fall into a murkier legal area in this regard, sometimes due to the intrinsic conflict between secular and ecclesiastical practices,[21] and it is prudent to become familiar with the relevant laws, which vary from state to state: Privacy invasion, like negligence, can be a legitimate claim against a church.[22] Confidentiality in counseling is handled differently at times within churches, and around issues of dementia, there are certain guidelines to keep in mind. Whether a claim of confidentiality breech is legally defensible or not, a parishioner would have valid reason to object if their confidences were revealed to other church members, whatever the benevolent intentions, without explicit permission.

Bear in mind that any form of dementia is a medical condition. Unless churches provide health care, which under certain circumstances could include pastoral counseling, they are exempt from the broad-reaching federal Health Information Privacy Protection (HIPPA) Privacy Rule. Many states, though, have laws meant to enforce an individual's right to privacy, and medical conditions are defined as protected information (therefore confidential) under HIPPA regulations.[23] Attorney David Middlebrook, co-author of *Nonprofit Law for Religious Organizations*, advises clergy to be mindful of HIPPA and its purpose, whether specifically bound by its provisions or not. "Rule of thumb," he cautions, "keep information confidential unless the individual or immediate family gives you permission to share."[24] HIPPA requirements do not for the most part apply to the publication of prayer lists, however, although guidelines have been developed that ensure privacy is respected when members desire it.[25]

Confidentiality is necessarily breeched in certain counseling situations, such as when the client discloses potential harm to self or others and abuse or neglect of those unable to protect themselves. Of course, exceptions to confidentiality should be clearly stated and discussed, if clarification is necessary, prior to the first counseling session. People with advanced dementia are usually elderly (sixty or older according to federal law) and considered disabled, meaning they have a mental impairment that significantly limits one or more major life activities, so potentially they are in two protection categories. In some states, clergy are mandatory reporters of elder abuse and neglect whether intentional or unintentional.[26] My own father was neglected in a care facility, and it contributed to his long, painful death. Left sitting motionless for hours on end, day after day, he developed infected pressure sores on his heels. People who are frail and unable to care or speak for themselves can quickly fall victim to bad practices, even in a professional setting. We feel deep compassion for caregivers and the challenges they face in providing for the needs of a person who in many cases cannot cooperate with, much less acknowledge, their care. Strength understandably fails, as it would for anyone, and outside support is needed to relieve stress or secure necessary resources, which may be educational or medical. Family caregivers aren't trained. They step into this daunting role because circumstances demand it.

Sometimes caregivers themselves are at risk. Cathryn, from chapter 2, said her husband once became irate when told he needed a shower. Towering over her, he grabbed her by the shoulders and forcefully shook her, "the way you'd kill a baby," she said, "back-and-forth and side-to-side."[27] A delicate woman in her late seventies, almost a foot shorter than her husband, she was justifiably scared. I've interviewed a caregiver who described her husband as a "monster," prone to violent outbursts despite the decent marriage they had shared for decades prior to his dementia. Her husband, she understood, was frustrated by his inability to comprehend his environment, which had been made as simple as possible. She understood, but she was scared of him. Although it's a hard truth to acknowledge, people who've lost the capacity for self-control and are living in a state of perpetual confusion can be unknowingly aggressive. Up to 20 percent[28] exhibit threatening physical contact, such as biting, hitting, pinching, and kicking caregivers.[29] Situations involving dementia can be volatile,[30] and members of the church staff may have a legal duty to respond if a person's safety is threatened,[31] matters of confidentiality and privacy aside. While it is necessary for professionals who offer counseling services to be apprised of and comply with these reporting duties, be aware that community support for families coping with dementia is often woefully inadequate,[32] meaning that such a report may not result in helpful actions. I know from experience this stumbling block is maddening and deeply upsetting.

## SACRED HOLDING: THE FOUR COMPONENTS

### Initiation: The Persistent Widow

We can move now into the parts of the sacred holding model, the first of which involves its sometimes unorthodox beginning. Churches differ from other counseling settings in that ministers see from the pulpit the main population from which their counselees derive and can sometimes discern the need before any words are said. Research has linked specific facial expressions (down to specifying the muscle groups involved) to the severity of depression.[33] Even without such commonsense research, most of us recognize stress and sadness in slumping shoulders, a downcast expression, agitated fidgeting, the effort to stifle tears, and other familiar gestures. In the case of dementia, the problems are often uncomfortably apparent. You met Michael and his wife Elaine in chapter 2. Michael tried to continue attending church with Elaine after her dementia became symptomatic. She waved her hands, whistled, and hummed, and he struggled to keep her in check, eventually abandoning the venture. Unlike therapists, who rely upon self-referrals from strangers, ministers have knowledge of and access to their parishioners, as well as an ongoing responsibility to observe them, and these differences have implications for the initiation phase of counseling.

But also unlike therapists, whose work is divided into discrete hours and for whom counseling is the main activity, ministers are inundated with tasks aside from pastoral care, which itself is multifaceted. It includes not only counseling but home visits, care for the sick and dying, memorials and marriages, and other consuming activities. A survey (albeit not recent) of more than a thousand randomly selected ministers indicates that counseling may understandably be low on the list for most. The median number of hours spent in it per week was limited to three.[34] Given the pervasive loneliness of our culture,[35] ministers who promote their role as counselor may well be flooded with takers who appreciatively grab the time slots at hand and clamor at the door. A minister, thus beleaguered, could hardly do more than react to those who present most urgently. It would be impractical to let other responsibilities slide for the sake of privately helping individuals, each requiring a relatively large outlay of time. Admittedly there is Biblical precedent for such extravagant love,[36] but we are all bound by mortal limits of time and energy.

I suggest, nonetheless and however idealistically, that a few of the few hours available for counseling be reserved for people coping with dementia and that, incongruent as it may seem, Luke's persistent widow[37] provides an example of how to initiate the connection. I had always thought of this character as a rather vengeful, self-interested person, subject to the declines of age and the helplessness of her low status. In other words, she is us. But I heard a sermon once in a tiny old church at the edge of a rural community inhabited by only a few hundred people in which the minister thoughtfully upended the obvious interpretation and placed God in the role of the widow, in dogged pursuit of his people despite our unworthiness. Similarly, ministers must at times, I think, become persistent widows in pursuit of those who are isolated by adversity or grief and too overwhelmed to ask for help.

A person confronted by a terrifying diagnosis needs support; caregivers whose lives have been radically restricted need support. When problems mount, a place to settle for an hour of confidential "casting of cares"[38] is a literal godsend. But whether this group of early-stage dementia patients and caregivers will seek counseling is uncertain, especially if it depends entirely on their initiative. Lack of initiative and difficulty planning are among the first symptoms of Alzheimer's, the most common form of dementia. Life eventually becomes, we've learned, a Sisyphean struggle in which common tasks are a complicated mountain to climb each day. Longstanding grief, lack of social support, stigma, and stoicism—all prevalent in dementia—are factors that affect help-seeking behaviors.[39] It's not such a stretch to compare this condition to a stubborn judge whose heart is not moved by the supplications of a needy plaintiff.

Making persistent, sincere attempts to connect conveys care. In a study of 950 Americans, more than a third reported serious loneliness and revealed that not one person in the recent past had taken "just a few minutes" to ask after them in a genuine way. Many expressed a need simply for this act.[40] In the book's introduction, I mentioned attending church after my brother died unexpectedly as he raked leaves, when he was fifty years old. Greg was my only sibling; we were born during the same calendar year and grew up like fraternal twins. For months afterward, I could not control my tears at church, though remarkably I was unable to cry anywhere else. I didn't shake or sob, but strange tears streamed from my eyes almost from the moment I sat down, every week in the same pew, about as far away from the minister as the length of two average dining room tables. At the end of the service, he shook my hand and moved me along, week after week. But I've been just as guilty of ignoring a friend's tears, wondering crazily if she'd had recent eye surgery.[41] We are human and subject to feelings of uncertainty and awkwardness. In a church, however, care is an expectation, and the failure to respond to evident suffering even in a minimal way compounds it. I felt invisible during those weeks—in need of simple acknowledgment. Invisibility hurts. Dementias are described as invisible illnesses early in the disease progression, when those with the condition are still able to express themselves,[42] and caregivers are described as the "invisible" second patient within the medical setting.[43] As my father's brain failed, I saw him slip further and further to the margins, where he was belittled and ignored, treated as though he was either invisible or a problem that might oblige an unworthwhile investment of someone's time.

Becoming that persistent widow who initiates a deeper connection may be a matter of consistently looking for chances to communicate this message in different ways: *I know what you are going through is hard. Come and talk with me, if it would help. I'm here for you, and I care about you.* If counseling doesn't result, the effort alone will make a difference. A similar message might be helpful if you suspect dementia in a parishioner, but no corroborating information has been forthcoming from the family. It's wise not to share such a worry without a specific reason, such as their performance on an important church committee.[44] Express general concern, and let the parishioner or family member fill in details if they wish: *Everything okay with you?* Or, *with you and Elaine?* It is more likely that you will fail—in the brief, intermittent encounters of church—to perceive the dementia with which a parishioner and family may struggle in private.

## Compassionate Listening: The Still Place

In the first years after my husband's suicide, I encountered two people who held me sacredly, one by her compassionate listening, the other by his willingness to be with me in grief—his witness. They inspired the next two components of this counseling model. I met the first through a friend who correctly sensed that my inner turmoil exceeded the limits of her (or any friend's) supportiveness, no matter how generous. Grief aside, I was grappling with a load of problems, from rotting wood in my house and a neighbor's nasty harassment to an account manager's financial exploitation of me. I had recently spent just under an hour and too many dollars talking to a therapist in a downtown office. I described some of what I faced, deliberately leaving out the parts that made me feel most vulnerable. I said I felt like a wolf caught in a trap, trying to chew off its own paw. She listened, her face increasingly perturbed. When I finished, she cast her eyes down for a few seconds, fiddling with her hands. Looking back at me, she said hesitatingly, as though unwillingly compelled by the truth of it, "Everywhere you look, it's all so huge. You must feel really trapped if you can't even kill yourself." It was an unwise confrontation. Among the details I had omitted was the plan I had for just that, should things become truly unbearable. Sometimes in those dark days, I could feel relief only by reassuring myself that I could, if I had to, escape the pain.

In this tenuous state, I was sent by my friend to meet a nun stationed in the auxiliary building of a Catholic church that sprawled across a neighborhood block. Although I never knew exactly what job Sister Pat had in this large church, I'm pretty sure it didn't include talking repeatedly to a desperate, bewildered Protestant with no aspirations of conversion. But I appeared week after week at her door, lugging my bin of "thrashing questions," each attached to a difficult story. She listened with unflagging compassion and the kind of shrewd intelligence that inevitably enjoins respect, and I felt held—like the sick, exhausted survivor of a shipwreck being towed slowly toward land. When we parted, I gave her a framed print of a ship in a storm.

I remember only the gist of our many conversations, although oddly one sticks in my mind that illustrates the gentle way compassionate listening happens. I was lying in bed, late the night before one of our appointments, the lights still on and the tens of thousands of seconds that comprise a night ticking away, one at a time. Insomnia during those years was a torture. I sometimes walked the street, too agitated to remain in the house, much less tossing in bed. My cat was sick. I could hear him vomiting and wondered, as it continued, if I should take him to the emergency veterinary clinic. I decided I could not; I simply could not wrestle this big, agitated cat, who could be vicious at the best of times, into a cat carrier and drive him into town in the middle of the night. Instead I took the Bible from my bedstand and began to leaf aimlessly through it, like I might an old magazine left in a bus station, trying, impossible though it was, not to hear the cat's heaving. Soon enough, I stumbled upon a passage of Isaiah that stirred me with its obvious relevance to my situation: "Sing, O barren woman, you who never bore a child, burst into song, shout for joy, you who were never in labor; because more are the children of the desolate woman than of her who has a husband, says the Lord. . . . You will forget the shame of your youth and remember no more the reproach of your widowhood. For your maker is your husband . . . "

I wasn't really praying in the thick of grief, but I felt the need to respond in some way to these words. I lifted my eyes, as though I might see God through the ceiling. "I want a divorce," I said, in all seriousness. "You aren't a good husband. You can't go out with me on Saturday mornings for coffee. You can't help me with the cat. I don't want you for a husband." And with that, I closed my Bible.

The next afternoon, I related this episode to Sister Pat, conscious as I spoke of the slender wedding band she wore, indicating her marriage-like fidelity to God.

"A divorce," she said, raising her eyebrows slightly, "from God?"

"Yes," I replied.

She hesitated for a moment. "Well, you can go ahead and divorce God," she said, "because God will not divorce you."

The central theme in my interactions with Sister Pat was that I could bring the terrible memory of Wayne at death; the thrashing questions, no matter how wayward; the problems that assailed me from, it seemed, every possible direction; my anger, inability to pray, unyielding grief, and fearful future; and my sense of injustice, abandonment, and isolation to God. I could bring even my unwillingness to live,[45] without making any of it into a churchy-sounding speech that would fail to correctly represent my heart. I comprehended that whatever I had to bring to God was enough, was already known. She helped me by taking seriously my questions, all of them, and listening with compassion and positive regard (or love, or whatever term we assign to deep acceptance), while refraining from any of the reactions she could have displayed with good reason: disapproval, rebuke, exhortation, superiority, impatience, piousness. She remained authentic. Without making me wrong, she revealed in her words, her biblical knowledge, and her way with me the God she knew, the one who would not divorce me, until finally my questions, though unanswered, were mainly at rest. In that close room, with a sad philodendron and furniture from an office supply store, I began to see the God who loves and loves and loves, no matter what this world slings out and who can work all things together for good.[46] Compassionate listening doesn't change circumstances or answer unanswerable questions, but it can help a person muddling through the worst losses and intractable problems find a still place where God is present,[47] and that in and of itself may feel like a miracle.

Sister Pat spent considerable time with me, and I realize most ministers cannot offer so much to a single troubled parishioner. But I also know the sacred holding of another person can happen in an hour or an instant, because I've experienced it both ways and from both sides. I was interviewing a man with a wife in mid-stage dementia unable to offer him anything, he felt, in return for his ceaseless care of her. I abandoned my list of questions and listened to him, reflecting back his sense of isolation, loss of friends, the restrictions caregiving imposed on his own life, and his need for companionship. After about an hour, as our time together wound down, he stood up, looking around in mild surprise, and said as if to someone else who might be in the room with us, "It helps to talk. I feel better. I feel lighter."

With dementia, we must recognize that compassionate listening may involve two people with opposing needs. In his unhappiness, this man supplies us with an example of the conflict in counseling that can arise between the needs of a caregiver and those of the person diagnosed with dementia, if she is still able to identify and express her needs. As the life of the caregiver becomes more circumscribed, the result is almost unavoidably the kind of loneliness he expressed to me. A research article, which identifies four increasingly difficult stages of caregiving similarly quotes a forty-nine-year-old woman caring for a husband with younger onset Alzheimer's: "When you are a caregiver, you are totally isolated. In its own way, it is a disease and sickness to be in one building with one person twenty-four hours, seven days a week, week after week. It is not healthy. It has gotten the best of me."[48] Caregivers begin to feel as though they work alone at a job that consumes every waking hour and threatens sleep. Years ago, I knew a caregiver who often described his wife and everyone else in her condition as "fat, dumb, and happy," meaning blamelessly ignorant of dementia's impositions on others. "It's not the person with dementia you need to worry about," he would say philosophically. "They're being cared for, and they don't know what's going on. We're the ones who suffer."

Well, maybe not so fast. For a time, people with dementia can make choices, even as their impairments increase, and there is no accounting for the grief of sensing a failure of one's own mind. Being deprived of appropriate autonomy, while steadily losing the ability to exercise it, causes discontent. It would for anyone. The youngish woman mentioned above began to take her husband to adult daycare so she could have some time for herself, and he reacted with resistance. A minister she consulted for help, presumably with convincing her husband of her need for relief, dismissed her out of hand: "You've said your marriage vows, for better or worse, until death do you part. You've had the better, this is the worst."[49] No big surprise that she felt unsupported.

I wonder if she'd have felt the same way, in spite of the same outcome, had this minister, who was caught between the couple's conflicting needs, said to her instead, "Tell me what a day is like for you," and then listened, trying to put himself in her shoes. Ministers can't bring about solutions to impossible problems any better than the rest of us can. But they can be honest both about themselves and God: "I want to help you, and I can talk with your husband. I don't think I can get him to change his mind about a situation he hates, though. Are there any other alternatives that would free some of your time? Can I pray for you both and for God to show us a way? God watches over our lives, every moment, day and night,[50] even though sometimes we feel very alone."

## Witness: Our Willing Presence

In Christian vernacular, the word *witness* means to profess one's faith, usually in an effort to persuade: *My story of God may help you to believe, and this is why I am telling it.* Witnessing can also be instructive: *Here are steps to take in approaching God if you're unsure; this is how to pray.* Groups who go out witnessing sometimes use pamphlets to eliminate the risk of becoming tongue-tied while attesting to a personal relationship with the unfathomable yet intimate Creator of everything, seen and unseen, as well as to leave behind a tangible, simple message—hopefully of truth. But in the context of this sacred-holding method of counseling, I use the word in a third way: to indicate instead our willing presence in the face of another person's emotion. Grief needs witness.

We live in a culture of self-sufficiency under an ongoing tacit mandate to renounce sadness, at least when in the company of others. The clichés, *keep a stiff upper lip* and *keep your chin up* exhort us not to tremble or collapse, to stay strong and proud. These ideas are not necessarily wrong, but if there is a place in which one should be allowed the expression of emotion, it is in counseling, where social conventions can be dropped. We find comfort in the promise that God counts our tears and keeps them in a bottle.[51] Putting a stoic face on grief is like going around in a costume. It's exhausting to pretend all is well when it's not. But we have to do this to live in a world that tells us, perhaps wisely, not to wear our hearts on our sleeve.

Dementia, as previously mentioned, can be invisible to others. Social skills are deeply established early in life, so a person, sometimes even in mid-stage dementia, can come across normally in a brief encounter when things are falling apart at home. Caregivers, perceiving the reality of it, are crushed (which is not too strong of a word) when friends say enthusiastically, "I saw your [husband, wife, sister, mother . . . ]. It seems like there's nothing wrong at all. They're doing great!" There are few replies to make beyond simply, "Thanks, we're doing okay," or "Actually, there's quite a lot wrong. You just can't see it."

Every suffering person needs at least one place where they are accepted and loved as they are, permitted to viscerally express pain that must remain hidden in our stoic culture. In the same way Sister Pat demonstrated with her compassionate listening the love of God, no matter what assails, the act of bearing witness in love to the evidence of emotional pain is "counting" it, as God counts our tears and keeps them in a flask. To count is to matter, and to matter is to find hope.

About a year and a half after my husband's death, and after Sister Pat, I went to a psychologist because he advertised a specialty in hypnosis. I couldn't see a way out of relentless insomnia and the horrific images that flashed into my mind without warning. I can remember crawling under my bed, holding my knees to my chest, trying to escape these images. Nothing helped. I felt as though I had been permanently torn inside into two people, one who wanted to live and one who—even in the presence of the loving God of my time with Sister Pat—still wanted to die. I understood for the first time how traumatized children in the vulnerabilities of immaturity develop dissociative disorders, because I felt such a level of division within myself in the struggle between life and death.

The psychologist didn't offer hypnosis to me, as it turned out, but instead he offered his willing presence, his witness, and his humanity, and I began to feel the two selves within me knit back into one, willing to live, although nothing changed in the outward circumstances that had provoked my wish for death. He did this by offering time, for free, at the end of the day, once a week, more often if I needed, when I could come and sit on the sofa in his office and cry. I did this over and over again. He sat across from me, not saying a word, until finally he asked one evening if he could wipe my tears away, just to help me feel close to another human when I was experiencing such profound sadness. He was careful with boundaries; there was nothing inappropriate.[52] But he sat in front of me, gently dabbing away at these unstoppable tears and pitching each soggy tissue, basketball-style, into the trashcan. As I write about it so many years later, I'm reminded of the table blessing many of us learn in early childhood, "God is great; God is good." I was being helped, I knew, by a great and good God who would put in front of me what I needed to live, as I needed it. Then, I needed a place with another person where I felt accepted in the unacceptableness of raw grief.

In the Jewish faith, the tradition of shiva acknowledges that grief is a time apart, and while shiva ("seven," in Hebrew) lasts only a week, the symbols of it—covered mirrors and simple clothing to convey the unimportance of appearance, low chairs to represent the disempowerment of grief, a torn black ribbon to represent the grief-torn heart—are ways of acknowledging the alternate world that grief creates, at least temporarily. A person facing a severe change must learn to live in a different world, a world that initially feels stripped of its prior assurances and comforting, motivating patterns. Nothing will ever be the same as it was, and this is hard to accept. Depending on what has been lost and how, the shift from a shiva-like world in which grief predominates to a new life with restored optimism can take quite a long time. In my experience, it happens more readily with a counting of tears—the perception that the loss, in its magnitude, has been witnessed.

Chapter 2 addresses some of the fears that people living with dementia experience. The word *fear* in this situation could be interchanged with *grief*. There is not a single area of life that isn't negatively impacted by loss of the ability to think. The grief of dementia is complex and protracted. It can be broken down into countless losses that accrue over many years, each of which requires a more exacting adjustment and each of which makes the person with dementia less capable of connection. It can be hard for a person on the outside looking in to see the many trees of loss for the forest of loss. Caregivers are not going to receive from their loved one a birthday card; they will not be comforted when a beloved pet dies; they won't be treated to a holiday dinner. They won't return home to the surprise of a clean house, a vacuumed car, or a repair made. A wise friend told me once that a relationship isn't as much about big things as it is about thousands of small, everyday decisions to demonstrate care by generosity and, more often than might be imagined, by self-restraint. Dementia upends this capacity. A caregiver's husband, diagnosed eventually with frontotemporal lobe dementia, gave her a box of artificial sweetener for her birthday one year, before his condition had been identified. "Why did you give me this?" she asked, startled by what she had unwrapped. "Because you like it," he replied, oblivious to the inappropriateness of the gift.

My father told me he loved me a few months before his death, but many with dementia can no longer do this, even in their most lucid moments. By the time death occurs, the opportunity to rectify past wrongs, to seek or give forgiveness, to express love, and to say goodbye are long gone, as is the chance in the end to laugh or revisit favorite memories together. Family caregivers grieve many deaths before physical death occurs, and they can struggle with feelings of guilt over an ambivalent wish that their loved one, so radically altered, *would* die. The caregiver's emotional experience has been described in research literature using the dispassionate terms "pre-death grief" and "post-death complicated grief," which are directly (not inversely) associated and related to the dementia-specific issues of serial loss, decline of the caregiver's own health, the burden of critical decisions, and a level of stress that is as great before the loved one's death as it is after.[53]

While living with dementia can certainly be made easier by a community of caring people, life with dementia is what it is, and it brings about anguish. The tears of grief are not bad. Weeping can be embarrassingly messy, hence our proclivity to shove over a box of tissues at the first sign of it. These tears help heal the hurt when nothing can change the reason for it. They signal both to the person who cries and to observers the significance of the precipitating cause—how much something matters. They serve as "exclamation marks," according to research on the function of human tears, and provide release from pent-up emotion.[54] Emotional tears, in contrast to the tears we shed in response to eye irritation, contain hormones and other toxins that build during times of stress. Tears release these chemicals in small quantities and stimulate the production of endorphins (a word formed by the contraction of *endogenous* and *morphine*).[55]

There are reasons for discomfort when another person cries. When it happens in public, crying may provoke concomitant embarrassment in onlookers and shame in the person whose composure has crumbled. Whether crying in front of another person, not a crowd, is cathartic depends on that person's response,[56] so counselors learn to view tears as positive, a sign of the transition from holding to releasing pain. Despite this, even the therapists among us may fret and fuss when another person cries, as though stopping the tears will solve the problem, which, according to psychology professor Jay Efran, is like "fixing a car by disconnecting the 'check engine' light."[57]

Scientists sometimes assign convoluted language to common processes. Crying becomes "a complex secretomotor response" involving "the lacrimal apparatus without irritation of the ocular structures," accompanied by "spasms of the truncal muscle groups."[58] But Charles Dickens may have said it best in *Great Expectations*: "Heaven knows we need never be ashamed of our tears, for they are the rain upon the blinding dust of earth, overlying our hard hearts."[59] As ministers, counselors, or friends, we do well to sit quietly through another person's tears, bearing witness to their significance and understanding that we all at times repeat the psalmist's disquieted prayer: "Hear my cry; do not be deaf to my weeping" (Psalm 39:13).

## Prayer

As mentioned earlier in the chapter, our four-component model assumes that pastoral counseling is restricted by other duties and may consist of a single session. Depicted graphically, it would look like the figure below, with prayer throughout the encounter, however long or short. You may notice that the "witness" component is drawn differently from the other elements. Prayer, initiation, and compassionate listening are a part of every counseling encounter, whether the encounter lasts for one session or many. There may not be tears, but witness, or openness to emotional expression, must remain throughout as suggested by its positioning in background of the inner circle.

Prayer occurs (as one might easily infer from the diagram):

A. Before initiation, with the minister's having been made aware of a need
B. Prior to each session
C. During the session, if called for
D. At the close of the session
E. As continuing informed[60] prayer, meaning that following a counseling session, prayer can become more specific given the minister's increased understanding of the situation

A review of the research literature on prayer published over an entire century discusses many types (mystical, prophetic, intercessory, petitionary, prayers of thanksgiving and adoration, and so on) and diverse motivations for it, ranging from neurosis to "a positive means of adjusting to an unusual or baffling situation."[61] Regardless of how we complicate the effort for academic purposes, at its most fundamental level prayer is communication with God. The content of a person's prayers reflects a relationship, necessarily unique and understood by God alone. The best we can offer of ourselves in prayer, according to our old friend Job, is the candid inclinations of our heart,[62] expecting that God most certainly knows, forgives, and loves what is there. We petition from our inmost selves, realizing that what we want is constrained by what we know, which is very little. We are not privy to the whole picture; we know only what we see, feel, and can meaningfully grasp. As the late writer and theologian Frederick Buechner put it, we are little-necked clams trying to understand the universe.[63] But we also pray in awareness that we are heard and that to pray is to build this sacred relationship, thus opening ourselves to ever increasing comprehension of its unspeakable meaning.

Two types of prayer may especially offer comfort to those living with dementia: prayer with awareness of self-limitations and prayer with awareness of God's limitlessness. A minister or pastoral counselor who prays in the conscious awareness of their limitations joins the person with dementia in utter humility: Their prayers are equally shared, offered by the "two or more,"[64] whether the one with dementia comprehends or not; in a true sense, neither does the minister, not fully. Praying with awareness of God's limitlessness infuses the simplest prayer with profound meaning, so the whole of faith is encapsulated in a word or two. Although a person with advanced dementia may no longer understand any prayer, however short and simple, the gentle repetition of a few prayerful words can become soothing and familiar. We trust God to add the missing words, in perfect knowledge of us.

## Awareness of Self-Limitations

Stooped in bed, with gray hair falling about her shoulders in unruly strands and hands like a sparrow's feet, my mother told again an old story about her first real attempt at prayer, the memory of its failure indelible after more than eight decades. She had a baby duck that died. Based on the teachings of her devout, Southern Baptist father, she thought she could pray for anything, and if she prayed with enough faith, it would be done. I don't need to finish this story. She clasped her six-year-old hands together and prayed all night for her pet to come back to life, and in the morning, she found a dead little duck in its box. She never quite got over it, but none of us do. We struggle throughout our lives with how to pray when our hearts are breaking, or we are swamped by worry and doubt. These emotions can overwhelm faith the way storm clouds roll in and occlude the sun, to use a trite analogy. We rely on others; in fact, we often beg others to pray for us—to bring their faith into the weakness we feel in defeating circumstances. The act of asking others for prayer in times of desperation is tantamount to saying along with that father of a mute son, "Lord, I believe. Help my unbelief" (Mark 9:24, NKJV).

When a person senses that her brain is failing, she may pray for healing, which is riskier than praying for strength or help. We must accept that God may be unwilling to heal, and in having asked quite so directly are left feeling bewildered and vulnerable. This is true in any relationship in which we risk asking for what we want, knowing that it may not be forthcoming in the way we hope. Sometimes it's easier not to ask. Nevertheless, we naturally pray for health, whether formally or within our intrinsic desires. It goes without saying, though, that most of us, praying with all the faith we can muster, are not the beneficiaries of visible miracles. Dementia is dementia, the way incurable cancer is cancer, and the course it follows is one of increasing dysfunction. While it is right to pray for healing—in trust of God's unerring goodness—it is certainly wrong to instruct a distraught person that coveted answers to prayer hinge on the amount of faith summoned to the action. Applying common sense to the mustard seed analogy,[65] taken as my grandfather took it, at face value, none of us has great hope of applying a mustard seed's worth of faith to prayers if Jesus's disciples, walking right alongside him every day, lacked even this much.

In the mid-1970s, I stumbled upon the book *Something More* by Catherine Marshall, which set me as much as anything else on a path of deliberate seeking. She writes about the death of her granddaughter, Amy, the second of her three grandchildren to die in infancy. In faith, she summoned a contingent of people to gather and pray intensely for the baby's healing, but Amy died with Marshall sitting beside her hospital crib, less than a week after birth, her body beset by the multiple tubes that had kept her alive for this short time. Marshall writes about the difficulty she had reconciling this death. After many years, she reached a profound, simple conclusion: God is in everything.

Such a truth should bring us comfort, but when we are confronted by tragic, distressing, unexpected, or frightening circumstances, we reach for hope like a life raft amid monster waves, often by beseeching others we perceive as faith-filled to pray for us. Knowing we are, as some say, "covered by prayer" is a comfort if those from whom we seek this help respond with compassion. My husband and I were beside ourselves with worry one night during our infertility saga, and we called a minister to ask him to pray for us. We were in one of those drab, extended-stay hotels, near a medical clinic far from home; we had just received deeply upsetting news. There was a long pause after we revealed the situation to him, the tension building as we hovered over the phone. At length, he said coldly, "I'm not going to pray for some miracle at the lab tonight. I'll pray you have peace about it. I'm willing to pray for that." We mumbled our goodbyes, feeling like we had been shoved in a ditch. I tell this story to illustrate that there is no need, God being in everything, to spell out what we will and won't pray for or to judge the worthiness of a prayer request made in sincerity, even an impossible, dead-duckling sort of prayer. We can keep our prayers simple, filled with compassion and the humility of our limitedness, leaving the rest to God:

> Lord, there is so much we don't understand about suffering and the struggles of this life, but we know we are not alone. You are above, beneath, and within everything. No matter where we go, however dark, or high, or hidden, or deep, you are there.[66] As you prayed to be spared when you faced unimaginable suffering,[67] so we also pray, realizing that we can only see dimly,[68] as we would in a mirror made of polished metal.[69] We may be unable to bring before you even a mustard seed of faith, but still we pray in faith for what we want in our hearts, knowing that as our own prayers fall short, you pray for us.[70] Help us to accept whatever comes, or doesn't, as being fully within your will as our loving father, and give us your peace, which is beyond what any of us can understand.

### Awareness of God's Limitlessness

Some years ago, I was struggling to pray about a specific situation in my life. I couldn't find the right words or bring myself to use the ones that did come to mind. In frustration, I mumbled, "you know," that annoying idiom we use so habitually that it seems more like a verbal tic than a comprehendible expression.

Although we insert the phrase into our speech thoughtlessly, these words aren't meaningless. We all want to be understood and wrestle at times with the limitations of language. Out of the two hundred thousand words at our disposal, we can't come up with an accurate few that don't feel too wrong or risky to say in certain situations. Taken literally, "you know" asserts the entreaty, "I can't figure out how to say what I mean, but you get it. You know. You understand me, don't you?"

As I said the words, I was impressed by a sense of God's knowing and my utter inability to perceive the magnitude of it. God does know. God knows my *very self*—my *inmost being*, when I sit and stand, my thoughts, travels, sleep, unspoken words.[71] God knows how I have existed across time and who I am in relation to every other person and every event, no matter how seemingly inconsequential. God understands my relationships, the origin of my fears, the consequences of my mistakes, my deepest needs. I remembered photos of magnified sand and feeling stunned by the way each grain was beautiful and carefully made.[72] God is beyond our capacity to understand and yet revealed in a grain of sand. I could say "You know" to God and have it mean everything. The words, so simple, became my most powerful prayer—a "grain of sand" that tells the whole impossible mountain. I sometimes say it meditatively, alternating emphasis between words, "*You* know, you *know*," adding a request: "Pray for me, because you know." *You know* is my prayer of petition and relinquishment when I can't find other words. It completes like a prism the words I do manage to say. It expresses my limitedness and God's limitlessness: God understands, I do not.

While this plain prayer helps me deal with my own inadequacies in prayer and could provide a person for whom language skills are slipping away with a means to pray, some people are able, even living with dementia, to pray boldly, pouring out words before God. I uncovered a compelling example of it in a scholarly journal (of all places) with an unusual article documenting the case study of a wife caregiving for a husband with frontotemporal lobe dementia.[73] Studies typically undertake the question of how "religiosity" impacts stress by correlating quantifiable variables, such as frequency of prayer and church attendance, with measures of stress, the more thoughtful researchers admitting the limitations of such an approach to assess with any true accuracy the sincerity of intimacy with God. This study, however, qualitatively assessed the couple's religious coping strategies, based on the caregiver's Catholic beliefs and faith experiences, as well as her husband's personal faith in as much as it could be determined given his condition. The caregiver was a cancer survivor who had not only been healed of her cancer during a Eucharist service, as she convincingly recounts, but also had been reassured by God that both she and her husband were in God's hands. As she remembered it, the words were, "I got you both."[74] Her husband was healthy at the time, so it was only years later that she realized the significance of the revelation.

Throughout her husband's illness, his wife relied on her faith, praying for everything from help with a parking place to coping with her many care-giving challenges. She prayed about becoming upset with her husband and then confessed her guilt, realizing that he did not in his infirmity deserve her anger. She called members of her parish to come and pray with her when her husband disappeared one day for a period of several worrisome hours. She asked the ethnographer documenting their lives to pray with her as she wept one day in frustration over her inability to cope with the many problems she faced alone.

But among the spontaneous prayers, the couple also prayed daily the same long, ritualistic prayer for healing of, literally, everything that could possibly go wrong with their bodies. The husband would hold a hand to his forehead, laying, as his wife explained, his own hands on himself for healing. He died four years after his diagnosis, with his illness progressing; his wife died a year later. But they prayed every day of those years, without discouragement, for a healing that did not come, knowing that God could bring it about at will—had, in fact, done so in their lives once before.

In a weekly address in spring of 2021, Pope Francis addressed the question of why some seemingly worthy prayers go unanswered, to our common discouragement and confusion. He makes the distinction between cultivating a relationship with God through prayer and praying to favorably influence God toward one's own bidding.[75] This couple, who were evidently not accomplished or well-off, at least not by worldly standards, found a way of praying for the miracle they wanted while never doubting the limitlessness of God or the goodness of God's provision. They petitioned God for all kinds of healing but unfailingly ended the prayer with an appeal to "[center] our entire beings with your presence, joy, and peace, and draw us closer to you every moment of our lives," not tempering the earnestness of this closing request by an expectation of the physical healing they desired.[76] They seemed to most fervently want to remain in relationship with God, which is the unassailable reason for prayer.

If it is too challenging for a person with dementia to pray as this couple did, in detail and without self-doubt, I offer another simple prayer I use when I'm beset by a problem or worry significant enough to intrude in my thoughts. I learned this prayer in Ireland, where I spent late summer into winter almost three years after my husband's death. I went there alone and stayed in a huge house overlooking the Loch Corrib, where the wind perpetually howled and rain spattered against tall windows, regularly drenching the load of peat I bought for starting fires. One morning, I discovered that a heavy trampoline had blown into the top of a tree and was left dangling over the garden like a huge broken bird. I was recounting the latest of my problems managing this property to a friend I'd met who was, in a word, powerful, seemingly in every way. "Leave it with me," he said quietly and repeated, "leave it with me." And I knew, without a doubt, that he would take care of the situation. So now when I flail and fret over troubles, I pray this prayer: *Help me leave it with you; I'm leaving it with you.*

## CONCLUSION

Kerrie Hide, a longtime lecturer in mystical theology at Australian Catholic University, confronts in her essay *Symbol Ritual and Dementia* the fear that complete memory loss will as a matter of course erase the ability to live with any conscious memory of God or, most grievously, to take part meaningfully in the act of Holy Communion; cognizant participation requires the memory of its purpose.[77] In explanation and comfort, she invokes the writings of Julian of Norwich, which describe to the extent possible the indescribable "oneness" we all have with God, existing within us as an unerasable memory.[78] Our goal in counseling as ministers and other helpers is to increase awareness, through means of our compassionate listening, witness of emotion, and prayer—our sacred holding—of the truth Hide relates:

> Although the fear of being considered *nothing* can be real in a society that has lost its sense of the divinity of our humanity, ultimately, we are not abandoned when we are most vulnerable. There is at the depth of our being an irrevocable relationship of *oneing* with divine love that can never be destroyed. . . . When people with dementia are supported and encouraged to express glimpses of their relationship with God, they experience a sense of deep connection, comfort, healing, joy, and peace. People with dementia can feel and know: *You hear my prayer* (Psalm 22:24)."[79]

Earlier in the chapter I mention that sacred holding "expands" on client-centered counseling. By this I mean it does not limit counseling to people who are able to participate in a traditional way or who will take the initiative to seek it out. It makes counseling accessible, no matter what. We can compassion-ately listen to anyone, even when they aren't making sense. I had meaningful conversations with Elaine (of chapter 2) although she was never coherent. We communicated through tone of voice, eye contact, and the light, familiar touches we learn to use with each other to convey care. Watched from a distance, it would have looked like normal conversation.

We can provide compassionate witness to anyone's feelings of sadness and loss. I remember a brief connection I had once with a woman who was approaching the mid-stage of Alzheimer's disease. She'd left her house and been found after several hours by the police, hiding in a park a mile or so away. Later that week she was being fitted with an identification bracelet she could not remove. Someone held up her arm; another person clipped on the bracelet; her husband stood watching with a look almost of satisfaction. When they had moved on, she sat, shoulders slumped, staring sadly at the bracelet, so I pulled up a chair beside her. "They thought I was wandering. I wasn't wandering. I was trying to get away from him," she said, cutting her eyes in her husband's direction. Having had some contact with her husband myself, I could readily sympathize with her need for escape. Our eyes met, and I shook my head in commiseration. "I know," I said quietly, "I know." In our lingering eye contact, we shared an understanding of what that moment had meant to her: She was losing both her mind and her autonomy, and she was at the mercy of a man whose interpersonal skills were limited. With dementia, these moments of connection are sometimes all that can be had, but they're just as real in the moment as an hour in a counseling session.

And any one of us benefits from prayer, whether we are the ones praying or for whom prayer is offered. In our "holding" of people who need it, we give tangible expression to that "irrevocable relationship" with divine love—the "oneing" which fully understands, fully accepts, and will fully redeem, and we can be the messengers, as Hide affirms, of connection, comfort, healing, joy, and peace.

## CHAPTER 4

# Preparing the Congregation
# for a Memory Ministry

We've considered dementia from many angles: its physical and emotional impacts, the stress it causes for caregivers and within families, the long-standing grief it brings about, the spiritual quandaries it provokes. It's difficult to cover the bases, spread as they are over the entire landscape of life. We've looked at how ministers and lay leaders can work directly in counseling with people who are coping with dementia. But we must shift now to the challenge of creating a safe haven within the church, where this group, often socially isolated, can come for love and acceptance and to offer their unique gifts.

As I said in the first chapter, I assume in this book that church leaders have made a decision to explore the avenues through which a church may become more dementia friendly. The goal of chapter 4 is to provide a method of assessing the congregation's readiness for the ministry and to begin the process of inspiring a church culture in which people living with dementia feel welcome. I use the word *challenge* because creating a dementia-friendly church will likely require a shift in attitude among members whose instinctive compassion may be overridden by awkwardness, unfamiliarity with dementia, and concern about how this change might affect their own experience of worship and other aspects of congregational life.

The church's commitment to welcome in and succor those who face all kinds of difficulties is not enough to ensure a smooth transition from a community where direct contact with dementia may be quite limited to one in which it is commonplace. Becoming a dementia-friendly congregation is different from, say, hosting a soup kitchen, despite the expense and complexities of such a setup: We can all identify with hunger; we run from dementia.

People over the age of 50 are often more afraid of it than they are of cancer, and this fear may be heightened by personal involvement with others who suffer from it.[1]

If an anticipated change arouses apprehension, it will also provoke resistance, according to Harvard Business School professor Rosabeth Moss Kantor, particularly when people are unprepared for it, or it is fraught with uncertainty and altered routines and programs.[2] Kantor advises anticipating the likely grounds for opposition and developing the plan accordingly, especially seeking input from those most apt to feel threatened.

Churches, like every other institution on earth, are populated by flawed people beset by their own needs and expectations. However, unlike other institutions, churches are guided by an authoritative text that commands love, forgiveness, and equality among people, no matter what their circumstances, and churches have well-established systems by which such ideals are encouraged and supported. While this provides an advantage from the standpoint of motivation, anyone in a leadership role who has tried with the wave of a hand to bring about a change that impacts people (unless it involves an increase in their freedom, time, or money), risks being pilloried. I can personally attest to this, having made the mistake myself. The parishioners are best brought on board before the sails of a new action are flung to the wind.

Dale Ryan, professor of recovery ministry at Fuller Theological Seminary makes a useful point, I think, about the need to establish a relationship between new ministries and the congregation. It requires assessing the political climate of the church, much as we may hate to admit the reality of church politics. "All congregations," he states, "have interest groups, age groups, particularly influential people, and people whose support is critical to the success of any endeavor in the congregation." Cultivating the blessings of these pivotal people and groups involves honest dialogue with the parishioners considered particularly influential in anticipation of their questions and concerns about how the ministry might impact the church.[3]

To move from a few key members to the congregation as a whole, it seems reasonable (in the interest of both ease and finances) to consider the readily available methods by which church leaders inspire positive attitudes and can gauge reactions from people. Worship bulletins are a mode of regular written communication; smaller groups, such as Bible studies and Sunday school classes, allow a forum for discussion; sermons provide a way of conveying a persuasive message to a majority of members. We'll look at surveying the congregation's readiness for a memory ministry, along with activities to involve the congregation in the initial stages of planning and at sermons as a motivating tool.

## A Word about Words

Before we go any further, however, I feel compelled to insert a caveat about the words used in discussing or referring to dementia during sermons, announcements, presentations, and casual conversations, as well as in written material distributed among members. Words matter. Words can unintentionally hurt and alienate.

In the book's introduction, I mention my ordeal with infertility, and I bring it up here to illustrate my point, because this condition brings about social challenges that are similar in some respects to dementia: Infertility is not necessarily obvious; it is isolating; the emotional pain of it causes heightened sensitivity to the reactions and judgments of others; it changes relationships; the awareness of it is constant. Some years after I had accepted the loss—I knew I would not have a child by any means after my husband's suicide, which derailed my plans for adoption—I found myself trapped one Sunday morning by people and their jackets, pocketbooks, and Bibles in the very middle of a pew, listening to a miserable sermon about Mary's elderly relative, Elizabeth. The disgraced Elizabeth, fruitless vine that she was, is a poster child for infertility. My memory is quite vivid due to my discomfort, memory being the inevitably flawed agency it is, I realize. Moments of hurt tend to stick in our minds like barnacles lodged on a rock, while the hours of contentment swim by like schools of fish.

The minister paced to a spot up front and faced us, reading from the book of Luke. "But they had no children because Elizabeth was barren; and they were both well on in years. No children," he repeated, "because Elizabeth was barren." He clenched his jaw for a second or two, as if mustering the resolve to go on, grim duty that it was, given the topic, and drew in a breath. "Barren," he intoned, almost with a flourish. Then, so we could fully absorb the significance of this plight, he became a living thesaurus: "Infertile. Sterile. Childless. Empty." He paused dramatically between each word. "She was incapable of conception," he concluded, with the finality of a judge delivering an awful verdict.

He swept, I guess, from that into a triumphant account of John the Baptist's miraculous birth, but it was lost on me. Each of his words about Elizabeth's infertility caused me to flinch inwardly; I couldn't stop the reflexive pain of it. I was infertile, sterile (by then, anyway), and childless. I felt an emptiness that seemed irreversible. Each word was accurate, but each, save the actual Bible verse, was unnecessary. We all know what the word *barren* means.

We can sympathize with ministers, expected to anticipate the sensitivities of hundreds of people who are essentially strangers, in spite of our metaphorical status as brothers and sisters—the children of one God. But as a people, we are beset by certain hardships common enough to be expressed as subsets of the population. Infertility is one of these. Dementia is another. Such categories should guide us when speaking to strangers. We realize we need help anticipating the sensitivities of others; we see things imperfectly, humans that we are, looking through the darkened glass of faulty perception.[4]

Throughout this book I describe a situation that causes legitimate suffering and produces sufferers. I've suffered because of it. I wouldn't call what my father did, or what I did, watching him waste away and die, anything less. The people we wish to serve suffer; they "suffer" because they have a "dementing disease" that can, as it progresses, "overburden" caregivers. But people do not like to be referred to as *sufferers* (when the term singles them out), or *demented*, or *overburdened*, or *diseased*. These words invoke pity, and no one wants to be pitied—treated with compassion, yes—pitied, no. To create an accepting culture, we must avoid expressions—*senile, impaired, afflicted* and the like— that could make anyone feel the way I did that Sunday so many years ago.

## SURVEYING THE CONGREGATION

Soliciting opinions in advance of a change not only makes the process more seamless but also generates a feeling of involvement from the outset. Survey research is one efficient way to accomplish this task. The main objective of an initial survey is to gain a sense of how prepared a congregation is to embrace the changes a memory ministry will entail. A church in which a large percentage of members have significant personal experience, as indicated by the answer to item one in the survey that follows, may need less preparation. An inexperienced group will require a slower start with more investment in education. As you will see, becoming a dementia-friendly church is a process, and it can stop at any point that seems reasonable for a given church and community. It may be limited to helping members understand what it means to live with dementia so they can better support fellow parishioners who are struggling with it.

If interest has been expressed in having a memory ministry, a logical next step would be for the church leadership to assess how widespread this interest is and whether it can be created among those who might not have considered the idea before. The task, then, becomes formulating discriminatory questions that will predict how members might react to an influx of new attenders living with dementia. Such a survey should be set in motion by a steering committee with an advance plan in place to enable interpretation of the results. While this point may seem obvious, according to Gallup Workplace, a global analytics firm, many organizations with good intentions collect data only to become trapped in "analysis paralysis" and fail to use it effectively.[5] No one wants to be sitting glumly at a conference table, sifting through an intimidating pile of completed forms with no decent way of synthesizing the information.

Think of the following sample survey as a starting point, revising it as necessary for your purposes. I advise conducting a small pilot study at the outset to determine whether the survey adequately answers the questions most relevant to the plans and ideas you have in mind. As designed, this survey contains items that will determine the congregation's familiarity with dementia, as well as their initial concerns and willingness to become involved. Be sure to set the stage for the survey by informing the congregation ahead of time of its purpose as an initial inquiry to gain information and gauge congregational interest. Have a caregiver speak in a brief "mission moment" about dementia caregiving to help members perceive the need for an initiative.

### Sample Survey: A Dementia-Friendly Church—Are We Ready?

*Questions for Members and Dedicated Visitors*

One of our purposes as a church is to love and serve our community. Our clergy and church leaders have become aware that many neighbors in our community are living with dementia. "Living with dementia" means either they've been diagnosed with a medical condition that causes it, or they are caregivers. We can share God's love by offering a comfortable place for these neighbors to come and worship with us, and for friendship and support. But we need your input as we consider how to become more dementia-friendly as a church. Please help us by completing this 5-minute questionnaire and placing it in one of the designated boxes on your way out.[6] Thank you for sharing your thoughts and opinions.

1. Mark the statement that best describes your experience with dementia.

_____ None, other than what I've learned through the media.

_____ I have a friend, relative, or acquaintance living with dementia. My contact with them is infrequent.

_____ I am providing (or have in the past provided) regular help to a loved one or friend living with dementia.

_____ I work professionally or volunteer with people who have dementia or are caregivers, or I have in the past.

_____ I am living with dementia.

*Fill in a different answer or add to your answer.*[7] _____

_____

2. Mark any questions below that are important to you. Make a star beside the one that is most important.

_____ Is *any* form of dementia contagious or transmissible between people?

_____ Will our worship services change? If so, how?

_____ How do I interact with a person whose dementia is noticeable? What if we aren't understanding each other?

_____ Will a memory ministry require any additional staffing or resources?

Do you have other thoughts, questions, or concerns?

_____

_____

3. Tell us how important it is to you to provide a memory ministry at this church.

☐ Highly important
☐ Moderately important
☐ Low importance
☐ Not important

4. Below is a list of service opportunities other churches with memory ministries offer. Mark any that interest you.

_____ Greeting, guiding, and assisting at worship services and other activities

_____ Volunteering in a respite program for people with early-stage dementia (*Note*: Respite programs provide short-term relief to caregivers by providing a safe, enjoyable place where they can leave a loved one for a few hours of care.)

_____ Helping with a caregiver support group

_____ Helping with dementia-friendly worship services

_____ Serving in coffee hours or luncheons caregivers can attend with their loved ones

_____ Visiting the homebound, delivering meals, or helping with home maintenance and tasks

_____ Helping to prepare or distribute educational and outreach materials

_____ Truthfully, none of the above

5. Would you attend a few educational sessions about dementia, if they were held during the Sunday school hour or at another convenient time?  YES  NO  MAYBE

6. Additional comments: _____
_____
_____
_____
_____

7. What is your age?[8]

_____ 12–17
_____ 18–35
_____ 35–65
_____ 65+

8. What is your gender?  MALE  FEMALE[9]

## Why These Questions?

The rationale behind selected items is explained below to help with interpreting the results:

1. *Experience with Dementia.* Knowing—even caring about—a person living with dementia is not enough to ensure that you can relate meaningfully to its hardships. I've had more than a few frustrating conversations with friends who knew the fact of my caregiving but nothing about the stress and problems involved. The majority of their comments about my experience began with the well-intentioned words, "Why don't you . . . ?", and the majority of my responses began, "because it would be impossible" or "because I've already tried it, and it didn't work." It was exhausting for both of us, like being trapped in the spin cycle of a washing machine. People who have not walked a mile in the shoes of a caregiver (the first two responses) cannot appreciate the demands of the role and will almost certainly need preparation before they are able to give support to those actually traveling this difficult road. Chapters 5 and 6 contain educational activities church leaders can use to provide this preparation.

2. *Questions and Concerns.* Item two assumes resistance to change based on certain identifiable factors. The choice of answers is limited to these factors, along with the option of an unstructured response. An alternative such as "I don't have any questions or concerns. I support this ministry" can be added, but it might invite a socially desirable if not completely candid answer. The choices included in this item cover reasons for resistance to change identified by Rosabeth Kantor: a genuine sense of threat, the differences the change may bring about, concerns about feeling incompetent, and fear of unanticipated consequences.[10]

   - **Is any form of dementia contagious or transmissible?** While revealing a deal-breaking source of resistance for some, the selection of this question also suggests misinformation. Progressive dementias aren't contagious by any common means. Creutzfeldt-Jakob dementia, which afflicts about one in a million people, has been rarely linked to neurosurgical instruments. Beta amyloid protein, one of the main cellular pathologies of Alzheimer's disease, has been found at autopsy in a relatively small group of people exposed during the 1950s to injections of contaminated brain tissue from cadavers meant to correct a severe deficiency of growth hormone during childhood and adolescence.[11] Research of late has linked (not yet causally) Alzheimer's pathology to microbes—specifically, spirochetes and common strains of the herpes virus—to which many of us are exposed in daily living,[12] and bits and pieces of this research trickle into nonscientific articles and interpretations, sometimes causing needless fear. If many people mark this question, their responses indicate the need to start a dementia ministry with basic education.

- **Will our worship service change?** The second option provides an acceptable way of expressing the concern that people with symptomatic dementia may occasionally disturb services. We like to think, of course, that we're above this sort of self-interest when the interference cannot be helped, but the fact is that people vary in their levels of distractibility. I recall being quite irritated one Sunday morning at two women who sat behind me and chatted quietly for the whole hour. I wanted, literally, to swat them with my church bulletin. If many members mark this item, it would underscore the need for church leaders to accommodate in their planning both people who can no longer sit in silence and those who require a quiet setting in which to worship.

- **How do I interact with a person whose dementia is noticeable?** This option addresses the awkwardness we feel when normal mores and the ways we connect interpersonally no longer apply. I took part in a radio program on Alzheimer's, and when we broke for a commercial, one of the sound engineers jerked off his headset and asked me with surprising urgency, "But what do you say if they're not making any sense?" His question and the unease behind it are common in those who haven't been around people with dementia. As suggested in the previous item, some are more able than others to simply go with the moment. But awkwardness can be largely allayed through education. Indeed, the idea underpinning all of my work is that understanding leads to comfort and acceptance.

- **Will this initiative require any additional staffing or resources?** The fourth option relates to trust and feasibility. Members of the planning committee that issues the survey will no doubt have considered in advance questions of budget and scope, as will be discussed in chapter 7, and how the addition of new programs might inadvertently affect the existing ones. This item on the survey indicates the need to make transparent the planning behind the initiative and the intention to gain approval from the congregation before making changes that will impact them.

3. *Interest in the work of a dementia ministry.* The success of any ministry requires participation from members who are engaged in the work of it, and a memory ministry will require a certain level of acceptance from everyone.

## Getting an Adequate Response

There are ways to encourage people to fill out questionnaires. Precontacting is a strategy that increases response rate. It could be an announcement or note in the calendar or bulletin the week before: "Next week you'll find a survey in your bulletin. Please allow a few extra minutes after the service to complete it. We are considering a new ministry to those in our community who are living with dementia, and your thoughts and opinions are important."

Another is by expressing gratitude openly and sincerely—having, for instance, an usher beside each receptacle into which completed surveys are placed, to thank every single person who deposits one, if they are collected after a large gathering. A recent study in the *Journal of Personality and Social Psychology* confirms that those who see others being thanked are more willing, themselves, to be similarly helpful.[13] If surveys are conducted by email, reply with a bright, visually attractive thank-you message. Small acts of appreciation can have big effects: Gratitude increases feelings of social value and the tendency toward helpfulness in the future,[14] a bonus to any new venture that requires the support and goodwill of others in order to be successful. Also, length matters. Keep the survey short, particularly if it is a pen-and-paper survey. People who are eager after a service to attend coffee hour or to leave are not likely to spend more than several minutes hovering over a form, no matter how grateful the ushers are.

# Administering the Survey

The method of administration depends on whether questionnaires will be extended to an entire survey population or to cluster groups within it. Conducting a pen-and-paper survey of a large church may be unrealistic even if a representative sample is drawn from the results to avoid an unwieldy amount of data. For a church of 1,000 members, for example, 278 randomly selected surveys would be necessary to ensure that the results are usable with some certainty.[15] There are mathematical methods that can be applied to achieve such a sample, thus providing generalizable results,[16] but the idea of initially surveying so many people may make the steering committee's collective eyes glaze over. Some churches are small enough to survey efficiently as a whole, but churches also have readily available groups with somewhat homogenous characteristics, such as gender- or age-based Bible studies, which enable a form of cluster sampling.

We will consider two methods, surveying the entire church or selected cluster groups within it, and how each method can be accomplished, realizing that we do not want to become bogged down in tedious research. Our goal here is only to gain a reasonably correct idea of church members' attitudes and to let the information they provide inform subsequent planning and educational efforts.

## Surveying Everyone

Most of us rely on the weekly worship bulletin to guide us through services: We are told when to sing, listen, pray, and read aloud. We find out about upcoming events and programs, budget shortages, and staff changes. We may find space for notetaking or pictures for restless children to color. It's an impressive role for one little leaflet. For our purposes, the bulletin can be used to convey a survey to fill out before leaving the sanctuary.

The pre-Covid church had already embraced certain media platforms. By 2018, 84 percent of Protestant churches had websites and Facebook pages.[17] Predictably, the larger the church, the greater the use of technology to disseminate information and exchange messages.[18] Social media methods that involve public posting must be used carefully, however, if at all, as a means of gaining insight into attitudes about dementia. Wrongly, dementia is "socially discrediting," to use a term coined by sociologist Erving Goffman, and the feeling, among those living with it, of being stigmatized, even by friends, is common.[19] Querying peoples' thoughts about dementia is best done privately, through a survey tucked into the time-honored church bulletin, emailing the survey to members individually, or providing a direct link to it from a digital communication to the congregation. Digital methods would make data analysis easier but might favor certain demographic groups.[20] As far as soliciting information through Facebook, Instagram and the like, it goes without saying that people can be astonishing (and astonishingly outspoken) in their viewpoints. I am reminded of an incident that happened well before social media provided us a means of delivering our impetuous opinions to the world at large. I was part of a church advisory committee, and we were thinking of ways in which church could be made more accessible. A soft-spoken, older man named Henry raised his hand.

"I think," he ventured, "that having Bibles in the pews, so we can follow the Scripture lessons better would be a good thing." You could have heard a pin drop. A woman sitting across the room straightened her back and pursed her lips.

"Well," she replied in a forbidding tone, "I frankly think all of this rifling through the Bible would be quite distracting." She shuffled some papers in her lap, as if to demonstrate. She must have held sway with the group (she would have had many online followers, no doubt). Henry's idea was quickly shelved. It isn't a leap of imagination to anticipate how she might have reacted had Henry suggested inviting potentially unquiet people with dementia into the weekly worship services or how hurtful her comments, broadcast over social media, could be to those living with the condition and their extended family in the congregation.

A questionnaire in which people are obligated to sit and think for a minute, sharing their ideas in longhand, may yield the most valid information. We've become accustomed to tweeting, liking, and commenting with little deliberation, and, as humans, we are primed to connect quickly, even to our disadvantage.[21] Research indicates that people are simply more honest with pen and paper in hand than they are tapping away online.[22]

## Using Cluster Groups to Conduct a Survey

If conducting a survey online or through worship bulletins is not doable, then Sunday school classes and similar church groups can be surveyed instead.

Use the survey questions to facilitate a discussion of views and experiences. Such breakout groups offer an advantage when seeking representative opinions, especially when an exchange of ideas is the group's norm. They're a handy microcosm of the congregation the minister observes from the pulpit, communicating through inexplicit indicators such as facial expressions and body language.

The following is an activity you can use to conduct the survey in a small group and use it afterward as a tool for discussion and prayer:

1. Administer the survey anonymously.
2. Lead a discussion based on questions one through five (assuming use of the sample survey supplied by this book):

   - **Experience with dementia.** (1) How many of you have a family member or friend living with dementia, or have had in the past? What is or was it like for them? For you? (2) Have any of you been caregivers, and can you describe the experience for us? (3) Dementia usually begins slowly, and the symptoms are not obvious at first. When we think about dementia, often we imagine a person at an advanced stage when many abilities have been lost, but dementia usually goes along slowly, developing over years and years. Ralph Waldo Emerson died with dementia, probably Alzheimer's. As he began to experience its symptoms, he wrote the poem *Terminus*. (Read the poem aloud, at least the last verse, or provide copies.[23]) What does it mean? How does the fact that Emerson could write it when he did fit with our ideas of dementia? What does it tell us about the gifts people with dementia can share?

   - **Questions and concerns**. (1) What concerns do you have about our church beginning a memory ministry? (2) What questions do you want to have answered? (Discuss and either provide answers to questions immediately if you can, or record the questions to supply answers as quickly as possible.)

   - **Becoming dementia friendly**. There are different ways of becoming a dementia-friendly church. The questionnaire listed some services other churches provide, but it can be a matter of simply learning more about it so we can support our own members who are living with dementia—as a person who's been diagnosed, a caregiver, a relative, or a friend. It may be developing new approaches to worship that better serve people with dementia. When you read the list of service options—helping with a respite program, leading a support group, hosting meals, helping homebound caregivers with tasks— were there any that especially interested you? Why or why not? If the church were to provide education, what would you most want to learn? (Make note of the suggestions.)

3. Ask: What are some Bible verses or concepts that can guide us as we consider ways to become dementia friendly at our church. Here are two examples. Can you think of others?

- *To guide us as we anticipate what people living with dementia can bring into our lives*: Henri Nouwen (1932–1996) was a Catholic priest who taught at the University of Notre Dame, Yale Divinity School, and Harvard Divinity School. He was a prolific, brave, self-revealing writer. After his teaching career closed, he chose to work caring for a profoundly handicapped man, Adam, until Adam's death. Reflecting on this experience, Nouwen mused, "I was facing once again my question, 'What do I believe?' Then I became aware that this was a question Adam could help me answer.... Adam, who never spoke a word, gradually became a true source of words for me to express my deepest conviction as a Christian, living at the turn of the second millennium. He, who was so vulnerable became a powerful support to help me announce the richness of Christ. And he, who could not expressly recognize me, would, through me, help others recognize God in their lives."[24] What does this quote say to you about our interconnectedness and need for each other. How does it show us a living example of God's promise, "My grace is sufficient for you. My power is made perfect in weakness" (2 Corinthians 12:9, NIV).

- *To guide us in our efforts to start any new ministry, whatever the focus*: "For I am the Lord, your God, who takes hold of your right hand and says to you, do not fear; I will help you" (Isaiah 41:13, NIV).

4. Close in prayer. This is a prayer I might say:

God, help us understand what you have to teach us about love and compassion. You ask us not to fear, but we do. We fear many things in this life. Some of us fear dementia. Help us, as we consider this new way of sharing and accepting your love, to know that we are never alone. You are helping us and guiding us into right actions, and feelings, and words. This life can seem so long, like an eternity when we struggle with our own pain and problems, but it's not long. We don't have long to do what you've asked us to do—to live in a way that shows your love—and we make a lot of mistakes. Help us do whatever you put before us, to run your race, our race, without becoming tired or losing heart.

## An Introductory Video Series to Follow the Survey

In a sense, I view my role in writing this book as a curator of materials currently available and easily accessed. The need for dementia-friendly churches that offer inviting places in which everyone can take part has been recognized and various teaching tools developed by individuals who've walked the walk, or as Kenneth Carder would put it, danced the dance of dementia. Carder is a retired bishop with the United Methodist Church and professor emeritus in Christian ministry at Duke Divinity School. He is the author of several books, including *Ministry with the Forgotten: Dementia Through a Spiritual Lens*.[25] Carder freely offers us a set of downloadable videos, running between eight and twenty-three minutes each, which provide a sensitive, insightful introduction to becoming a dementia-friendly church. An accompanying study guide outlines an hour-long teaching session for each video. The study guide takes the guesswork out of presenting the videos: An instructor can preview videos and use the corresponding section guides to prepare. These materials are based on Carder's twelve years as caregiver to his wife, Linda, who died with advanced frontotemporal lobe dementia.

His book, entitled *Ministry with the Forgotten*, enlarges upon these educational sessions, and I recommend its addition to the church library. Information on Carder's book and a list of other suggested books for the library are in appendix 1.

Carder found himself transformed, as he lived through the changes in Linda, into a person who could love without an expectation of reciprocity or even a response, and in this, he says, she gave him one of the most important gifts of his life. "I wasn't dependent on her responding, so that I just . . .," he hesitates, his voice trailing off, "loved her."[26] As Linda lost her ability to feed and dress herself, to brush her teeth and comb her hair, and as she progressed through stages of aggression and paranoia when she failed to recognize him, he realized that her acceptance of his continued love was, in and of itself, an act of love.

He learned that Linda was his teacher, that through her, his concepts of love and self-worth were expanding. Carder overturns the notion that we, as church members, should serve "these poor folks" with dementia through cookbook-type programs: They are, he says, a means of grace to us. We worship *with* not *for* or *to*, looking beyond the messiness and pain of dementia, and perceiving the ministry as a mutual blessing. There is not a better starting point for such a ministry. The video series walks its viewers through basic information about dementia and the theological underpinnings of such a ministry. To download *Alzheimer's/Dementia: Ministry with the Forgotten*[27] videos and the study guide, conveniently available in both regular and large-print editions, follow this link: https://encoreministry.org, and navigate to the resources page.

> What are the gifts that people with dementia offer to the church? Their very presence exposes our idols of intellectualism and personal autonomy and reminds us that the essence of human identity and worth lies in God's grace. Their authenticity and genuineness strip away our own pretense and rigidity. They teach us the value of each moment and call forth our empathy, compassion, and patience. They break down the distinctions of age, class, race, and capacities, which routinely separate us, and help to form us into the body of Christ, a visible sign of God's reign of compassion, generosity, hospitality, and justice. —Kenneth Carder, (*Ministry with the Forgotten*, 106)

## SERMONS

From this book's introduction, you might gather that I've listened to many sermons, given by many ministers. I have even listened to sermons in French, Portuguese, and Italian, none of which I speak. Sermons are one of the main ways ministers inspire churchgoers and thus should be central in the effort to create a dementia-friendly church culture. A passionate sermon that rings true can change the way people think and feel toward each other. For a 14-minute demonstration of it, watch Bishop Michael Curry's sermon about the transformative power of love, made to the auspicious congregation present at Meghan Markle and Prince Harry's royal wedding in 2018. Summing up "everything God has been trying to tell the world," Curry said, as though talking to his closest friends, "Love God, love your neighbors, and while you're at it?" He paused and added in a hushed voice, "Love yourself."[28] They were charmed by him and challenged, or so it seemed.

Admittedly, dementia is a harder topic to tackle than love, no matter what the disposition of the listeners. Love is something people desire, not a dreaded condition most expect to face but are loath to contemplate before circumstance demands it of them. According to the 2019 World Alzheimer's Report, 95 percent of people believe they could themselves develop dementia during their lifetimes, yet many with the condition reported feeling shunned and rebuffed by friends and strangers alike.[29] Even in medical settings, where knowledge and experience are relatively high in comparison to a church, patients with dementia experience isolation and discrimination.[30]

And we know that entrenched attitudes are hard to sway. Our attitudes are integral to our self-concept and have actually been compared to physical possessions we cherish and would presumably defend.[31] But sermons are meant among other aims, to confront attitudes lodged in ignorance, discomfort, and fear. Rather than helping us feel good about our lives, Jesus tells us he came into the world not to bring peace but a sword.[32] Change that demands a revision of self-protective beliefs and comfortable habits inevitably causes uneasiness.

Based on research examining the persuasiveness of sermons, ministers would do well to help their parishioners envision the ways in which a dementia ministry can further the church's identity as a place where people in trouble obtain comfort and help.[33] There is optimistic evidence, though not without contradiction,[34] that people are, in fact, changed by what they hear from the pulpit, particularly in their willingness to reach out to others who are lonely or in need,[35] and that these changes are encouraged by use of specific approaches, such as storytelling and personal appeal on the part of the minister.[36]

The Bible says little about dementia[37] upon which to base a sermon, but sermons about any affliction can be built around the myriad verses telling us to love, comfort, and care for the vulnerable, to bear patiently with each other, and to act out of selflessness. Here are verses that I believe could be used more specifically in a sermon about dementia, and why:

- "You yourselves are our letter, written on our hearts, known and read by everybody. You are a letter from Christ . . . written not in ink but with the Spirit of the living God, not on tablets of stone but on tablets of human hearts" (2 Corinthians 3:3, NIV). Taken in context, this verse is Paul's comparison of the new covenant to the old, but it also tells us who we are in God, beyond words and laws: We are living letters. Think of the verse speaking to us about our role among people with dementia, who have lost (or are losing) the ability to understand language: *If I have dementia and can no longer speak and read, you are my living letter from Christ. I still understand love. I can see and feel your love in the way you look at me and interact with me.*

- "He defends the cause of the fatherless and the widow, and loves the foreigner residing among you, giving them food and clothing. And you are to love those who are foreigners, for you yourselves were foreigners in Egypt" (Deuteronomy 10: 18–19, NIV). Many of us have had an "Egypt" in our lives, a circumstance in which we felt powerless or unwelcome, and from which we wished to be liberated. We've been to foreign countries where we couldn't figure out how to use money or where to buy what we needed. For people with advanced dementia, the familiar world becomes a foreign place, where nothing makes sense. Fundamentally, these are the people we are told to defend, protect, welcome, and love in gratitude for God's care of us.

- "If I say, 'Surely the darkness will hide me and the light become night around me,' even the darkness will not be dark to you; the night will shine like day, for the darkness is like light to you. For you created my inmost being; you knit me together in my mother's womb" (Psalm 139:11–13, NIV). We see a person with dementia, or we imagine ourselves with dementia, and it's hard not to perceive mainly what has been lost. We associate loss and grief with darkness. But where we see darkness, God sees light. In Psalm 139, God describes seeing our unformed bodies in the darkness of the womb and all of our days, laid out, before even one day has been lived. We can't understand this kind of seeing, but we can see people living with dementia, especially in the later stages, as existing outside bodily restrictions, which are temporary in the eyes of God, who promises to make everything new.[38] For God, one day is like a thousand of our years;[39] the eighty or ninety years we live on earth are barely a fragment of eternity.

- "For just as we share abundantly in the sufferings of Christ, so also our comfort abounds through Christ" (2 Corinthians 1:5, NIV). In an earlier section of this chapter, "A Word about Words," I discuss the reason to avoid terms that separate and marginalize, and one of these is "suffer." But words like *suffer* and *affliction* are used throughout the Bible. They don't stigmatize when used to refer to the human state, rather than uniquely to people living with dementia. We all suffer in this life, some more than others. And if our lives are relatively easy, we still feel the threat of loss. As Christians, we've been given the example of ultimate suffering and the gift of ultimate redemption. There is no shame in suffering, because we know the one in whom we trust, and in whom we've believed.[40] Suffering unites us in our shared condition of fragility and dependence on God. As God's people, we are called to help each other through hard times, to be "like a shelter from the wind" (Isaiah 32:2). We can become more sturdy shelters for others by learning something about circumstances they face that we have not, ourselves, been through. We learn about dementia, not to single out those who live with it as "sufferers," distinct in some bad way, but to claim our common humanity and need and to offer meaningful comfort.

- "For I was hungry and you gave me something to eat, I was thirsty and you gave me something to drink, I was a stranger and you invited me in, I needed clothes and you clothed me, I was sick and you looked after me, I was in prison and you came to visit me. Then the righteous will answer him, 'Lord, when did we see you hungry and feed you, or thirsty and give you something to drink? When did we see you a stranger and invite you in, or needing clothes and clothe you? When did we see you sick or in prison and go to visit you?' The King will reply, 'Truly I tell you, whatever you did for one of the least of these brothers and sisters of mine, you did for me'" (Matthew 25:35–40, NIV). If I were giving a sermon to support the idea of becoming a dementia-friendly church, I would base it on this passage from Matthew because it allows me to share how I've come to understand God through the experiences of my life. More importantly, though, when we look at a person whose brain has failed, we tend to see only a person who can no longer feed herself, or speak, or read, or go for a walk alone. I want to encourage people, instead, to make a conscious effort to look beyond the limitations and see nothing less than God, who lived confined in a human body, during a human lifetime, and who continues to live intimately with us, experiencing our restrictions as his own, working within and though our lives, no matter what. I've written the sermon; you can find it at the end of this chapter.

## CONCLUSION

Research indicates, as we've seen, that organizational change is accomplished more easily when it furthers the organization's identity.[41] To encourage support for a memory ministry in your church, be sure to emphasize how it will increase the church's outreach to the community and provide loving fellowship to people who need it—sometimes desperately. The survey and related activities of this chapter are meant to help you determine what information parishioners may require in order to better understand dementia and to feel, when confronted by it, compassion rather than awkwardness or resistance. They are not intended to convey the sense that becoming dementia friendly will make the church different, only more in keeping with its central mission. I would encourage the term I use, *informed compassion*, to explain why we must engage in advance learning and preparation rather than by simply leaping in: Unless you've lived with dementia yourself in a meaningful way, you may have little ability to comprehend the struggle of it. The next two chapters focus on further preparation for the congregation and individuals who will work closely within the ministry in whatever ways it may unfold.

\* \* \*

## SERMON TO ENCOURAGE A MEMORY MINISTRY

In the name of the Father, and of the Son, and of the Holy Spirit. Amen.[42]

Ages ago—it almost feels like a different lifetime—I worked for several large school systems, and in my role, I visited many elementary school classrooms. I went into a fourth-grade class one day, and to my surprise, the children at their desks were divided into two groups with a mark made out of tape down the floor, separating them as though by means of an imaginary fence. I glanced from one group to the other and then at the teacher. She walked over, stood beside me, and drew an apologetic breath. "You're wondering why the room is set up like this," she began and swept her hand toward one group, "Well, these are the doers." There was a laudatory list of what the doers did: "They pay attention in class, they do their homework, they cooperate." She paused to drive the point home, then swung around with narrowed eyes and pointed to the other group. "But these are the do-nothings. They do nothing because they are nothing." She emphasized the words "are nothing." There was a list of the ways these children had failed.

I was appalled and saddened for those children sitting glumly in the do-nothing group. You are, too, most likely. But you see the parallel, crude though it is, between the passage we just read and this class. In frustration, the teacher had separated her students into sheep and goats. It's easy to condemn her—correct, we know, to condemn that particular behavior—but in doing so, we also condemn ourselves.[43] Very few us go through life without a hint of sheep and goat mentality, whether we admit it or not. As adults, we try not to impose this kind of harsh judgment on children, but we do judge, and our judgments deliberately push certain people toward the margins.

Look at what we value and respond to in others—beauty, wealth, intelligence, power, competence. In our society, these are the more obvious wellheads of status. I'm as guilty as anyone else. I look at the way people dress, although I am most often wearing jeans and sneakers; I make snap judgments based on minimal, even inaccurate information about people, while wishing I could deflect, by explaining myself, that same kind of judgment from others.

Join a group of any size, and you may find yourself subtly appraised according to some covert standard and nudged into one of two pens, sheep or goats. I spoke with a single mother who homeschooled three children ranging in age from five to fifteen, while working to support these children. She told me that within her local community, she felt snubbed because she used readymade lesson plans, instead of creating them herself. It was a status symbol among the homeschooling parents to eschew use of the generic plans readily available online. Why? There's no logic in such an idea, but we humans do this kind of sorting, whether it makes sense and is kind and reasonable, or not. In today's passage, God—who alone has the right to judge—does the sorting.

But here's the difference: God uses only one discriminatory measure, and it's not based on how you look or what you have. It's based only on the failure of compassion, on God's ability to see through to the heart, to our deeper motivations.[44] God tells us in today's passage to *act* with compassion toward those with evident needs; He tells us in an earlier chapter in Matthew's gospel that we have neither the right nor the ability to judge.[45] We learn from this passage how close God is to us in our suffering. He identifies with people who are hungry, thirsty, lonely, sick, naked. He says to us: This is who I am; I live within your suffering; I experience it with you.

God's merging, binding identification with suffering separates Christianity from other religions and from other ways of being spiritual—the suffering in our stead, for our sake.

I became a Christian, I thought, when I was in my early twenties, following some years of soul searching. I had always felt drawn to God. As a child, I knelt beside my canopy bed and tried to teach myself how to pray. And it worked. I said little prayers, and I memorized the Apostles' Creed. I learned to sing all four verses of "Holy, Holy, Holy." But just before I went to college, I experienced one of those sharp moments that you remember: They mark a turning point, one road or the other that you have to choose. I was standing in our kitchen at home, holding the refrigerator door open to look for a snack, and a strong thought broke into my consciousness, seemingly from nowhere: Is there really a God? Is God real?

I knew instinctively that the answer to this question would determine the rest of my life and that I had a choice about whether or not to answer the question. I sensed that the answer might be dangerous. I sensed the power of the answer—one way or the other. So, the choice was, do I look, or do I turn away from the looking?

The short version of it is that about five years later, I answered an altar call at my home church, where, disarmingly, they made everything about religion seem very comfortable. There was a long green velvet cushion that ran down the length of the altar, so you weren't kneeling on the hard floor, and a place to rest your elbows when you prayed. But I remember saying with all the sincerity I could bring into it, "I give you my life," and feeling both the gravity and the release of making that statement.

Of course, I learned that this doesn't just happen once; your whole life isn't given in one breath or one utterance, even though it felt that way, that day. It's a matter of many choices every day. The commitment is to the God who gives us the choices and forgives when we don't make the best ones.

Twenty years passed before I stepped into the fuller meaning of what it is to be a Christian. I had, over the relatively short course of about eighteen months, experienced multiple losses, and everything I didn't lose, it seemed, was threatened: Both of my dogs died; I suffered a head injury in a horseback riding accident; my father had the first of the strokes that would leave him, in the end, suffering from vascular dementia. I miscarried my only pregnancy—after five years of infertility treatment; I went through a fourth failed IVF, this one done surgically, in an operating room across the country. My husband had a nine-hour brain surgery—also three thousand miles from home—for a rare type of brain tumor. We were uncertain in the aftermath how full his recovery would be; he struggled continually with complications brought about by a severed nerve. I had a botched surgery that left me with no hope, then, of having children, ever. My husband died by suicide two months later, and I found his body hanging from a doorjamb. That's not all, and it didn't stop there. I remember once holding a pillow up to my face a couple of years later, screaming into it, over and over.

After my husband's suicide, I felt like I had been eviscerated, everything about my body was numb and cold for weeks on end—like I had ice water running through my veins, and I would never be warm again. I believed I would never smile again. For a long time, I couldn't even go into our bedroom. I couldn't wear clothes that reminded me of places we had gone. When I could finally enter the master bedroom, I resolutely avoided Wayne's closet. I left it shut, wouldn't touch the doorknob. But one day, I thought, I have to open that closet. I can't go on living in this state of avoidance, trying to control and contain pain. The grief was so intense, my heart physically hurt, ached, every minute of every day, as though it was caught in a vice. I reasoned; how much worse could it be? Can I hurt more than this?

Well, the answer was yes, I could.

I opened the closet door, and there were Wayne's shoes, where he had left them. His ties, the one he had last worn still tied, his shirts. His closet had a window with wooden blinds that had gotten very dusty, and the particles of dust were sifting steadily through shafts of sunlight, almost as though marking time, as if you could see time pass, inexorably but far too slowly. Everything was just like he had left it, like he might be coming home soon. I fell to my knees, and crossed my arms over my chest, trying, literally I thought, to keep my body and soul in one piece; I felt like I was coming apart, that I was being torn apart. And I said out loud, without thinking, from somewhere deep inside, "God, Almighty. I could not worship a God who hadn't suffered." That was when, I think, I became (using the word more poetically than literally) a Christian. In that closet, in my grief.

Fleming Rutledge, who is a prolific author and one of the first women ordained by the Episcopal church, wrote a book entitled *The Crucifixion* that left me, as few books do, in a state of true awe. Over six hundred pages long, and I felt myself almost clinging to every word. And I am an easily distracted, critical, impatient reader—the kind of reader book authors can't stand. Her writing is never clearer than when she describes the experience of crucifixion, with its excruciating physical pain and the intent on the part of the executioner to dehumanize—to strip away, through this unspeakable punishment, the humanity of the person undergoing it, to relegate the victim to a lower species. It's hard to read and impossible to imagine.[46]

We worship a God who has suffered and who suffers with us, who asks us to express our love for him by reaching out to people who need help, in utter humility—without letting your right hand know what your left hand is doing.[47]

In this church, we're contemplating a broad outreach to people who are struggling with dementia. Dementia isn't easy. It isn't so much about physical needs, like hunger or thirst. It's more about understanding and reacting with compassion to people who are becoming strangers within their own minds, within their own homes and neighborhoods. They can feel stigmatized, cut out and pushed to the margins, even by friends. It's about helping caregivers who are going down this hard road alongside a loved one, caring for them, eventually, day and night.

We can quibble and debate—many biblical scholars have—about what our sheep and goat passage means exactly: Are "the least of these my brethren" Jesus's disciples, are they persecuted Jews, or the poor in general? Does "all the nations" refer to gentiles only or to all people, every one of us, in end times?[48] And what's so bad about goats, anyway? As theologian Ian Paul points out, in rabbinic literature, goats are at least as valuable as sheep.[49] I personally am most bothered by the image of the "eternal fire prepared for the devil and his angels,"[50] imagining myself sitting squarely in the middle of those do-nothing goats, if my salvation hinges on good behavior (and as I would have been in fourth grade, careless student that I was). But worthwhile as it is to be precise and to call into question our understanding of Scripture, we don't want to miss the forest for the trees by getting too caught up in these questions.

This is what I think the God of my late husband's closet would say about what we are trying to do: *I am right in front of you, in every person who suffers. Look at me. Take care of me. Learn from me.*

*I'm the one who is humming and whistling. I'm the one who doesn't understand the sermon. I'm the one who can no longer use my fork. I might use my fingers.*

Or *I'm the one who is facing that kind of decline, who fears it. I've feared. I feared so terribly once that I sweated drops of blood.*

Or *I'm the caregiver who just wants to get away, so tired I can fall asleep in a boat, in a violent storm.*[51]

*Look at me. I am right in front of you. And I suffered and died for you—for every single one of you—equally.*

AMEN.

# CHAPTER 5

# Educating the Congregation

A few years before his death, my husband was elected to a term as an elder in our church. Just after his confirmation, we were at coffee hour following a worship service in which the "Special Choir" had sung. This choir consisted of about fifteen people from a group home in the neighborhood. They attended church almost every Sunday and apparently relished most especially the few Sundays of the year in which they robed and served as our choir. The music was tuneless and unintelligible, but it was undeniably joyful. As my husband and I stood balancing our cake and coffee, we noticed a man, a wealthy, prominent man, torpedoing his way through the crowd toward us. After a cursory greeting, he glared at my husband with flinty eyes.

"I come to church," he said, through jaws almost clenched in annoyance, "to be edified. I don't come to listen to disabled people attempting to sing. Those people do not belong in the choir loft." Wayne, the newly powerful, was thus tasked with fixing the problem.

Despite our best intentions, we are all mired in wrong attitudes informed by fear and selfishness. Dementia is more disconcerting to us after a certain age than brain disorders present at birth, such as beset those choir members: We are aware of the distinct possibility of it in our own lives. That man's aversion may lurk in many who are threatened by the evidence in others of cognitive impairment but who are less candid about admitting it. In frank language, Andrea Gillies, author of the memoir, *Keeper*, describes her mother-in-law's dementia as "a [daily] scene from an amnesiac horror movie."[1]

In starting a dementia ministry, we must take into account the possibility of parishioner fear, which is not irrational,[2] and the reality that advanced dementia can be difficult to witness. It's important to strike a balance between educating the congregation, so they feel more comfortable in the presence of people with dementia, and overwhelming them with disconcerting facts and stories. Some of us are repelled, to use a hard but honest word, by the eventual muddling of language, loss of self-restraint, or erosion of manners and grooming. Cathryn, from chapter 2, said that by the time her husband reached mid-stage, she could not bear to watch him eat: He drank sherry straight from the bottle, blew his nose in his napkin, and stuffed food into his pockets to hide later beneath the toilet brush. She struggled to feed him three times a day for years, and her resolve eventually broke under the strain of it. Mine would, too, I expect. Confronting misguided attitudes in a church and encouraging compassion—a cultural shift—can be accomplished without forcing upon everyone the grim realities of incontinence and the eventual inability to use, for example, tissues to deal with a runny nose or a spoon and fork to eat.

Arguably, we should all be willing to enter into a more complete understanding of dementia's ordeals, our disinclinations aside. Jesus requires no less of us, as the one whom, at our best, we emulate, but Jesus knows, as well, our significant shortcomings. Our main goal is to create a culture within the church that welcomes and provides for people living with dementia, and in order to do so, we must work within the congregation's sensitivities. Depending on how the ministry is structured, there may be limited opportunities for contact between parishioners and people in later dementia. Most ministries limit participation in respite programs, for instance, to those who can still eat without assistance, take care of their own toileting needs, and interact amicably with others. People with advanced dementia often become unsettled when they're away from home or separated from their main caregiver. They may resist such situations, thus limiting direct participation in church, even in activities tailored to their needs.

A "shift" may not be necessary in every culture. In some cultures, people do not tend to react with fear or aversion to advanced dementia. Feelings about the condition are often determined by the extent and type of news coverage (or the lack of it) within a given culture.[3] Researchers Alexandra Hillman and Joanna Latimer point out that while Westerners consider dementia not a part of normal aging, and hope is defined mainly in terms of a cure, this perception isn't the case in some places. In parts of rural India, for example, dementia wasn't regarded as a problem until the media portrayed it as one and began to market products and services to help with it: People with dementia were just old, not unwell. Much of the related research has been aimed at determining why certain cultures have either a higher or lower incidence of dementia, instead of how they differ in their views of it and how this affects behavior.[4] While noting a few exceptions within our culture,[5] Hillman and Latimer concede that cultural depictions of dementia are generally negative, underscoring the need for dementia-friendly communities that encourage living well with it, awareness campaigns, and further study to determine how culture impacts our reaction to it.[6]

The educational materials provided in this chapter are designed to challenge stigmatizing thoughts and to teach ways of helping people in the early stage, specifically, of Alzheimer's disease[7] feel comfortable and accepted. They can be used in Sunday school groups, presentations, or special services in which the whole congregation is invited to participate. Activities encourage participation and dialogue, based on a boatload of research confirming that adults respond best to structured experiences that allow for open conversation.[8] Appendix 2 contains supplementary activities you can use if you wish to give extended practice or more in-depth information, as suggested by data from the survey described in the previous chapter. Each lesson is preceded by supplemental information for the group leader to use in planning and group discussion. However, there are likely people in the church who are living with dementia and would be willing to share their stories and experiences; they will be your best teachers, activities aside.

## LESSON ONE: CONFRONTING STIGMA

### *Leader Preparation*

The stigma of dementia, we've learned, is perpetuated by a larger culture that esteems power and intelligence and unconsciously impresses upon us the tendency to marginalize those who struggle in these areas. But when dementia is concerned, even well-meaning people can fall into a trap of judgmentalism. We see a white-haired woman rocking a doll, unable to comprehend the difference between plastic and flesh, and we (in our inescapable humanness) think, "I don't want to be like that. I hope it never happens to me or anyone I love." This isn't a lack of compassion, but it is a judgment, albeit an almost impossible one to avoid. To relate compassionately to people living with dementia, we must try to reframe these reactions within our own minds, actively replacing automatic thoughts with higher truths, while understanding that we, unlike Cathryn and other full-time caregivers, are free to come and go within this difficult circumstance.

God asks that we control our thoughts;[9] the tongue, linked inextricably to the mind, is likened to a horse's bit and a boat rudder, manageable at will.[10] Cognitive therapy, one of the five leading psychological approaches, is based on the premise that we can change our lives for the better by identifying and correcting faulty thinking. We can certainly change for the better the lives of people living with dementia if we become aware of the stigmatizing ideas and reactions we harbor toward them, sometimes beneath consciousness and certainly intent, and work to change ourselves. Stigmatizing results in feelings of shame and self-devaluation, isolation, and sometimes in the actual shunning of families caring for a member with dementia.[11]

These are some common examples of stigmatizing thoughts, with suggested replacement thoughts and concepts for discussion:

- **Stigmatizing thought:** "Thank God I don't have dementia."

  **Replacement thought:** "I am no different. I didn't make myself. We live, breathe, and have our being through God, who created each of us in his image, no matter what our abilities."

  **Concept:** We can take appropriate pride in accomplishments resulting from hard work, but we need to remember, continually and as an unceasing prayer, who dispenses our talents and the opportunities we do not control: "We are the clay and you are our potter. We are all the work of your hand" (Isaiah 64:8, NIV).

- **Stigmatizing thought:** "People with dementia are different."

  **Replacement thought:** "People with dementia are people. We are different parts of the same mystical body, each with an equally valid purpose.

  **Concept:** Consider the image of yourself as one minute part among the diverse, almost uncountable parts of a complex, perfect system— organs, bones, muscles, 724 trillion cells—all working together toward a common end, an end ordained by God that continues across the millennia.[12] Paul almost humorously tells us not to look at one another and make comparisons based on human value systems: "The eye cannot say to the hand, 'I have no need of you' And the head cannot say to the feet, 'I have no need of you!' On the contrary, those parts of the body that seem to be weaker are indispensable, and the parts we think less honorable, we invest with the greater honor" (1 Corinthians 12:21–23, NIV).

- **Stigmatizing thought:** "I can't be friends with a person who has dementia."

  **Replacement thought:** "If any person who has ever lived knows the pain of abandonment, it is Jesus Christ, whose friends slept, denied, betrayed, and scattered during his time of greatest need, when he couldn't give back in the way they expected, and they were scared. I have a chance to react differently."

  **Concept:** As Christians, we are asked throughout life to make choices in which we subordinate our desires to accomplish a greater good, understanding that all such choices matter and all are reciprocated in the end. It may require a different effort and a different set of expectations to be friends in this circumstance, but this is not a reason to avoid it. God promises that the benefits work both ways: "If you pour yourselves out for the hungry and satisfy the desires of the afflicted, then shall your light rise in the darkness, and your gloom will be as the noonday. The Lord will guide you continually; he will satisfy your desire with good things, and make your bones strong. And you shall be like a watered garden, like a spring of water, whose waters fail not." (Isaiah 58:10–11).

- **Stigmatizing thought:** "People with dementia are like children; dementia means a return to childhood."

  **Replacement thought:** "People with dementia may be forgetting how to care for themselves, but they've borne children, fought in wars, flown planes, climbed mountains, and done, every one of them, a thousand things I will never know. They've experienced life."

  **Concept:** There's an old analogy that likens the brain riddled with dementia to a failed television set—the broadcasts are out there, meaning mature consciousness is still present, but the receiver is not working. The brain, much as we value it, is seldom mentioned in the Bible. When God connects with us in the metaphorical language of the Bible, it is through our hearts: "My flesh and my heart fail, but God is the strength of my heart and my portion forever" (Psalm 73:26, NIV).

- **Stigmatizing thought:** "Alzheimer's is a fate worse than death; it means a person is losing her mind."

**Replacement thought:** "She has been diagnosed with Alzheimer's. Many years may lie ahead for her. Even as the condition worsens, I can do much to help her feel happy and in control, and I can help her caregiver by staying connected."

**Concept:** It goes without saying that we are all going to die, and dementia is one of the harder ways to do it. As we've learned, the condition is usually progressive; it will get worse in increments. It lasts for a relatively long time. Although these facts are true, dementia does not mean the end of life or the end of meaningful life. We can learn to live more fully in the present moment, alongside people who can *only* live in the present. We remain secure in the knowledge that even if a person forgets her own name, God will keep her identity and her place, no matter what befalls—deep waters, fire, separation from family, blindness and deafness—secure within his provision and plans: "But now, thus says the Lord, who created you, O Jacob, and formed you, O Israel: Fear not, for I have redeemed you; I have called you by name: you are mine" (Isaiah 43:1–2, NAB).

- **Stigmatizing thought:** "People with advanced dementia should stay at home or in a special facility; they don't understand what's going on anyway."

**Replacement thought:** "People with advanced dementia may still enjoy certain social situations, and their caregivers need places to take them, where both can enjoy the company of others. I have the chance to learn some of the most important lessons in life by opening myself to friendship with people who are living with dementia."

**Concept:** There are different ways of understanding. People with dementia may no longer understand complex ideas but perfectly understand a place or person as safe and accepting. While it seems odd to observe a grownup waving his hands or calling out aimlessly, if he is not in distress and is okay with where and who he is, you can be, too: "As God's chosen ones, holy and beloved, clothe yourselves with compassion, kindness, humility, meekness and patience. . . . Above all, clothe yourselves with love, which binds everything together in perfect harmony." (Colossians 3:12–14).

- **Stigmatizing thought:** "People with dementia can no longer think."

  **Replacement thought:** "The human brain is the most complex, robust organ in all creation, and progressive dementia is due to a long, slow disease, like Alzheimer's, in which the changes occur gradually."

  **Concept:** The preclinical and early stages, when most of the brain is still functioning, can last for many years, and a person is essentially the same as always, although with increasing memory problems. Even in the later stages, certain memories may be retained, as does the ability to sense love and comfort. Dementia doesn't override any of God's promises to us: "And I am sure that he who began a good work in you will bring it to completion at the day of Christ Jesus" (Philippians 1:6, ESV).

## Activity

[*Note*: You may need to break this activity into two sessions in the interest of time and attention span, which begins to fade in the most determined students after about half an hour.[13] If you have less than an hour, do the discussion (numbers one and two below) as the first session and the group project (number three) as the second session.]

Objective: To help parishioners recognize and change their stigmatizing thoughts about dementia.

Materials:

- Set of five cards, each printed with one of the stigmatizing thoughts and its replacement thought listed above ("Concept" is for your purposes as group leader.)
- Bible for each breakout group, preferably with no more than five participants each
- List of verses (see below)
- Paper and pen for each group

<u>Time Required</u>: Approximately an hour, perhaps longer depending on group size and enthusiasm

<u>Process</u>:

1. Discuss the following questions: [*Note*: Bracketed material is for the leader, to help with facilitation.]

   - A stigma is a characteristic or condition about which we are ashamed. If it can be hidden, we hide it, and we refrain from talking about it. We fear being regarded negatively if others know about it. People who live with dementia often feel stigmatized. It's hard to admit the diagnosis if you expect others to change their positive opinions of you and begin treating you differently. What are some other circumstances that are stigmatizing in our culture besides mental health issues? [Poverty, lack of education, obesity, certain types of cancer, having been in prison—anything that causes you to stand out in an undesirable way.]

   - What problems are caused for the person who feels stigmatized? [Isolation, either self-imposed in order to avoid pain and embarrassment or brought on by others' avoidance; feelings of unworthiness; fear of rejection, devaluation, and pity.]

   - As a society we sometimes use shame to dissuade undesirable behavior. We no longer use formal public shaming, but we do react with suppressive psychological tactics as a means of control. How is stigmatizing different from deliberate shaming? Does it have the same effect?[14]

   - Stigmatizing can extend to dementia caregivers and family members. What are the reasons we feel such discomfort with dementia? How does our reaction to people living with it compare to our reaction to women who have had surgery for breast cancer and are coping with a changed body or people who have smoked excessively and developed lung cancer?[15]

   - Is stigmatization ever imagined (when it's not really there) by people who feel marginalized? Is it possible that it doesn't exist to the extent that it is perceived? Can a few bad experiences reflect on all of us,[16] and how do we, in a church setting, provide a safe place that over-rides the common experience?

- Think of a secret, personal characteristic, condition, or past experience that you feel excessively private about because you are afraid it would change people's regard of you. What if everyone knew and began to act differently toward you? Imagine yourself pushed away, hear yourself being discussed behind your back, see your friends' new reactions to you, as though you've become odd, and they don't know how to relate to you anymore. How would you act and react? What would give you a feeling of freedom from the fear of having others know this secret, or condition, or past experience? [Realizing that, as with dementia or any mental health condition, there is no reason for shame; having people simply accept the knowledge without judgment; being treated with compassion instead of avoidance; feeling deeply valued by others.]

2. Explain that changing habitual thoughts is difficult and requires effort: Think of it as exercising psychological "muscle" that may have gotten a bit flabby. We know from research that thought suppression doesn't work; trying not to think undesirable thoughts only makes them more intrusive.[17] Thought replacement, on the other hand, in which these thoughts are consciously replaced with healthier, more functional ones is a classic technique in behavioral therapy.

   - Divide into small groups. Give each group a Bible, a card with one of the stigmatizing thoughts listed in the leader preparation section above and its replacement thought, and a list of the following (or other) verses: Job 19:19, Psalm 25:1-2 / 16-17, Psalm 31:11-12 / 14, Psalm 46:1-3, Psalm 73:26, Psalm 139:15-16, Isaiah 43:1, Isaiah 64:8, Jeremiah 10:23, Jeremiah 31:3-4, Luke 6:31-33, Acts 17:28, 1 John 4:12.

   - Ask each of the groups to consider the thought card they received: Is there any truth in it, and, if so, does this truth justify or excuse stigmatization? Do you agree with the replacement thought, or is there another that would be equally or more effective for you? Select a Bible verse that supports the new thought.

- Moving from group to group, share (1) the stigmatizing thought, (2) the replacement thought, (3) important points from the group's discussion and the selected Bible verse or verses chosen. Explain that going forward in these lessons, we will work to change our stigmatizing thoughts about dementia. Discuss whether this task will be difficult: How hard is it, really, to control our thoughts? Think of Paul's struggle with himself: "I do not understand my own actions. For what I want to do, I do not do, but I do the very thing I hate" (Romans 7:15, ESV). How does Paul's confession encourage us to persist in trying but also to feel comforted in our failure?

## LESSON TWO: EARLY-STAGE OR MILD ALZHEIMER'S

### *Leader Preparation*

The initial symptoms of Alzheimer's disease are subtle, so much so that they are easily ignored or denied. We've all experienced episodes of brain fog due to stress, lack of sleep, poor nutrition, the consumption of impairing substances, or other reasons. We don't panic and assume the worst. We know that as we get older and our brains age, we are more prone to pesky senior moments. It becomes worrisome, however, when a recognizable pattern emerges.

Alzheimer's can mimic normal aging at first. Think of this: In our fourth and fifth decades of life, eyesight typically worsens. Vision stabilizes at some point, and we are able to cope with the decline by using glasses. It does not continue to the point of blindness, not in the absence of an actual disease or disorder. With Alzheimer's, the brain breaks down in a way that can initially seem to be within the scope of normal aging, but this process continues relentlessly until the brain is "blind," so to speak. It happens gradually, over time. But even after the disease becomes symptomatic, much more of intellect remains intact than is affected. It is important to remember that people in early-stage AD (or any progressive dementia), while coping with troubling, inconsistent neurological changes, are essentially the same people they always were, and they have not become insensitive to insult. Being avoided, ignored, or treated with a lack of respect is hurtful. Dementia doesn't change this reaction. None of us want to be excluded.

In the early stage, we often refer to caregivers as "care partners." Caregiving, meaning active help with tasks of daily living, is not needed until self-care skills have begun to unravel or safety is a concern, and care *partner* is a more accurate, dignified way of expressing the relationship at first. Care partners help their loved ones stay on track. Similarly, think of yourself, when you are with a person in early-stage dementia, as a "social partner," who can subtly ease difficulties by simply remaining alert to signs of confusion or actions on the part of others that could seem dismissive. People with mild dementia say that others often begin to behave as though they've become invisible, talking about or around them, as though they cannot hear or understand. Some deal with this behavior in their closest loved ones, much less the people they encounter in more casual settings. The job of a social partner is to quietly keep it from happening.

There are ways to help a person in the early symptomatic stages of dementia feel comfortable and fully a part of social gatherings. In the preclinical or very early stage of dementia, there is little need for accommodation.[18] Bear in mind that Alzheimer's begins to affect the brain fifteen to twenty years before any discernable symptoms appear.[19] Alzheimer's disease becomes evident to others in the breakdown of short-term memory, confusion with directions, decreased initiative, and problems with language. Additional symptoms are likely present early on, as well, such as difficulty with planning, handling finances and bills, keeping track of possessions, and sticking to a schedule. While deeply troublesome, these symptoms are not as noticeable to others. The activity that follows will help ensure comfortable, confident social interactions and smooth transitions between activities and locations within the church.

The relationship suggestions in this and later chapters are adapted from my earlier book, *Alzheimer's: A Crash Course for Friends and Relatives*.[20]

- **Address the person with dementia directly** (instead of deferring to the care partner), and keep questions and comments clear and focused. Allow more time than you normally would for a response. If you see signs of uncertainty, you can repeat yourself, but don't increase the volume of your voice or pause between words, as though you are talking to a hearing-impaired person or a child. For example: "Jenny, would you like a cup of coffee?" *Not*: "Jay, would Jenny like a cup of coffee?" or "Jenny, we have coffee, tea, orange juice, and water. And I think Serena Baker brought her famous coffee cake today. Can I get you any of those? We're so happy you're joining us for social hour! We have it every Sunday, right after the eleven o'clock service." [*Note:* While the latter would set a welcoming tone, remember that you can create this same effect with less risk of confusion by smiling, maintaining eye contact, leaving out the extraneous details, and pausing between questions: "Coffee, okay. Do you like it with cream or sugar? Just cream? Good. I'll get you a piece of coffee cake, too."]

- **Help with word finding.** One of the most common symptoms of early Alzheimer's is the inability to recall common words, and odd, seemingly uncontrollable word substitutions or the use of descriptive phrases rather than the forgotten word: "I've lost my handkerchief. No, no, not that . . . the thing with a handle that I keep money in." It's okay to help quietly, without any show of impatience or amusement: "Do you mean your handbag? I'll help you look for it."

- **Tell, don't ask, about the recent past.** Alzheimer's begins around a paired structure, the hippocampus, named for its seahorse shape (from the Greek words meaning "horse" and "sea monster"), located in the medial temporal lobe of the brain. The hippocampus enables the formation of memories and the ability to maintain proper orientation in space and time. As this part of the brain is affected, remembering the recent past becomes more difficult. When you are talking with a person in the early stage of dementia, refrain from asking questions about recent events. Instead, make statements: "Jay tells me you went to the beach last week, Jenny. Did you have a nice time?" [*Note*: "Did you have a nice time" is a general question, easily answered with a simple yes or no. Jenny can elaborate if she is able, but she's not put on the spot with a question that demands recall of specific details, such as, "How was the weather?" or "Did your son make it down for a few days?"]

- **Be inclusive in conversations.** People in early-stage dementia may find it challenging to follow conversations between three or more people. Group conversation requires the ability to keep track of what each person has said and to quickly formulate thoughts and reactions. Choosing to remain silent rather than risk the awkwardness of a mistimed or inappropriate response leads to being ignored, hence to the sense of invisibility. You can help by making frequent eye contact, which is a way of showing that you are aware of a person's presence without putting her on the spot. And if you notice that she isn't participating, refer to her by name (rather than asking a question) whenever it seems appropriate: "Yes, that's true! Jenny and I live near each other.

The traffic is awful in that part of town." *Not*: "Jenny, what do you think of the new traffic calming devices? Aren't they annoying?"

- **Don't call attention to mistakes.** Gracefully smooth over any conversational glitches, such as repeated comments, without a raised eyebrow or an awkward pause, adhering to that practical British adage, *Keep calm and carry on*, as though nothing unusual has occurred.

- **Help with directions**. With more advanced dementia, one's own house can become a disorienting maze. Initially the problem tends to be episodic. People in the early stage have reported sudden confusion when driving familiar routes or having gone miles off course without realizing it. A church building, with its typical warren of hallway passages, stairways, and rooms leading off the main sanctuary can be daunting to a newcomer, much less to someone with a flagging sense of direction. Discreetly escort a person with dementia where she needs to go: "Jenny, Jay is over at the fellowship hall. I'll take you there." *Not*: "Jenny, Jay is at the fellowship hall. Just go through those double doors. You'll see a stairway to the right. Go down and take a left. Then you'll go out the exit, under the covered walkway and into the foyer. The fellowship hall is behind the kitchen, which you'll see. You can't miss it."

## *Activity*

Objective: To develop skill in communicating with people who have mild or early-stage dementia.

Materials: [*Note:* This activity consists of a skit that needs to be rehearsed a few times in advance. If this cannot be arranged, at least give the players a chance to read their roles and make copies of the script to use while acting.]

- Seven copies of "If You Could Hear Me Think" (see below)
- Playbills that set the scene, present the cast (below), provide space for notetaking,[21] and list five communication tips demonstrated in the skit:

  o Address the person with dementia directly.
  o Help with word finding.
  o Tell, don't ask, about the recent past.
  o Be inclusive.
  o Assist with directions.

- Pens, if needed
- Also see setting, props, and costumes (below)

Time Required: About 40 minutes

Process:

1. Discuss: Have you ever had a friend with a problem that made you want to avoid them? You didn't know what to say or how to help. You felt compassionate, but you also felt awkward. Introduce the concept of informed compassion:[22] You have "informed" compassion when you've learned enough about another person's hardship that when you reach out, you actually do bring comfort. You know what to say and do, instead of inadvertently adding to the person's distress and sense of disconnection from normal life. Taking the time to learn about a difficult circumstance you do not fully understand—because you have not faced it yourself—is an expression of love. In this activity we'll learn some ways to interact with a person who is experiencing mild dementia, so we can help them truly feel welcome.

2. Distribute playbills. Instruct the group to watch for signs of dementia in Jenny, the main character, for communication tips to help with dementia, and for characters' attitudes toward Jenny. Make note of these on the space provided.

3. Present the skit.

## "If You Could Hear Me Think"

**Synopsis:** Jenny helps us learn a few communication tips about early dementia she wishes everyone knew.

**Setting and Props:** A church fellowship hall, during the coffee hour after the service. Use any available props to simulate.

**Costumes:** "Thought" should dress entirely in black or dark gray.

**Running time:** About 15 minutes.

**Characters:**

- JENNY: a woman with early-stage or mild Alzheimer's disease, at a first visit to coffee hour; Jenny has just begun to reveal her diagnosis to others.

- JAY: Jenny's husband and care partner

- IMA: friendly but awkward church member, who has been assigned to greet Jenny and Jay.

- WORTH: church member with a relative who has dementia

- THOUGHT: character who expresses what other characters are thinking

- NARRATOR: the group leader or a character who helps the audience understand what is happening [*Note*: If necessary, 'Thought' and 'Narrator' can be played by the same person. Move to the side when acting as narrator, so the two characters are not confused.]

- ASHLEY: young church member

- EXTRAS: additional people to simulate an after-church crowd [*Note*: the skit can be performed without these additional characters.]

**Scene:** Jenny and Jay, alone, off to one side. Other characters in groups and pairs, drinking coffee and talking among themselves.

\* \* \*

**Jay:** (*touches Jenny's hand*) Is this okay for you?

**Jenny:** Of course. But we don't know anyone. What are we supposed to do? Just stand here or go out and try to meet a few people?

**Jay:** We'll pretend we're potted trees. (*lifts his hands like stiff branches and looks straight ahead*)

**Jenny:** Oh, stop it.

**Ima:** (*walks over, smiling and extends her hand to Jay; she pointedly looks at Jay while speaking, glances occasionally at Jenny*) Hello there! Good morning! Are you Jay and Jenny London? (*pauses*) My name is Ima Dismissen, and I'm chairperson of the newcomer's group. Frank, our minister, told me you called earlier this week, Jay, about the memory group for Jenny. We are so very happy to have you join us! This is a very nice church, and Frank is a nice minister, as you'll see, but I wish he wouldn't wipe his brow so much. You'd think it was summer all year! I don't know why he does that.

**Jay:** Good to meet you, Ima. Dismissing? That's an unusual surname. I've never heard it before.

**Ima:** (*laughing lightly*) No, not dismissing, like 'I want you to go away.' (*pronounces slowly, emphasizing the end*) Dismiss—en. It's German, I think. And Ima is actually a Japanese name! Did you know that? It means 'now' or 'present.' London is an interesting name. Is it English?

**Jay:** (*smiles in amusement*) Well, yes, most likely. I think it means my ancestors came from that grand city, something like that.

**Jenny:** I have Alzheimer's disease. We found out about it a little while ago.

**Ima:** Um . . . Frank did mention . . . of course, but you look so . . . you look so nice. What a pretty dress. I would never have guessed. I mean known. No, I mean . . . (*4-second, awkward pause during which Ima looks embarrassed and shifts her eyes back and forth, as though searching for something better to say, and then turns to Jay*). Goodness, I see you don't have any coffee! Can I get you some? Jay, would you like coffee? (*hesitating*) Would Jenny like coffee?

*All players freeze in place. Thought steps up and places his hand on Jenny's shoulder.*

**Thought:** (*incredulous, hurt*) Why can't people talk to me and look at me? I am standing right in front of this lady. As soon as someone knows I have dementia, they start treating me differently. I'm still myself. I just have trouble remembering things. My words feel like they're stuck in thick molasses. And sometimes I can't remember what I've just said or tried to say. But I know what coffee is, for goodness' sake! I can answer a simple question like that. (*Players unfreeze. Thought steps down and backs away.*)

**Jay:** Ima, Jenny's here. (*puts his arm around Jenny*) You can ask her.

**Ima:** (*awkwardly*) Of course, of course, Jenny. Do forgive me! Would you like a cup of coffee? It's not bad here. Not great, but at least it's not instant. I used to go to a church that only had those packets of granulated junk, and some places make it so weak, it tastes like wet carpet. And we have real cream. Actually, it's half and half, not real cream. Sugar, cream? Black? Would you rather have tea? (*blinks her eyes rapidly*)

**Narrator:** (*stepping forward*) What do people do when they feel awkward? They talk either too little or too much. (*looking at Ima*) Just take a deep breath, slow down, and be yourself, the way you would with anyone you've just met. Be like your name, "Ima," meaning present now, in the moment. Give Jenny a chance to talk.

**Jenny:** (*eyes widen, glances at Jay and back at Ima*) What?

**Jay:** That's okay. We'll each have a cup of whatever hot thing you have, Ima. Both with cream. It's good of you to get it for us. (*Ima looks relieved and walks away; Jay and Jenny stand alone for a moment, then Jay elbows Jenny and speaks under his breath*) Uh oh, incoming . . . incoming. Here comes another one. Brace yourself.

**Jenny:** You are terrible.

**Worth:** (*walking over*) Ah, newcomers to coffee hour. I'm Worth Gayhardt, and I'm the unofficial welcoming committee—all one of me.

**Jay:** I'm Jay London, and this is my wife, Jenny. We're glad to meet the one of you, Worth. Jenny and I are mainly here to check out the memory ministry.

**Jenny:** I have Alzheimer's. We've known for about a year. I . . . I wanted to come to church to see if I could meet some new, some new . . . (*pauses, tilts her head to one side, thinking*). Darn it, the easiest words and thoughts slip right out of my mind. It's maddening. (*shakes her head in frustration*)

**Worth:** (*looking at Jenny*) Some new friends? (*waits for a response*)

**Jenny:** Yes, that's the word I wanted—friends. I want to meet some new friends.

*All players freeze in place. Thought steps up and places a hand on Jenny's shoulder.*

**Thought:** It's a relief when people help me with words, but not when they make jokes or 'come-on-get-it-out' hand gestures (*cranes neck forward a bit and beckons with one hand*). I accidently said the wrong word, a stupid word, in a store. I told the clerk I wanted some gunk instead of gum, and she laughed at me. I may not remember things very well anymore, but I remember that. I felt so dumb. He (*gestures at Worth*)—can't think of his name—gave me a chance to say, yes, 'friends.' That was my word. He didn't assume he had figured it out. (*players unfreeze, Thought steps back.*)

**Worth:** (*again, making eye contact with Jenny and speaking to her*) I bet you find friends here, Jenny. So many people are living with dementia, in one way or another. My brother-in-law was diagnosed a while ago, too. He recently stopped working.

**Jenny:** It's hard. It's a hard disease. (*using the same tone and expression as when she first said it*) I wanted to come to church so I could meet new friends.

**Jay:** We know people from our support group, but we don't meet many who have Alzheimer's, not when we're out and about. We feel like we've been stranded alone on an uninhabited island.

**Jenny:** (*ruefully*) *Gilligan's Island*, only all by ourselves, no professor and Mary Anne.

**Jay:** Watch it, Jenny. You're showing your age. (*gestures around the room*) I bet half the people here have no idea what *Gilligan's Island* is. I'm beginning to feel positively ancient.

**Worth:** Maybe you'd enjoy meeting my sister and brother-in-law. Would you like that, Jenny?

**Jenny:** (*looks confused*) Um . . .

**Worth:** My brother-in-law has Alzheimer's. I think he would like to meet you. Would you want to meet him and my sister sometime?

**Narrator:** Worth is asking Jenny a question she should be able to answer. He's not asking her about a recent event that she may have forgotten. He asks how she feels about a suggestion he just made. When he realizes she has lost track of his earlier comment, he repeats it.

**Jenny:** Yes, we would. (*same tone, as though she has not already said it twice*) I wanted to come to church to meet some new friends.

**Worth:** Church is a good place to meet people. Definitely better than Facebook or a bar.

**Jay:** I wonder what became of Ima and the coffee?

**Worth:** Ima Dismissen? She knows every person in the room and all their cats and dogs. Ima could talk to a fence post (*glances around the room and spots Ima*). Well, here she comes now, and is that steam still rising from the cups?

It's a Sunday miracle. She's made it in record time. (*Ima arrives and hands cups to Jay and Jenny. Ima and Worth exchange greetings. Ashley and another person join the group. A conversation begins. It can be about anything—the sermon, a scheduled church clean-up day, the absurd cost of new choir robes. Ad lib for a minute or so, with everyone except Jenny participating. Jenny remains silent, looking from person to person, and finally down at the ground.*)

*All players freeze in place. Thought steps up and places a hand on Jenny's shoulder.*

**Thought:** Group conversations are hard for me. I can't think fast enough to keep up, and I lose track of what different people have said. (*wistfully*) I used to love dinner parties. I must have given a hundred of them. Now I worry that I'll say something crazy if I try to jump in. Conversations swirl around me like bats. But I wish people would look at me, at least—not stare, but just look at me now and then. I feel invisible. (*Players unfreeze, Thought steps away. The conversation dies down, and suddenly everyone looks at Jenny.*)

**Ashley:** Jenny, weren't you and Jay at church last week, too? I remember seeing you up front, I think. You had on that terrific purple sweater, right?

**Narrator:** People with Alzheimer's lose short-term memory, meaning that they often cannot remember things that happened recently, like yesterday, or last week, or even a few minutes ago. Alzheimer's first affects the part of the brain that receives and holds information for a while, before it's forgotten or converted to long-term memory. It enables us to keep in mind a new phone number long enough to dial it, or the face of a person we've met and expect to see again. It helps us remember appointments and plans. When you are with a person in early Alzheimer's, make a comment about the recent past, instead of asking a question. Ashley (*gestures to Ashley*) could have said, "I believe I saw you in church last week, Jenny. This isn't your first Sunday here. I'm glad you came back!" and Jenny wouldn't have been confronted by a question she might not be able to answer. Think of this jingle: Tell, don't ask, about the recent past.

**Jay:** We were here last week, but we didn't stay for coffee hour. Jenny and I met at church when we were in college, but we got out of the habit of going a long time ago. Selfish about our Sunday mornings, I guess.

**Jenny:** We wanted to come to church to meet some new friends.

**Ashley:** (*smiling, sincere, touching Jenny's arm*) Well, It's nice to meet you.

**Jenny:** Can you tell me the way to the restroom?

**Ashley:** Sure! It's out that door (*pointing across the room*). Go down the hall and to the right. You'll go by some Sunday school rooms. It's at the very end, beside the fire escape.

**Narrator:** The same part of the brain that enables new memories to form also helps us follow directions and make sense of where we are in space. When you are asked by a person with dementia for directions, offer to escort her (or him). Unobtrusively do this, even if they decline. (*shrugs*) You can always say you need to go there, too.

**Jay:** I'll go with you, Jenny. (*Jenny and Jay leave the room. Worth, Ima, and Ashley stand together with Thought close by. Others move away.*)

**Worth:** Did you know that by the age of eighty-five, one in three people has Alzheimer's? It starts decades ahead of when you first realize it. Look at us, standing here. One in three. (*pauses*) Wonder which one it is?

*All look at each other, then freeze. Thought steps forward and places a hand on Worth's shoulder.*

**Thought:** (*shakes his head*) I don't know how my sister and Glenn will keep a roof over their heads. They were both planning to work for another several years. Glenn changed jobs when he was fifty because his company failed. This is such a hit financially, not to mention everything else. (*Players unfreeze, Thought steps away.*)

**Ima:** (*looks askance at Worth, speaks sarcastically*) Well, aren't you just a ray of sunshine this morning, Worth. One in three? Well, I do hope it's not *me*.

*Players freeze. Thought steps over to Ima and places a hand on her shoulder.*

**Thought:** I'm so worried about getting Alzheimer's myself. I'm forgetting a lot of things I used to be able to remember. Names and faces. I keep forgetting where I parked my car. I wish I weren't scared of it; I wish I hadn't been so awkward around Jenny. (*Players unfreeze, Thought steps away.*)

**Ashley:** Ima, this is something we need to be familiar with, so we can be the kind of friends who understand. My grandma has dementia. She hardly knows who I am, but she likes it when I visit her.

*Players freeze. Thought moves beside Ashley and places a hand on her shoulder.*

**Thought:** Is it hereditary? Will I get dementia when I'm older? What is it really like to be my grandmother? It makes me sad that she doesn't know my name anymore. But I love her, and I had lots of good times with her. (*resolutely*) I can be her memory keeper for some of her lost memories, like that time we made fingerpaint out of shaving cream and food dye. (*smiling*) What a mess. (*all walk away, Jenny and Jay reenter*)

**Jay:** Well then, my love, what did you think of church this morning?

**Jenny:** I don't really remember a lot of it, but it was okay, I guess. Who was that funny lady who kept talking so much?

**Jay:** That was Ima. Ima trying-hard-not-to-be-dismiss-ing. (*emphasizing the "ing"*) I think they are trying, Jenny. Let's try, too, you and me. We can all help each other. That's what friends do, right?

**Jenny:** (*pensively*) I will lose a lot with Alzheimer's, but I hope I don't lose people who care about me. I hope I'll always have friends. (*pauses*) Friends— that's one of the most important words. I may forget it with my brain, but I'll never forget it with my heart.

### The End

4. Discuss these questions:

   - Would you really have noticed Jenny's dementia, if you were with her for only a few minutes, and she didn't tell you? Did she stand out in a conspicuous way?
   - What indications of dementia did you see? [Repeating herself, forgetting (inconsistently) a common word, losing the thread of a conversation, not recalling whether she was at church one week prior, needing help to follow directions]
   - What could you tell about her personality? [She has a sense of humor; she's friendly and open. She has feelings that are normal and easy to understand.]
   - What communication mistakes did Ima make? [Saying too much at one time, talking to Jay about Jenny instead of directly to Jenny, reacting with awkwardness to Jenny's condition]

- What did Worth do right? [He talked to Jenny and gave her a chance to think. He kept his statements short and to the point. He did not call attention to her repetitions.]
- What did Ashley do right? [She reached out to Jenny in a natural way, as she would to anyone.] Which communication tips did you note?

5. Encourage the group to watch the 26-minute video,[23] "Christine and Paul Bryden on Living with Dementia," (https://christinebryden. com—Open the Resources page, and scroll down to *Videos*), made by Christine, a scientist and former advisor to Australia's prime minister, and her husband. Christine was diagnosed with younger-onset Alzheimer's at the age of 46, when she was raising two children as a single parent, just after she and her former husband had divorced. She has lived with dementia in a relatively high-functioning state for an almost unprecedented twenty years, writing five books after her diagnosis and speaking internationally as an Alzheimer's advocate.

## CONCLUSION

We've discussed Richard Taylor, the psychologist who spoke, almost until his death, about the need for societal understanding of people with dementia. He wanted others to see him as himself, as Richard, even as he struggled with his losses. "I am Richard," he'd insist, sometimes repeating it several times, "I am Richard." This association between name and identity is not without meaningful precedent,[24] but Taylor is referring to the reality that dementia often results in depersonalization and social exclusion by people who think you are no longer yourself. It's an agonizing form of isolation.

The first activities in this chapter tackle the tendency we may have to stigmatize people who are living with dementia. It happens early on, hence the unwillingness to divulge the diagnosis. When people with dementia come into the church, they are not asking for anything different from what we all want, whether they can still express these needs or not: *Get to know me. Recognize my self-worth and value. I don't want your pity; I want your acceptance, respect, and understanding.*

## CHAPTER 6

# Preparing Leaders and Volunteers

It almost seems reasonable to consider people like Christine Bryden, whose video is recommended in lesson 2 of the previous chapter, and Richard Taylor, and imagine that dementia may not be so terrible in every case. Years after they faced the diagnosis and were coping with symptoms, they wrote books about living with dementia and spoke many times to international audiences. Taylor did this until his death; Bryden continues. They've done more than most of us who are living *without* dementia manage to do.

But these people and others like them are the exceptions and not the rule. The tendency to minimize the difficulties of dementia when things look okay on the surface is common. Caregivers often report that others, even medical professionals, make wrong judgments on the basis of brief encounters that reveal nothing about the hardship of living with it around the clock. When Elaine, whom we've encountered several times in this book, remained quiet in social situations, she appeared perfectly normal, even friendly and interested. No one would suspect what her life or Michael's was like behind closed doors.

Dementia wreaks havoc as it moves beyond the early stage, and this fact should be foremost in the minds of church and lay leaders as they plan a ministry around it. Chapter 6 contains activities meant to educate those who have little firsthand experience with dementia about its hard truths, focusing, as with the previous chapter, on Alzheimer's disease. Ministers, lay leaders, and volunteers who work directly with caregivers or people in later stages need to have a reasonably correct understanding of what living with dementia means as it worsens. Whether the congregation at large would benefit from exposure to such a sobering portrayal is a judgment call. We've already learned that dementia is a worry to people on the cusp of elderliness, and many churchgoers are.[1]

You may wish to use the activities to develop workshops only for selected groups. The lessons that follow furnish a sequential course of study, building on the material of chapter 5 to illustrate the stages of Alzheimer's from the middle-stage symptoms to the end. As before, each contains activities preceded by background information for the group leader.

## LESSON ONE: UNDERSTANDING MID-STAGE OR MODERATE ALZHEIMER'S

### *Leader Preparation*

As the early stage of Alzheimer's gives way to more severe symptoms, the care partner must become, in a true sense, a caregiver. Retrogenesis, a widely recognized theory developed by Dr. Barry Reisberg of New York University, maintains that over the duration of symptomatic Alzheimer's, which can be as long as twenty years, skills and abilities are lost at about the same rate and in the same order that they are gained during childhood and adolescence; in other words, the process of normal human development is reversed. A person with mild Alzheimer's is losing functional skills acquired between ages eight and nineteen, such as the ability to engage in work and handle simple finances; a person in the moderate stage loses the skills of middle and early childhood, such as the ability to shower without assistance, select clothing, fasten buttons and zippers, and use the toilet privately.[2]

Behavioral difficulties not related to loss of skills arise in mid-stage Alzheimer's. Sundowning syndrome, for example, is a pattern of agitation and restlessness that begins in early evening and lasts into the night. About 80 percent of people with dementia exhibit one or more difficult behavioral or psychological symptoms, which can include disinhibition, aggression, agitation, psychosis, and impulsivity.[3] Such symptoms complicate the tasks of caregiving. Caregivers manage a constellation of unpredictable problems in addition to the stageable regression in skills.

These changes increase dependence on the caregiver and give rise to insecurity when they are not present. The inability to express needs clearly and have them met triggers outbursts of frustration and bouts of sadness. I spoke with a caregiver whose mother wailed intermittently in the years before her death, reacting, it seemed, to a phantom itch that could not be brought under control. When only long-term memories of a spouse are retained, and the present is lost, it causes understandable confusion: How many of us look the way we did thirty years ago? Recent events pass by like cars on a freeway, without leaving a trace of memory. At my father's funeral, an aunt with moderate dementia, unable to make sense of his absence at a family gathering, asked my mother over and over again, "Well, now, where in the world is Jack?"

But despite the losses, an adult struggling to operate a coffee maker or wandering the neighborhood in search of a childhood home is still an adult, a fact we must honor despite the temptation at times to do otherwise. A twenty-something woman, relating the frustration she feels over her grandfather's uninhibited behavior in public, remarked, "I scold him like a child, because that's how he's acting!" She pointed her finger and looked at me with stern, narrowed eyes, as if to demonstrate. "I just say, 'Stop it, Grandpa! People don't act like that! You know better!'"

"How does he react?" I asked.

"He looks sad," she said, and she looked sad, too.[4]

The differences between people at this stage can be substantial, and so can an individual's behavior from one day to the next. This variability makes it almost impossible to teach communication methods to use across the board, but there are certain strategies that apply widely enough to serve as a guide:

- **Accept. Don't argue or correct**. By middle stage, confusion on major fronts is a persistent state. Seasons of life ("I have two young children, ages six and ten"), place ("Are we at home?"), and familiar people ("Are you my Aunt Rachel?") are like fragments of a dream or scattered puzzle pieces that don't fit together. Trying to set things straight with the facts ("You don't have young children anymore; We're not at home, we're at church; I'm your niece, not your Aunt Rachel") will only result in frustration.

- **Stay calm**. This can be hard when a person is being paranoid or adamantly insisting on an incorrect set of facts, but if you give in to feelings of irritation or anger the situation will escalate. React by acknowledging the person's emotional state (sadness, worry, threat, loss, frustration) and trying to distract her: "I can tell you're upset about your lost watch. Was it one of your favorite things?" *Not*: "Of course I didn't steal your watch. How can you accuse me of doing that?"

- **Remember that what you say is not as important as the way you say it.** The nonverbal component of communication accounts for over 65 percent of a message.[5] Body language and facial expressions can often be understood by a person when their capacity for language is lost. I've had conversations with people in middle-stage dementia that made no sense as far as words go, but it didn't limit our understanding of each other. Once, I drew an evening with Elaine to a close by saying, "Elaine, I'm glad you came to dinner tonight." She smiled, touched my arm, and replied warmly, "It wasn't yesterday when I found you can't try if your hair blows."[6] We meaningfully expressed our pleasure in each other's company, and we could each have been speaking a different foreign language.

- **If conversation is still possible, talk about the distant past, not the recent past.** Unlike Elaine, many people in middle-stage Alzheimer's can speak coherently and even accurately but only about more stable memories of the distant past: a childhood home, one's wedding day, the first job after college, a beloved pet.

- **Ask closed questions and keep comments short and to the point.** From the early stage on, Alzheimer's causes increasing language dysfunction. This problem affects auditory comprehension. Ask closed questions that offer a choice ("Would you rather have water or ginger ale?") and keep statements simple and concrete, allowing about fifteen seconds—which can seem like a long time, indeed—for a response. Supply an answer if necessary ("I will get you a glass of water. Would you like some water?")

*A note to the reader*: Activities in this chapter rely on online resources, which may not always be available. If you cannot access them or other links for activities in the book please visit my website (www.allweatherfriend.org) for alternative materials to use.

### *First Activity*

Objective: To observe how the stress of dementia affects relationships and families; to consider ways of showing compassion to people who are struggling to live with it.

Materials:

- Equipment to show the 8-minute YouTube video, *"Experience 12 Minutes in Alzheimer's Dementia,"* https://alzheimersweekly.com/2014/05/experience-12-minutes-in-alzheimers-on/[7]
  [Note: This is a 2009 video, and the quality is not great. But unlike other dementia simulation videos, it sets the experience in a family, and this family provides a disquieting but sadly realistic portrayal of Alzheimer's. It's hard to watch and not be moved to compassion and for this reason is worth the small technical glitches. Be sure to mention to the group that the news story was first aired almost 15 years ago, and the announcer states that more than five million people in the United States have dementia. The current figure has increased by a million.[8]]
- A large dry erase board or chalkboard
- Handout: "Stages of Alzheimer's Disease" fact sheet produced by the Alzheimer's Association: https://www.bu.edu/alzresearch/files/pdf/StagesofADAlzAssoc3.pdf.[9]

Time Required: About 30 minutes

Process:

1. Review a few of the symptoms and communication tips for mild or early-stage dementia. Ask if anyone watched the Christine Bryden video (see page 108), and can compare Christine to "Jenny" of last week's skit. [Christine has had symptomatic Alzheimer's for longer than the fictitious Jenny, and her speech is slower. Like Jenny, she frequently relies on her caregiver for help but seems to have a good grasp on what is happening around her. Christine's disease, as we said last time, is progressing much more slowly than is typical.]

2. Explain that Alzheimer's progresses in overlapping stages based on human development. While the disease is different for every person,

there are certain indicators of each stage, and these emerge within a general time frame. The breakdown of stages is based on this understanding of the disease. Distribute the handouts and allow reading time.

3. Introduce the video featuring Lawanda Wilson,[10] who has Alzheimer's and lives with her son, Blane, and his new wife, Georgia. Blane participates in a simulation exercise in which his ability to see, walk, and use his hands is deliberately impeded. He wears distracting headsets that create continual confusion,[11] to enable him to experience for himself what his mother may be going through. We can identify with people who are hungry, vulnerable, ill, impoverished, blind, and in most other common circumstances of need, so we understand what to do when the Bible tells us to help them. Dementia is not so easy to imagine. We can close our eyes or refrain from eating to the point of true hunger, but we cannot shut down our brains or otherwise bring ourselves to a physical sense of what having dementia is like. This is why illnesses that cause it are often described as invisible and why simulation exercises are helpful.

4. Watch the video and discuss, using the following questions:

   - It's hard to blame Blane and Georgia for their frustration.[12] Do you feel greater empathy for Lawanda than for her son and his wife, or similarly for everyone involved? If you had to take the place of one of these people, who would it be, and why?

   - Think back to our discussion on stigmatizing as it relates to Lawanda, in whom we see moderate to moderately-severe dementia. Here are a few of the stigmatizing thoughts we considered previously, applied to her:

     o I'm glad I'm not like Lawanda. I hope it never happens to me or to anyone I love.
     o Lawanda is different from most people who are about her same age.
     o I couldn't be friends with Lawanda.
     o Alzheimer's is worse than death.
     o Maybe she should stay in a facility.

We talked about the possible truth in these stigmatizing thoughts but the need, nonetheless, to reframe them. Did you find yourself able to use replacement thoughts to help you see beyond Lawanda's losses? Can we accept God's providence and plans and see God working, still, in Lawanda's life? What can we learn from her?

- Recall the nine fruits of the Spirit (Galatians 5:22–23), and list them on the board: love, joy, peace, patience, kindness, generosity, faithfulness, gentleness, and self-control. Consider our responsibility, according to John's gospel to "remain in me, as I remain in you. Just as a branch cannot bear fruit on its own, unless it remains on the vine, so neither can you, unless you remain in me" (John: 15:4, NABRE). When we are with Lawanda and others like her, how do we "remain" in God? What does it mean to remain in God? How could our love, gentleness, patience, self-control, and other fruits of the Spirit lead, in Lawanda's situation, to outcomes we would not likely see? [The church's support could help Blane and Georgia with the stress of caregiving and Lawanda with her isolation. This help would carry over into their private lives—to Blane and Georgia's care of Lawanda and each other.]

- What strengths can we observe in Lawanda? [She still recognizes her son; she expresses and accepts love; she's mobile and can remember how to drive and do other complex activities.] What lifestyle factors make Blane and Georgia's caregiving difficult? [They apparently cannot afford an adult sitter when they're not home or just need a break from caregiving. They are not well-informed about dementia and its limitations. They live in a small space that hasn't been retrofitted to make it safer for Lawanda, so she seems frequently to imperil herself there.] We can see tension and resentment developing between Blane and Georgia and between Georgia and Lawanda. How realistic is unconditional love for any of us, as the flawed, unforgiving, self-interested, problem-ridden men and women we are (if we're being honest)? How did Blane show love for his mother? What comfort can we find in verses like, "The steadfast love of the Lord never ceases, his mercies never come to an end. They are new every morning" (Lamentations 3:22–23, ESV).

- What would improve life for Lawanda, Blane, and Georgia, given the family's apparent limitations? Imagine this family joining our congregation. How could we support each of them? What do you think they need from a church?

## *Second Activity*

Objective: To increase skill and confidence communicating with people in moderate stage dementia and to view these skills as a means of showing grace.

Materials:

- A large dry erase board or chalkboard
- Four copies of "Say This, Not That" scripts (see below)
- Two chairs
- Playbills which set the scene and synopsis, give the cast (below), and list the following communication tips, with space for notetaking:

  o Accept, don't argue or correct.
  o Stay calm. If the conversation is headed in the wrong direction, offer reassurance, then try to change the focus.
  o Talk about the long-ago past, not the recent past.
  o Remember that what you say is not as important as how you say it.
  o Ask closed, easy-to-answer questions
  o Look to the caregiver if you need help.

Time Required: About 25 minutes

Process:

1. Review the handout middle-stage symptoms of Alzheimer's and distribute the playbills. Introduce the skit: It would take place about three to seven years after the first skit when Jenny was in the early stage of Alzheimer's, depending on how fast her disease is progressing. We'll be watching sample conversations to identify correct and wrong ways of communicating and to learn why certain responses are more likely than others to help a person with middle-stage dementia feel comfortable and safe.

2. Make these three points: (1) We can adjust; they cannot. We must work cooperatively and compassionately with whatever *they* bring

to the interaction. (2) *Correct* does not mean *true*, not in this circumstance. It means this "correct" way of responding will help the person feel secure. *Wrong* does not mean *bad*. It means this "wrong" response may cause agitation. With dementia, truth does not refer to fact but to the more important reality (the higher truth) that dementia causes people—without exception—to confuse time, facts, faces, and places and to misinterpret information, hence our first directive: Accept, don't argue or correct. (3) If you need help, look to the caregiver, who should be nearby and is familiar with the way his loved one communicates her needs: "Jay, Jenny and I would appreciate your help. We don't seem able to connect this morning. Can you join us?"

3. Introduce the characters and present the skit. [*Note*: Choose the three volunteers before the session begins, to allow time to read lines in advance. Practice in advance if possible. The group leader should serve as narrator.]

**Characters:**

- JENNY: from the first skit; parishioner who now has moderate or middle-stage Alzheimer's
- IMA: wrong-way character
- ASHLEY: correct-way character
- NARRATOR: the audience's interpreter

**Setting:** Two seats in a fellowship hall: Jenny is sitting in one chair, Narrator is standing nearby.

## "Say This, Not That"

**Jenny:** (*happily, as Ima approaches her chair*) Oh good, there you are! You're my favorite neighbor. I haven't seen you in a long while. Where have you been? Do you have those pecan cookies you make? I love those cookies.

**Ima:** Hello, Jenny. (*sits down beside Jenny and pats her knee*) I'm glad to see you, too, but I don't live near you, remember? I'm your friend, Ima—like Ima glad to see you!

**Jenny:** (*confused*) I'm, Ima . . . glad? What?

**Ima:** (*loudly, speaking very slowly, and patting her chest*) I'm not your neighbor. My name is Ima. I go to church here with you and Jay.

**Jenny:** (*leans back at the sound of a raised voice*) Church? This is church? I didn't know we were at a church. (*shakes her head*) I don't like it here.

**Narrator:** When Ima corrects Jenny and suggests a mnemonic to help her remember the name "Ima," Jenny becomes more confused. Then Ima raises her voice. It's the annoying thing we do in foreign countries, too—speak our terrible French or Spanish, *very loudly*. But speaking loudly only works with a person who's hard of hearing, and it makes Jenny react with displeasure. Let's watch a different way to talk with Jenny. (*Ima steps away, Ashley approaches.*)

**Jenny:** Oh good, there you are! You're my neighbor, Evelyn. I haven't seen you in a long while.

**Ashley:** Hi, Jenny. I'm glad to see you!

**Jenny:** Hi . . . hi . . . hi . . . (*with voice trailing off, becoming confused*). Are we at home? Where are we?

**Ashley:** We're at church.

**Jenny:** Church? I thought we were at home. How did we get here?

**Ashley:** We came here in cars. Church is a place that feels like home, sort of. (*making eye contact, keeping her voice steady and calm*) Tell me about your home, Jenny.

**Jenny:** (*sighs and looks into the distance*) Home. . . . Big, wide streets. Tall trees. It's called Fairmont Hills. I love to ride my bike on those hills. Feels like I'm flying. I ride sometimes with the children. They're both into bike riding now. Got bikes last Christmas. (*laughs lightly*) I'm afraid Jay and I might wind up on welfare if we keep giving them such expensive gifts!

**Narrator:** Ashley doesn't correct Jenny. She simply responds as a neighbor might and lets Jenny steer the conversation. Jenny begins to talk about the distant past, as though it's occurring in the present: She has young children; she goes bike riding with them. And this is okay; it's good. She feels happy talking about this part of her life. Now let's see what is happening between Ima and Jenny. (*Ashley steps back, Ima sits down beside Jenny.*)

**Jenny:** (*agitated*) Church? This is a church? I didn't know we were at church. I don't like church.

**Ima:** You don't? I like church. Church is a good place to be (*nodding affirmatively and speaking as though to a child*). Good, and nice, and fun.

**Jenny:** I want to go home. There are too many people here!

**Ima:** (*firmly*) No, no, there are only a few. Look (*points to each*), you, and me, and Jay, your caregiver. See? Right over there.

**Jenny:** No! There are some people coming over here. I can see them. (*Holds her hands up, palms facing out, as if to make them stop*)

**Narrator:** Jenny might be hallucinating, which can occur with more advanced Alzheimer's and in other forms of dementia, too. Or she could also be misinterpreting what she sees. Ima becomes uneasy, and she contradicts Jenny— again. How do you think Jenny is feeling right now? Call out some words. [Let the group respond.] We'll go back to the conversation and look at a different way to handle this situation. (*Ima steps back, Ashley sits down beside Jenny.*)

**Jenny:** Big, wide streets. I love to ride my bike on those hills. Feels like I'm flying sometimes.

**Ashley:** I like to ride my bike, too. I have a purple bike. What color is your bike?

**Jenny:** (*in a small, worried voice*) I don't know; I don't know. Why are there so many people here?

**Ashley:** (*calmly*) Do you see people? I don't see them, but I'll tell them to go away. You people, go on! Go somewhere else. Jenny and I are talking with each other. (*waits a few seconds*) Let's turn our chairs a little bit, so we don't see them anymore. (*moves her chair so it partially blocks Jenny's view of the room*) Is that better?

**Jenny:** Yes.

**Ashley:** We were talking about bicycles, Jenny. What kind of bicycle do you have?

**Jenny:** I don't know. I want to go home now. Can I go home?

**Ashley:** (*in a concerned voice*) Are you cold?

**Jenny:** I want to go home!

**Ashley:** Let me get Jay for you. Jay? I think Jenny may need you . . .

**Narrator:** Ashley doesn't argue with Jenny. She keeps her voice low and maintains friendly eye contact. When Jenny begins to get agitated, she tries to redirect the conversation with an easy question: *What color is your bike?* But Jenny insists: I want to go home. So Ashley asks if she's cold. A person with dementia might ask to go home because of a physical need: They're hungry, or cold, or in need of a restroom, and home represents comfort. When Jenny persists, Ashley calls for Jay, her caregiver. The caregiver will be around. If you're not sure what to say or do, it's okay to ask for help. Always ask for help when you need it!

**The End**

4. Discuss the skit:

- What differences can you see in Jenny now, compared to when she had mild or early-stage Alzheimer's? [She's confused about where she is; she doesn't recognize people she has known for a while; she talks about things that happened decades ago as though they are occurring in the present; she misperceives her surroundings; she's anxious.]

- What did Ashley do that worked for Jenny? [She accepted Jenny's reality. Without saying "Yes, I'm your neighbor," she accepted the role Jenny assigned to her, and she let Jenny control the conversation. She kept her comments and questions simple, without treating Jenny like a child, and relied on nonverbal cues (smiling, making eye contact, using an engaging tone of voice) to communicate more complex messages of security and positive regard.]

- Why was it important for Ashley to get Jay when Jenny asked to go home? [Because Jenny is unable to express her needs clearly and was becoming agitated. Church is different from day or residential dementia care, in which trained employees care for people with advanced dementia without a family caregiver present. In church, the caregiver will be close by, unless the person with dementia feels secure enough to cope with being left in the care of others for a while.]

- What did Ima do wrong? [She corrected and contradicted Jenny. When Jenny became apprehensive, she did, too. She raised her voice in an effort to help Jenny understand, but a raised voice may imply anger to a person who cannot comprehend the accompanying words. She addressed Jenny in babytalk ("good, nice, fun"), and Jenny shut down: "I want to go home. I don't like it here."]

- What did Ima do right? [She was sincerely trying to be with Jenny. She's not avoiding her.]

- How could Ima "remain in God," instead of yielding to her own discomfort? [She could stay gentle and quiet, no matter what; she could pray for herself and for Jenny. She could gratefully accept what Jenny has to offer: her presence at church, her willingness to engage in conversation, her responsiveness to indications of love and patience, her unique way of helping Ima and others accept and express the gifts of the Spirit we discussed earlier.]

### *Third Activity*

Objective: To develop empathy for caregivers; to learn ways of helping to ease stress.

Materials:

- Three copies of *"What I Said, What I Thought"* script (see below)
- Two chairs
- Playbills that set the scene and synopsis, give the cast (below), and list the following communication tips, with space for notetaking:

  o Listen; don't advise.
  o Keep away from criticism.
  o Avoid platitudes, even spiritual ones.
  o Reflect the caregiver's emotions.
  o Offer practical help if you can.

- Pens
- Slips of paper, each containing one of Jay's lines, [*Note*: See number 4 below for specifics.]

Time Required: About 30 minutes

Process:

1. Explain: This final skit demonstrates how caregiver stress can be exacerbated by a conversation in which the "church friend" does everything wrong (pretty much) with Jay, Jenny's caregiver, whom we met in the first skit. Caregiving to someone with moderately severe dementia, like Jenny at this point in the story, is complex. The solutions we might automatically imagine, such as securing additional help, may be impossible for many reasons, among them a loved one's inability to cope with it: The middle stage can bring about personality changes, depression, apathy, wandering, hoarding and hiding items, hallucinations, paranoia, and disinhibition—not always, but often. Dementia caregivers, for the most part, are doing their best in an overwhelming situation. Caregiving can be rewarding. It can also be isolating and physically, mentally, and emotionally exhausting.

2. Review the fruits of the Spirit: love, joy, peace, patience, kindness, generosity, faithfulness, gentleness, and self-control. We learned in the first activity that a person with dementia can help us learn to remain in God. We have the opportunity to express these qualities, or fruits of the Spirit, as we are pulled into unfamiliar interpersonal experiences. But caregivers may continually struggle with common human feelings: grief, anger, frustration, boredom, fear, envy, loneliness. Although we all experience and can relate to these feelings, our reaction to them in another person is often to problem solve, project, advise, minimize, or cajole—or to simply avoid the person altogether. Caregivers need for us to listen with kindness, patience, gentleness, and self-control. They need our empathetic, nonjudgmental presence. They need our companionship. And like the loved ones for whom they care, *they* need to guide *us* in how we can best help.

3. Distribute the playbills and explain how this skit differs from others: We are going to watch and participate in a conversation with Jay and a friend from church. Jay is also speaking with his "silent voice," a

character who expresses what he would like to say but can't, out of politeness. The skit will pause periodically, so we can discuss how Jay is feeling and how the conversation could have gone differently had his friend kept in mind the qualities we just mentioned.

## Characters:

- JAY: caregiver of Jenny, who is now approaching the late stage of Alzheimer's
- SILENT VOICE: character representing Jay's frustration
- FRIEND [*Note*: The script is written for a male character but can be easily adjusted.]
- NARRATOR [*Note*: Do not read the discussion points and answers in brackets. Pause and discuss; use the suggested answers to guide the discussion if needed.]

**Setting:** Two seats in a fellowship hall, with "Silent Voice" standing behind Jay

## "What I Said, What I Thought"

**Jay:** Like I said, Jenny is changing so much. I feel like I'm losing her altogether. I can't ask her a question. Simplest things, do you feel like eating spaghetti tonight? She stares at me with a blank face. Jenny, who loved to cook. She could make her own pasta from scratch. She doesn't have any idea what spaghetti is anymore.

**Friend:** Why don't you just make the spaghetti without asking her?

**Silent Voice:** (*impatiently*) I *know* I can make spaghetti without bothering to ask Jenny. That's not my point, is it? The point is that Jenny no longer knows *what* spaghetti *is*.

**Jay:** I usually give her two choices, so she won't have come up with anything herself. Every effort has to be minimal. This is hard for me. I was an accountant before I retired. I'm used to having things add up evenly, logically. I've always been a good problem solver. I've had to accept that it isn't a problem I can solve. (*sighs, hesitates*) It's a mess to manage.

**Friend:** (*critically*) A . . . *mess*? Do you really mean a mess? Wonder how poor Jenny would feel about that?

**Silent Voice:** Yes! A mess. I don't know how to talk to her anymore. She doesn't talk back. She follows me around, humming and asking questions that don't make sense. "Is Barbara here? Is Barbara here? Is Barbara here?" Well, who in the world is Barbara!? Sometimes she makes sense, but it's about what our children did thirty years ago, like it's now. I've started calling the pile of laundry Mount Washmore—I get one load done and add two more to the heap. It's so hard to keep her and everything else clean! We eat canned food for dinner most nights because I can't cook with her right beside me. It's all I can do to mix up six things for Chicken-of-the-Sea casserole. She needs help with everything, and everything takes a long time. Helping her brush her teeth takes a long time. "Open your mouth, Jenny. No, keep it open. Look, just please open your mouth." A *mess*? (*adamantly*) Yes, It's a mess.

**Jay:** Well, not a mess. I mean it's more of a challenge, I guess.

**Narrator:** Let's go back to what Jay said: "I've had to accept that it isn't a problem I can solve. It's a mess to manage." We'd rather hear him talk about his love for Jenny, despite her dementia, or about how his faith is helping him cope, wouldn't we? Instead, he describes his life in a desperate way. His life is a mess. He's frustrated and overwhelmed. Think of those conversational gifts he needs to receive from his friend: gentleness, self-control, kindness, patience. Think, too, of what he doesn't need, which is criticism or to have his problems minimized. How did his friend show disapproval? [With his tone of voice and his chiding questions]. How could the friend have responded differently? [The friend could have asked, *Do you want to talk about it? What is it like, living with Jenny now?* It wouldn't change Jay's circumstances, but how would compassionate listening have made him feel?]

**Jay:** That's it. A challenge. Definitely the biggest challenge of my life.

**Friend:** Well, remember, God doesn't give us more than we can bear.

**Silent Voice:** (*incredulous*) *Really?* What has God "given" you to bear, spending your retirement traveling around with a wife who can actually pack a suitcase and order from a menu? I wish God didn't think quite so much of me!

**Jay:** What do you mean, God doesn't give us more than we can bear?

**Friend:** Just that he's there for us, helping us through our troubles. You aren't alone.

**Silent Voice:** I am alone. I don't know what to do.

**Narrator:** How is the friend affecting Jay? [He's making Jay feel defensive and pressured into optimism.] Did it help Jay to be told God will not give him more than he can bear? [Allow time to answer.] First Corinthians 10:13 is the verse people refer to with that adage,[13] but in literal translations of the Bible, this verse is talking about *temptations*, not *hardships*. It's not a promise that our suffering will be made bearable. Think about it. Christian martyrs have been stoned, beheaded, skinned, and even grilled to death. What could the friend have said, instead, to comfort Jay? [He could have said, "You aren't alone. God is with you, and we are with you. We want to help; how can we help you and Jenny?"]

**Jay:** I don't mean to complain, but I'm tired. Jenny doesn't sleep through the night. She wanders around. I've put slip-locks on the outside doors. She doesn't understand how to open them, thank goodness. I don't worry about her getting out to the street in her pajamas, but she doesn't sleep, so I'm always half awake. The other night, she pulled all of the sheets and covers off the bed. I don't know what got in her mind. I had to make the bed up and coax her into it. By then, I was wide awake.

**Friend:** Can't her doctor give her sleeping pills?

**Jay:** We've tried that. I tried sleeping pills, too. They made me a zombie the next day.

**Friend:** Surely there's a silver lining here somewhere! What are the good parts of living with Jenny?

**Silent Voice:** I need to get away from this person. He's so clueless.

**Jay:** I'll always love Jenny, but the love is so different.

**Friend:** There, see? It's not all so terrible.

**Jay:** I didn't say it was *all* terrible. There were so many good times with Jenny before the dementia, I can't even begin to count them. (*shakes his head in disbelief*) Even now, she's some company, at least. I haven't ever lived alone. Part of me doesn't want her to go to a care facility, even though we're really struggling to manage.

**Narrator:** What is the friend doing wrong? [Again he's pressuring Jay into optimism and suggesting easy solutions to Jay's problems.] When is problem-solving more of a hindrance than a help? [When the other person has not asked for this kind of help, when you don't know what you're talking about, and when there isn't a solution—the problem of Jenny's dementia cannot be solved.]

**Jay:** My daughter told me she'd never allow her mother to live in a facility, as though it's entirely her decision.

**Friend:** I can see why. Some of those places are terrible, and it must be lonely for people, being taken care of by strangers in an institution.

**Jay:** I'm a stranger now to Jenny. She barely knows who I am. She pushes me away when she gets upset.

**Friend:** She knows you on some level. She seems to need you all the time. Do you realize how anxious she got, when you left the fellowship hall last Sunday?

**Jay:** She's becoming bothered by people. Wants to be at home and not go anywhere. She sits around sometimes for hours like a lump on a log, and I hate to admit that's it's a relief. I can't leave her with anyone—I'm afraid she'll fall. Then we might wind up in the emergency room. Good gosh, those places can be awful for a person with dementia. Jenny depends on a walker because of her bad knee, but sometimes she can't figure out how to use it. She collapses in a heap on the floor and won't get up.

**Friend:** Can your daughter stay with her?

**Jay:** With two kids running around? Ellen works part-time, volunteers for the literacy council. She coaches a youth league. We talk once a week, but it's not enough to give her a sense of how hard this is. She doesn't want to hear anything bad about her mother. Caregiving has taken over my life. Ellen's life consists of racing back and forth in her Volvo, if you can race in a Volvo. But that's her choice.

**Friend:** Well, keep your chin up. We're all praying for you. I have to get going. My wife and I are having some folks over for dinner, and she won't speak to me for a week if I don't help her get things ready.

**The End**

4. Depending on the size of the group, break into as many as five smaller groups or into pairs, and give each group one of Jay's lines, listed below. Tell the groups to (1) identify his emotions and why he feels the way he does, and (2) think of a response that reflects the emotion and demonstrates gentleness, patience, kindness, and self-control. [*Note:* "Emotions" and "Responses" beneath the lines are for only the group leader to use in guiding the discussion.]

○ **Jay (line 1):** "She's becoming bothered by people. She wants to be at home and not go anywhere. She sits around for hours. I can't leave her with anyone—I'm afraid she'll fall and we'll wind up in the emergency room."

Emotions: *Isolated* by Jenny's needs and changing response to others, *bored and lonely* spending long days with a person who can no longer be a companion, *anxious* that Jenny will hurt herself, *apprehensive* about the threat of a sudden episode in a hospital.

Responses:

— "Hospitals can be scary even when you know what's going on. The emergency room would be awful for Jenny—and for you, with her."
— "The days are long for you, at home alone with Jenny, aren't they?"
— "As hard as you try, there's so much you cannot control."

○ **Jay (line two):** "I'm a stranger now to Jenny. She barely knows who I am. She needs help with everything, and everything takes a long time. Helping her brush her teeth takes a long time."

Emotions: *Grief* over his loss of Jenny's companionship and their previous relationship, *frustration* over how much time is taken by activities we normally do without thinking.

Responses:

— "It hurts to lose a spouse or partner. Jenny was your best friend, and now she can't fill that role for you."

— "We take for granted that we'll always be able to brush our hair and teeth. All of those simple things are a challenge now for Jenny. You never expected this."

- **Jay (line three):** "My daughter told me she wouldn't allow her mother to live in a facility, as though it's entirely her decision."

Emotions: *Misunderstood* by his daughter, *troubled* that if he has to place Jenny elsewhere for care, he'll have to do it over his daughter's objections (which will make a hard decision even harder), *guilty* for wanting Jenny to live somewhere other than in her home.

Responses:

— "Your daughter doesn't realize what you are going through, day after day, taking care of her mother,"
— "It must add to your stress to have your family telling you what to do; they aren't the caregivers."
— "Choosing a care facility has to be one of the most wrenching decisions to make. Do you have anyone to talk to who's gone through it before?"

- **Jay (line four):** "I don't know how to talk to Jenny anymore. She doesn't talk back. Sometimes she talks, but it's about what happened thirty years ago, like it's now. I'll always love Jenny, but the love is so different."

Emotions: *Resigned* to a relationship that no longer meets his physical and emotional needs, *sad* that Jenny is unable to respond to his care, maybe *worried* that no one will be around to take care of him, should he need it.

Responses:

— "You miss the way Jenny was. It would be impossible not to."
— "You love Jenny, because she's still Jenny inside, but you hate what this disease has done to her. I hate it for you, too."
— "You miss her love for you and having her care about you. Anyone would."

- o **Jay (line five):** "Like I said, Jenny's changing so much. I feel like I'm losing her altogether. I can't ask her a question. Simplest things, do you feel like eating spaghetti tonight? She stares at me with a blank face. Jenny, who loved to cook. She could make her own pasta from scratch."

  <u>Emotions</u>: *Powerless* to help Jenny with her constant problems understanding anything, *uncertain* of how to relate to her.

  <u>Responses</u>:

  — "You miss the Jenny you knew and could count on."
  — "Alzheimer's must seem like a wall that keeps getting higher and higher, cutting Jenny off from you."

5. Going in the order of the lines, have each group share Jay's line, his feelings, and the new response. The leader should guide the discussion using the suggested emotions and responses if the groups are coming up with ideas that are understandable but not helpful, such as, "I don't know how you stand it. I'd go crazy," or "I totally get why you'd put her in a home. I would, too!"

6. Consider the friend's departure. It was not only a brushoff but an insensitive comparison of Jay's life to his own: The friend is able to have a dinner party with his wife; he has a social life. Have you ever faced a difficult experience when your friends didn't know what to say and somehow made it worse?

7. How can you be sensitive, when the circumstances between you and a friend are very different, and yours are better? You don't want to walk on eggshells, afraid to say anything positive about your own life for fear of making your friend feel left out. [You can make an ongoing effort to imagine yourself in your friend's place, and you can be willing to hold back on the happy details of your own life that correspond directly to your friend's loss or difficulty: "We're doing well enough. I was excited over my son's promotion. He worked hard for it, with all of those nightshifts." *Not*: "We're doing well enough. Sue and I are going on a cruise to the Cyclades Islands. Did I tell you about that? We are so excited!"]

## LESSON TWO: UNDERSTANDING LATE-STAGE DEMENTIA

### *Leader Preparation*

In the skit from the previous lesson, "Jenny" is entering late-stage dementia: She requires continuous supervision and help with almost every activity; she's having difficulty managing a walker; she no longer consistently recognizes her spouse; she cannot communicate any of her needs. She may be unable to control her bowels and bladder. If she lives to the end of Alzheimer's, she will not remember how to swallow. A daughter describing her father, just before her mother's death, said he would stroke her mother's throat with his fingers to help her eat, begging, "Please, not yet. I'm not ready for you to go." And this followed years of intermittent combativeness, in which the woman unknowingly cursed, spit, and hissed at him.[14] Alzheimer's is ugly in its destruction of the brain, but sometimes caregivers show an equivalence of beauty in their displays of love and commitment.

We learned in chapter 2 not to make comparisons between caregivers: We all have different abilities, and some are more able than others to sustain love through the changes of dementia. Most dementia caregivers, myself included, have broken down. We've said and done things we regret, too many times. As needs intensify, problems become thornier and more complicated. Decisions are not clear-cut and must sometimes be made in concession to conflicting demands.

While thinking through how to help parishioners understand if they've never witnessed late-stage dementia in a loved one or friend, I heard a sermon,[15] given by Josh Bascom, the minister mentioned in this book's introduction. His words contained a suggestion. The sermon was about Lazarus's return from the dead, rotting flesh restored, still wrapped in burial linens.[16] This story is notable, Josh said, not only for what Jesus did—weep—but also for what he did not do, which was hand Mary a box of tissues and spout platitudes about loss. I would add, as well, that his tears simply and sincerely expressed his love for Lazarus. No one felt the obligation to comfort Jesus. He was quietly present with Martha and Mary in grief, much as Josh was present for me in the week or so before my father's death.

I was aware of the similarities between Lazarus, entombed, his body beginning the process of disintegration, and people in the last ravages of dementia, with brains atrophied and limbs rendered useless, as though bound by strips of cloth. Jesus, in spite of his ultimate power over death, wept. If we allow ourselves to enter viscerally into the world of a person dying of dementia or a caregiver witnessing this death, we cannot help but have our own emotions aroused, and in the sincere sharing of pain, there is comfort and relief, even in our powerlessness to change the situation.

### *Activity*

<u>Objective</u>: To learn compassion for people in the late-stage of dementia and their caregivers, friends, and loved ones; to learn ways of meeting practical needs.

<u>Materials</u>:

- Computer or other means of listening to two 10-minute NPR stories,[17] "Tom Debaggio's Journey Continues" (https://www.npr.org/2005/05/19/4658784/tom-debaggios-alzheimers-journey-continues) and "A Decade of Alzheimer's Devastating Impact " (https://www.wrvo.org/2010-06-16/a-decade-of-alzheimers-devastating-impact).

- Handouts or a large chart listing the symptoms of late-stage Alzheimer's. There are many reliable organizations, such as the Alzheimer's Association (www.alz.org), that provide this information. However, for a concise, printable summary,[18] access the web page "Severe (Late-Stage) Alzheimer's Disease," from *Alzheimer's News Today*, a division of the digital media firm BioNews, Inc: https://alzheimersnewstoday.com/severe-alzheimers-late-stage/.

<u>Time Required</u>: About 45 minutes

<u>Process</u>:

1. Using the handout, review the symptoms of late-stage Alzheimer's: What do you think would be the most challenging part of caregiving for you if you had a loved one in this stage? [Not being recognized; personality changes; erratic, unpredictable, or irrational behaviors; the difficulty of addressing basic needs, such as eating and bathing when these necessary acts are met with resistance and incomprehension; the lack of companionship; the isolation; the challenges of securing alternative care; being misunderstood, possibly, by other relatives; the anticipation of death]

2. Share the story of Tom Debaggio, an herbalist and nurseryman diagnosed with Alzheimer's disease at age fifty-seven, and his wife and caregiver, Joyce. Debaggio authored three award-winning books on gardening and two memoirs about his life with dementia, *Losing My Mind* and *When It Gets Dark: An Enlightened Reflection on Life with Alzheimer's*. Wikipedia has the basic facts on Debaggio's work. At his death, the *Washington Post* ran an obituary about his life.[19] He was known for his cultivation of herbs (particularly rosemary) and in later life for his advocacy for Alzheimer's, his openness about his condition, and his sense of humor.

3. Listen to the first NPR interview. What characteristics do we see in Tom that indicate his condition? [His speech is slow and hesitating; he is confused with directions; he has lost the ability to read.] Discuss these points:

   o We've learned that Alzheimer's is a progression backwards in terms of the competencies we acquire during normal human development. Where do you see Tom fitting into this scheme? [He seems to have skills that would be expected in early to middle childhood but is not, otherwise, childlike. He allows us to see regression in skills accompanied by a simultaneous retention of adult sensitivities. Notice the way the reporter talks *to* Tom clearly, without talking *down to* him and abandons questions he does not know how to answer.]

   o Think back to an incident with "Jenny" in the first skit. Through the thought character, Jenny describes being embarrassed in a store, when she mistakenly asked for "gunk" instead of "gum." She remembers these details, although forgetting much of the recent past, because it attached to the strong emotion of shame. Where do we see this happening to Tom? [He vividly remembers getting lost in his car. The memory persists because of the fear he felt.]

   o Why is it important to realize that our emotions play a part in memory? [Because it frees us from dependence on language. Understanding of gestures, tones, and facial expressions that bring comfort and pleasure remains intact almost to the end. The qualities we've been discussing throughout these activities, the fruits of the Spirit, may thus be communicated nonverbally, even if language is lost, through a gentle touch or a kind voice. We can show patience nonverbally, and this is especially important in late-stage dementia: A person in late-stage Alzheimer's may sometimes smell of urine; she can no longer use silverware or a napkin. If such lapses are hard to tolerate, this is when can we pray to receive true gifts that will override our sensitivities and enable us to show unconditional love.]

4. Listen to the second NPR interview, in which Tom is near the end of his life. His wife has placed him in a facility due to the impossibility of caring for him at home. He is no longer able to communicate using language.

    o In the skits we've watched, some of the characters had their thoughts revealed, and we were given a deeper view into how each was feeling and why. If Tom could step outside his dementia and talk to us, what would he say?

    o Until Tom went to a nursing home, Joyce Debaggio was caring incessantly for a person who could not talk, or feed himself, or sit on a stool for bathing, or use a toilet, or understand that a bed is for sleeping. She tells about her caregiving in heartbreaking detail in a later interview (no longer available) with BBC News.[20] Joyce says with obvious reluctance, "I didn't have any [help]. . . . When he became incontinent, it became really difficult because I was constantly cleaning up after him. He would pull down his pants and go to the bathroom anywhere. And I found that too difficult to deal with." It was her breaking point: Tom's care had become too difficult for her to manage. How could we, as a church, support caregivers, in both practical and emotional ways, through years and years of such hardship?

## CONCLUSION

The lessons in this chapter and the previous one are meant to help people who haven't lived with dementia develop a sense of its challenges and learn to interact with compassion throughout the difficult journey. We've considered the ways people, even those with advanced dementia, can help us experience God's love and provide for us a way of expressing it ourselves, through gifts of the Spirit. In this lifetime, we know, there is no greater joy available to us. We've learned, hopefully, to recognize and try to set aside preconceived notions and reflexive responses and to see ourselves on equal footing with everyone as members of God's church, no matter what.

I want to close with an example from my own life of what fruits of the Spirit may mean, when the fruit is both a product of will and of our ongoing connection to God, our "remaining," as John uses this word.[21] I was keeping vigil with my father at the hospital where he died, and, by then, was beyond much meaningful interaction. Every one of his 20,000 breaths a day was labored, as though drawn through a pinhole. I had been at his bedside for weeks, and my shoulders constantly burned with the effort of sitting for so many hours at a stretch and from the stress of witnessing this long death. A nurse came to check on him, and we exchanged a few words about his condition. She looked at me for a long moment, then walked around the bed, and, standing behind me, began to rub my shoulders. I felt suddenly a sense that I wasn't alone, that someone was aware and watching, and tears ran in two silent, insistent streams down my face and neck. I don't remember whether she said anything else, but I remember her gentle, loving touch and the release of those tears. I think this nurse must have acted with compassion countless times, until these gestures became instinctive to her, without conscious intent or thought, like fruit emanating from who she was in God, as a gift of the relationship. This is what we want to bring to those who are suffering, whatever the cause: our willing compassion and our "remaining."

# CHAPTER 7

# Programs That Work

There are several ways churches can plan dementia-friendly programs that bring together their members and residents of the surrounding community, many of whom likely struggle with dementia in one way or another. As we learned from Kenneth Carder in chapter 4, such a ministry is provided *with* not *to* people with dementia, and the rewards stream in both directions. In this chapter we'll look at six programs, most already running successfully in churches: The good news is that there's no need to reinvent the wheel. We only need to prepare a place in which existing wheels can easily turn.

Whether these wheels turn in a particular church setting depends on how well matched the ministry is to the congregation's readiness. If a ministry will be comprised mainly of groups, such as caregiver support groups or respite programs, in which interested parishioners can choose to participate, the preparatory work described in previous chapters can be discerningly provided to those who are interested. As a case in point, this chapter will look at the highly successful dementia program provided by First United Methodist Church in Montgomery, Alabama (FUMC). FUMC's ministry includes three activities in which members participate if they want to. Many do, given the pleasure of these activities for everyone involved.

If the goal, on the other hand, is to affect a cultural shift within the church, in which all members develop informed compassion toward people living through dementia, educational efforts will need to be comprehensive and in-depth. Caregivers and their loved ones may then participate in any facet of church, to any reasonable extent, in a context of acceptance and understanding.

As discussed, however, advanced dementia is disturbing. Recall Thomas Debaggio's wife in chapter 6 describing her husband's inability to use a toilet. If the aim of a ministry is to create programs in which people with earlier stage dementia mingle with volunteers for social activities, exposure to such hard stories might be counterproductive. Some of us are better able than others to cope with the physical realities of disease.

The ambition of this book is to provide a toolkit of information, materials, suggestions, and ideas. Like any toolkit, the tools must be used selectively, depending on what, specifically, is being built and how. We've looked at the problems and progression of dementia to better understand what people in this situation face from day to day, year to year. Now we shift to the joyful business of making a difference in the most realistic ways possible for various church situations and communities.

At least some of the isolation brought about by dementia can be alleviated through the social opportunities churches offer. Many communities have little in the way of activities and affordable services that support caregivers and their loved ones. Churches with viable, welcoming programs become magnets to people who might otherwise live in secluded hardship.

We'll consider six program options, each of which would contribute in a different way to a dementia-friendly church environment: respite, caregiver support groups, social cafes or breakfast clubs, adapted worship services, comfort rooms, and practical help. By reducing stress and isolation, any of these will help both the person who has dementia and the caregiver. A caregiver, for example, who attends a regular support group is less likely to experience depression and more able to cope,[1] and these advantages will impact the quality of care he or she can provide.

It goes without saying that to start small, follow the example of others, and build upon success is a sensible route to "loving" wisdom, as femininely personified in Proverbs, thereby engaging her useful protections.[2] No one wants to forge by trial and error into efforts that may collapse for lack of proper preparation, funding, leadership, or involvement. Thankfully, solid houses have been built already in these areas, for the most part, and blueprints provided.

Consider how each might fit into a strategic plan that defines the scope of the initiative at your church, its timeframe, and the process by which it will be executed. According to advisor Juan Riboldi of Forbes Coaches Council, there are seven planning steps businesses should take when initiating new projects to increase success, unite people around common objectives, and guide decision-making.[3] Although churches do not share the secular motives of businesses, these seven steps can be adapted to the church setting, to draft a plan that can expand and change over time:

1. **Assess.** Chapter 4 contains a short assessment tool to ascertain the congregation's knowledge and readiness, suggesting how much advance education may be needed to encourage the compassionate culture we seek to inspire. Chapters 5 and 6 include resources and teaching tools to use as the building blocks of an educational program that can be as brief or detailed as needed.

2. **Ascertain strengths and weaknesses.** How much space does the church have for a respite program—to use this as an example—and is there a restroom located near the space? Is adjacent parking available? Is signage required to provide easy directions to the space, bearing in mind that people with dementia will need these directions every single time they attend? Is the lighting along the route adequate? Is there an existing group or committee that could readily provide volunteers to start the program? Is there a qualified person interested in serving as director?

3. **Define the initiative in terms of mission.** Resistance to change can be overcome by helping those most affected by the change envision the ways in which it will actually facilitate an organization's longstanding missions.[4] In other words, the change is natural, given its relevance. To use respite programs as an example again, a new activity that regularly ushers in a potentially large group of people needing to be entertained and perhaps served lunch can be seen either as daunting or as yet another exciting way to further an important purpose, depending on how the undertaking is framed by its organizers.

4. **Set goals.** Think about the programs described in this chapter. Which would fit most seamlessly into your church's mission statement, available resources, and the congregation's interests and needs? Following the necessary education, would it be logical to proceed first with a monthly breakfast club? A caregiver support group? Set goals to accomplish one workable measure first.

5. **Define objectives and initiatives.** Riboldi advises limiting the number of proposed actions related to the goals, so that all may be accomplished in no more than a year's time. Expansion can happen incrementally, and this is a better strategy than biting off more than can be chewed, an idiom which originally (in a word to the wise) implied a mistake with tobacco that could be fatal.

6. **Figure out funding.** Respite programs usually involve a daily charge per participant, billed monthly, that offsets or eliminates costs. Caregiver support groups do not, but they also entail nothing more than a private meeting place with coffee and snacks. Dementia cafes or breakfast clubs may assess a small fee at the door. There are likely costs involved in publicizing activities within the greater community and in making necessary changes within the church building, a topic that will be discussed later in the chapter. Additional insurance may be required for certain activities, increasing the premium cost. These are issues to resolve in advance to eliminate any challenge to the church's budget.

7. **Develop a means of periodic evaluation.** Evaluating at intervals allows for tractable corrections if the program begins to flounder. When FUMC began a worship service for people with dementia, it eventually fell flat. This didn't happen due to flagging interest, overlong sermons, bad music, or lack of volunteers. It happened because it was scheduled at an inconvenient time for caregivers. When the time was changed to coincide with the respite program, it succeeded brilliantly: Everyone who wanted to participate was already there.[5]

## RESPITE PROGRAMS

The respite program at First United Methodist Church (FUMC) of Montgomery was started by Daphne Johnston, author of *Reclaiming Joy Together*, and is staffed by "an army of volunteers."[6] The program is like a cross between adult summer camp, the local coffee house, and a family-style restaurant, where church members mingle happily with people in the mild-to-moderate stages of dementia, and a good time, it appears, is had by all. But it's more than a daily event that will be quickly forgotten by some; it's a setting where fear, shame, embarrassment, inequality, and awkwardness simply are not part of the experience. Everyone is on the same footing, as evidenced by nametags bearing only a first name, exactly the same for volunteers as for participants. Through this program the church provides a place for caregivers to bring their loved ones, knowing they'll be assured a "respite" of absolute acceptance and fun, while the caregiver, thus relieved of responsibility, is given time for a much-needed break. Respite programs have *tremendous* potential to make a difference, both within the community and the church itself. FUMC's program has generated, from the start, nothing short of unbridled enthusiasm. Eager volunteers (not participants) must be turned away at times, and caregivers with deep pockets have surprised Johnston with unsolicited, generous gifts, which she's parlayed into an impressive movement. She easily brushes off her personal success, describing the whole venture as "a God thing."

Johnston's mission is for the program to spread. She realizes that respite programs work best when they occupy different locations throughout a given geographic area, making the service easily accessible to caregivers, who must do the driving.[7] The more respite programs lodged in churches, synagogues, and other places of worship, the better. To this end, Johnston offers local training and has by means of a substantial grant created a set of purchasable videos that outline exactly how to implement the program, from financial planning to training the "buckets" of volunteers who will emerge, she says, given an inspiring vision. She describes respite as joyful, a place with open doors: Anyone can attend, as long as they are comfortable in a large group, can use the restroom independently, and are capable of feeding themselves. "We 'blur the line' between everyone's talents," Johnston explains, "Everyone belongs here. Everyone can serve, can have a group and can be a part of things."[8]

Although the program at FUMC runs from ten to two o'clock, Monday through Thursdays, many churches start with just one day a week. The 2022 fee for attending (reduced or waived at any mention of financial strain, no verification required) was forty dollars per day. With fifteen paying participants, a one-day-a-week program can generate $30,000 per year—even without the donations that Johnston predicts will flow from grateful caregivers, relatives, and volunteers, if her experience is at all typical.[9] This revenue can be used to cover the salary of a part-time director and all other expenses. It's a financially sustainable program that meets an overwhelming community need: Almost six million family or unpaid caregivers provide dementia care in community settings in the United States; 8 percent of older adults living in communities have dementia, and this statistic, compiled by the national

Department of Health and Human Services, probably excludes many people with mild cognitive impairment (MCI) and early-stage dementia.[10]

To get started, Johnston advises researching the Respite for All Foundation website (https//www. respiteforall.org), which contains information about the instructional videos mentioned above. She lists three essentials a church must have: an available space[11] in which to operate, a part-time director (salaried or paid an hourly rate), and a food source, such as a caterer. The "roadmap"[12] of videos details the steps that were used to develop twenty-five successful respite care programs. Johnston realizes the process is intimidating. The hardest part, she admits, is getting started. Her book,[13] which is blissfully easy to read, gives practical advice down to a list of suggested supplies and is a good initial resource for interested churches. But the instructional videos provide the complete set of tools. Her goal is to have the program replicated. At the time of this writing, Johnston has (trustingly) listed her phone number and email address on the foundation website, and she's willing to help anyone who contacts her. Be prepared, though: It's difficult not to be swept up by her enthusiasm.

> Is there a Biblical remedy for the isolation and desperation often experienced by those with dementia and especially by their families? What does "the priesthood of all believers" mean when we are dealing with Alzheimer's? Through hands-on participation with individuals and families, respite ministry enables us to experience for ourselves a theology of creation, a theology of redemption, and a theology of hope. —Daphne Johnson, (*Reclaiming Joy Together*, 75)

## CAREGIVER SUPPORT GROUPS

As part of their dementia ministry, First United Methodist of Montgomery (along with thousands of other churches and service-oriented groups)[14] hosts a caregiver support group. It began on the unlikely evening of a blinding thunderstorm that extinguished electricity at the church. Twenty-one caregivers braved this storm and met in candlelight, so great was the need in their lives for people in the same boat, from whom they could gain comfort by sharing their stories.

Dementia caregiving is like trying to sail continually through just such a storm, while a recalcitrant crew scurries around shooting holes in the boat's hull. It's heartbreaking, frustrating, exhausting, inconstant work with no end in sight other than the death, one skill at a time, of the loved one for whom this care is given. There are, of course, bright, sweet moments, and we trust God to bring it all to good, revealing to us its gifts along the way: Kenneth Carder provides us with an example to follow. But no matter how optimistic and faith-filled a caregiver's perspective, dementia caregiving is hard, and friends and family don't always get it. They do not comprehend the overwhelming responsibility, the grief, and the insolvability of many problems it causes. A support group in which caregivers can commiserate and exchange ideas, while feeling deeply understood, is reminiscent, somehow, of Jesus telling the wind to be still,[15] at least for a while. Some support groups bond and form a circle of relationships that compensates for a prior social life that caregiving has upended.

Starting a caregiver support group requires a plan, competent leadership, a private space to meet, and members who understand the group guidelines. Some support groups are highly structured, but the groups I have led, or in which I've taken part, consist of people with a related concern who want to be in a safe, confidential place in which difficult experiences and feelings can be shared. Many full-time caregivers are with a spouse or parent, day and night, who cannot carry on a coherent conversation. Support groups are thus an outlet for adult social interaction. Although guest speakers addressing relevant topics are beneficial from time to time,[16] support groups are mainly for open, nurturing communication between people who must cope with dementia and want to talk about it.

## Planning a Support Group

1. **Define the purpose.** Is the purpose to provide a place where caregivers, whether church goers or not, can help each other in a safe setting, as described above, or will the group be religiously oriented, since it is under the auspices of a church? If the group is composed only of church members, an opening prayer offered by the group leader may be comforting, as well as the sharing of prayer requests.[17] Community members who aren't religious may feel disingenuous, however, if swept unexpectedly into a sacred activity they regard with indifference or disagreement. Communicate the group's purpose in a way that correctly guides the expectations of prospective members.

2. **Determine the meeting time.** Caregiver groups are best scheduled when caregivers can attend, and unfortunately, caregivers are often anchored at home for most of the day. People with advanced dementia cannot safely be left alone. They require either an adult sitter (not always easy to find) or a care arrangement, like the respite program described above, whenever the caregiver wishes to leave them even for a couple of hours. You can assign a meeting time and hope for the best, but consider putting out an inquiry first by email or a notice in the church bulletin: "Our memory ministry team is planning a dementia caregiver support group for church and community members. If you are interested, or know someone who might be, please contact the church office and tell us your preference for a meeting time (morning, afternoon, or evening) and frequency (once a month or twice a month). More details to come."

3. **Decide how you will train support group leaders and recruit two leaders per group of seven or more members.** The initial inquiry mentioned above should yield an idea of how many people may attend. The optimum number for a support group, based on my experience, is ten, give or take a few in either direction. If many more sign up or show up, either offer two separate groups at the outset (recruiting more volunteer leaders as needed), or arrange to split the large group in half on the night of the meeting. Enlist two leaders for each group. Leading a support group can be deceptively difficult, depending on the personalities and needs of the participants. Having two leaders not only allows for larger groups to be divided if necessary but allays the tension that may be felt by one, should group dynamics prove challenging.

4. **Plan for group leader training.** Some people are naturally gifted group leaders: They are compassionate, confident, sensible, outgoing people who relate well to others and can subtly keep control of a group. Most of us, though, need a bit of direction. If there is a psychologist or counselor in the congregation who works with families and groups, count your blessings and try to persuade them to accept the role of training support group leaders. Alternatively, seek out a local expert from the community or regional Alzheimer's Association. See appendix 3 for a guide to use in developing your own training workshop, should neither of these options be available.

5. **Work out the logistics.** Support groups generally meet for sixty to ninety minutes, depending on how many are present on a given day. Participants need comfortable chairs arranged around a table or in a circle, in a quiet, private room, where there will be no interruptions (for example, not next to the sanctuary when the organist may show up to rehearse). Drinks and snacks are nice if the budget allows. Full-time caregivers often have little chance to get away for a good cup of coffee and a special pastry, and this is a way of "caring for the caregiver," to use a well-worn phrase, the importance of which cannot be overstated. Small kindnesses matter when life is hard.[18] If the church can afford it, go the extra mile to make caregiver groups special.

6. **Clearly state the group's intention.** Develop a written statement to provide to each group attendee, which includes the purpose, a disclaimer (which may be important for legal reasons)[19] and the expectations, for example: "Caregivers Comfort is a monthly support group for caregivers and family members of loved ones with dementia to share their experiences, feelings, and suggestions in a compassionate setting. We do not provide group therapy or professional advice, just a safe place to be with others who understand. *Safe* means we expect that we can trust each other to keep the group confidential, we allow everyone enough time to talk, and we don't criticize, judge, or give each other unwanted advice."

7. **Promote.** Announce the group, its purpose (see item 1 above), and the date and time of meetings, perhaps with an invitational flyer. Depending on how wide you wish to cast the net, send it as an email to all church members, and post it in libraries, senior centers, and other places where people visit community notice boards. Make announcements at worship and church functions. Include a notice in the church bulletin. Ask active parishioners to spread the word. Make use of social media.

8. **Plan a fixed agenda.** The following is a sample 90-minute agenda along with a brief explanation of each item. An agenda encourages appropriate contributions, provides a tool to review the group's purpose (third item below), and helps to keep the group on task.[20] It should be shared at the group's beginning and perhaps posted in view during group meetings.

- <u>Arrival</u> (about 10–15 minutes): greetings to each other, refreshments
- <u>Opening</u> (3–5 minutes): welcome, prayer or devotion
- <u>Review the group's purpose and introduce new members</u> (about 5 minutes)
- <u>Checking in</u> (about 45 minutes): Each person is given the opportunity to share what has happened since the last group.
- <u>Review and focus</u> (15–20 minutes): The group leader asks about any past concerns, directs more attention to individuals who may need it, or asks questions to encourage discussion around a common theme or problem.
- <u>Closing</u> (5 minutes): prayer requests or thoughts before ending.

## SOCIAL CAFES/BREAKFAST CLUBS

Respite programs in churches, as mentioned, are usually for people in the early to early-moderate phase of dementia, who are comfortable being apart from their caregiver. Lay volunteers are not equipped to help with toileting and feeding or to cope with separation anxiety and other difficult emotional states. Although Johnston concedes that some who participate in FUMC's program wear incontinence garments and must be hand-fed, she says they've aged into this stage while participating over a period of years; as long as they're happy enough to be there, they are allowed to remain. However, a few toileting mishaps in a row, she says, would be cause for a conversation with the caregiver about whether continued attendance at respite is appropriate.

What can be done, then, by a church for people further down the road of dementia, who cannot manage their basic needs without help, even for the short period of a few hours, or feel insecure if separated from a caregiver? One answer is to provide a social venue for caregivers and their loved ones to attend together, and one way in which people have connected since time immemorial is over food. We eat to survive; we eat in fellowship to develop friendships. A study in the UK linked staggeringly important benefits to regularly sharing meals with others, irrespective of age or sex: increased satisfaction with life, happiness, health, community engagement, trust in others, and supportive friendships. These benefits were enhanced if the shared meals involved laughter and reminiscing,[21] which is important for everyone but most especially people with dementia, for whom long-term memory, what remains of it, eventually becomes the only toehold on reality.

A church-organized meal such as a breakfast or lunch club can provide caregivers and loved ones a place to eat out with others, away from home, in a setting that caters to their needs. It can be at the church or at a restaurant that can accommodate these needs.

## Hosting at a Restaurant

For several years I ran a breakfast club for the Alzheimer's Association, attended by caregivers and their loved ones. We met once a month at ten o'clock, at a local hotel that offered a breakfast buffet for a nominal cost. Five or six couples came regularly. With two volunteers, we managed to get everyone through the line and seated, although not always easily. (Based on the experience, I recommend no less than one volunteer per couple in a situation that involves making food choices, serving oneself, and balancing a tray containing multiple items, one of which is hot coffee in an unstable paper cup.) A late breakfast was more convenient than lunch or dinner because few hotel guests were milling about at that time of day, and caregivers had several hours to manage morning tasks: It is frankly impossible for a caregiver to rush away early with a person whose emotions are unpredictable and for whom time has become irrelevant. Planning in advance was unnecessary, an advantage that provided caregivers the flexibility of opting out at the last minute on difficult mornings.

Because caregivers are present, breakfast club can be more lenient than respite, but there are still some restrictions due to its setting. The club I organized was open to participants who were comfortable away from home and able to eat with inconspicuous assistance, such as cutting food into bite-sized pieces or helping to get a fork in hand. I made new friends in this club, and everyone, I think, appreciated the sense of normality and the enjoyment of time away from home. As dementia grinds on, caregivers may have few opportunities to eat at a restaurant, and even an ordinary hotel dining room was a treat.

Here are a few things to consider, if you are planning a breakfast or dinner club at a restaurant:

1. Choose a quiet restaurant or hotel with easy parking and buffet—or cafeteria-style service. Such an arrangement will eliminate the confusion of ordering from a menu and sorting out a flurry of different checks at the end. If possible, arrange for the caregiver to pay at the desk upon arrival.

2. Secure the proprietor's permission in advance. This can best be done with a visit, in which the program and its purpose are explained. On posted flyers or written communication, thank the establishment for their generosity in hosting the program and use every opportunity to support it with good reviews and a good word around the community. Always call a day ahead to ensure there will be an adequate number of tables reserved in a dedicated area, preferably not in the middle of the room or near the kitchen.

3. Meet at an off-time for other diners: mid-morning breakfast, late lunch, early dinner.

4. Try to have sufficient volunteers to greet each couple at the door and usher them to the dining room, and to help throughout the meal.

5. Require the caregiver to sign up initially to allow for minimal screening and to make expectations clear: The caregiver must stay the whole time; the person with dementia must be comfortable away from home, able to sit through an hour-long dinner, and feed themselves using a fork or spoon.

6. Have a few easy conversation topics in mind to gently redirect in case the discussion veers into areas that might cause discomfort, hurt feelings, or exclusion—for example, politics, the difficulties of caregiving,[22] or chronic complaining.

7. Always thank both the caregiver and loved one for making the effort to attend. Jot down a few notes for the next get-together to foster a sense of care and continuity: "Jay, last time we met, you and Jenny were planning to visit your sister. Were you able to go? Did you have a nice time?"

*Hosting at the Church*

As an alternative, host the meal at the church by engaging an inexpensive caterer.[23] Dinner could, of course, be provided by the casserole brigade or a Sunday school group, and most churches have kitchens. However, you might start out with a caterer until you have a good sense of how many will attend and how demanding the activity is. There are definite advantages to hosting at the church. People with dementia can be prone to odd behaviors. Michael, whom we've discussed, said that Elaine was apt to enthusiastically embrace strangers whenever they went out in public. Michael was mortified, mumbling excuses as he tried to pry her arms away. In a church, these hugs could simply be reciprocated. Elaine was only expressing her lifelong love of people, absent the ability to discriminate between her own friends and family and everyone else.

Here are some issues to take into account when hosting a meal at the church:

1. At the church, with the caregiver present, you may allow for greater dementia-related differences. The caregiver can offer more obvious help with eating. Behaviors can be accepted that might not be permissible in a restaurant. Decide whether you will open the event to anyone (at least for a trial period) as long as the caregiver is prepared to handle difficulties that arise, or will exclude people with, for example, a tendency to become aggressive when frustrated or overstimulated by a noisy environment.[24] Again, have the caregiver register in advance so these issues can be discussed.

2. Decide how to handle the cost: Will it be a flat fee that covers either catering or food prepared by church members? If so, determine the lowest amount per person needed to keep the program solvent.

3. If you permit people with more advanced dementia to attend, the food provided should be easy to eat (no steaming hot lasagna or overstuffed burritos) and table settings made as simple as possible (no patterned tablecloths or plates, only one piece of cutlery or food that can be neatly eaten with the fingers).

4. A restroom with enough space for two should be either very near the dining room or the route to it marked by clear signage. Equip the

restroom with the following items: Depends or other incontinence products in medium and large sizes, disposable undergarments, a box of disposable wash towels, a large, lined, lidded wastebasket, and a few articles of extra clothing that can be used if needed for a mishap and not returned (unisex or gender-appropriate shirts, pants with adjustable waistbands, a cardigan or sweatshirt jacket that does not pull over the head). Add a café curtain that can be pulled over the mirror, which may be needed if mirrors are no longer understood by a persona with later-stage dementia as a reflection of self.

5. As before, have at least one volunteer friend present per caregiver couple.

If planning a full meal is too great a challenge, try a morning coffee or afternoon tea with drinks and snacks, perhaps centered around a reminiscing activity, such as making a memory book.[25] A memory book is a chance for a person to share who they've been, whom they've loved, what they've done and achieved, where they've traveled, and so on.

Here are a few ideas for a memory book:

1. Ask the caregiver to bring clippings and copies of photos that show children, life events, pets, and favorite places. Representative photos could be cut from old magazines, as an alternative, but it may be difficult to manage collage-making while drinking coffee—best in this case to have an afternoon event with bottled water, soft drinks, and no sticky donuts. Cutting and pasting is a good way to involve a person with dementia in a tactile activity, even if the finished product is a bit messy. Do whatever helps the group have fun, revising the plan as needed. It's hard to anticipate what will work best. Stay flexible and creative, and keep your sense of humor.

2. Assign a volunteer to each caregiver couple to help with food and drinks, encourage story-telling about the photos, and write an entry that highlights the life of the person with dementia. If making a memory book is to be an ongoing activity, center each coffee hour around one topic, such as *Accomplishments*. For example, I could write this entry about my father's career: "Jack McDaniel, MD, practiced obstetrics for fifty years. He delivered more than 10,000 babies,

enough to fill the whole indoor stadium where he lived, during a career he has always described as joyful. He was known for singing while he delivered babies, usually the song by Patti Page for which he named his farm, *Mockingbird Hill*. 'It's a wonderful thing,' he always said, 'a labor of love. You feel young when you deliver a baby.'"

3. If appropriate given the group's size and attention span, go around at the end, and allow each pair to share their contribution for that day: "Dad loved his work, didn't you? Do you want to tell us about it? My dad is an obstetrician and surgeon, and he delivered more babies than twenty times the number of people who come to this church, even on Christmas and Easter. This is a picture of him in his surgical scrubs. He practiced medicine for more than fifty years."

4. With caregiver permission, put out the books or make a display with the material to share these stories with other church members.[26]

## ADAPTED WORSHIP SERVICES

Lynda Everman and Don Wendorf served as senior editors for a collection of essays on meeting the worship needs of people with dementia, entitled, *Dementia Friendly Worship: A Multifaith Handbook for Chaplains, Clergy, and Faith Communities*. Everman and Wendorf, now married, were both dementia caregivers to their late spouses for a number of years and have been passionately involved in dementia advocacy. The book crosses many faiths and includes theoretical material as well as personal stories contributed by people with dementia, which provide a unique window into its challenges. Much of it covers how dementia-friendly worship services can be planned and conducted according to clergymen and others who've successfully done it, to great personal reward. This book truly is a handbook, with easily implemented suggestions, designed to help tailor worship services to the specific needs of people living with dementia.

Everman lobbied without success for her book to be entitled *The Soul Shines Forth*, to convey the sense, through imagery, that no matter how dementia may change the way someone comprehends, feels, or behaves, the soul is not altered. We connect at this level regardless of any physical differences between us. But as a person becomes less able to understand language and sit through an hour of worship, she needs to be involved in a shorter service that attaches meaningfully to remaining memories and strengths. "The whole idea," says Wendorf, a retired psychologist, "is that rather than just standing up here performing—doing something 'for' people—[dementia-friendly worship] is oriented around maximum engagement, connection, stimulating memories, getting people to participate, getting people to tell stories, and providing all sorts of visual aids."[27] In these ways, worship can be made into a shared experience, where, as Daphne Johnston put it, the lines are blurred between people. Everyone is simply worshiping, in the most mutually accessible way possible, the God to whom we all belong.

The single most important element in dementia-friendly worship, according to Wendorf (somewhat surprisingly), is nametags. Names are our fundamental means of identity, linking us inextricably to our culture and past. To use each person's name, pronouncing it properly and clearly, while making friendly eye contact, communicates, almost universally (at least in the West),[28] a desire for connection and an acknowledgment of respect. It underscores the importance of the preposition "with," as in a *worship service with*, not *for* or *to*.

The approach to worship will depend necessarily on the stage of dementia experienced by most of the people participating. At an earlier stage, more complex issues of faith can still be addressed. Those with advanced dementia will need conceptually simpler services with more sensory engagement: using large pictures, familiar music, and objects to touch. Across the board, dementia-friendly services include several common elements, outlined below in the sample worship service by Reverend Jonathan Currier.[29]

I. One familiar hymn: Currier advises a single verse of a hymn that an elderly person would have sung in her youth. Print the verse or verses to sing (words only) in large type on a song sheet.

II. A short prayer or collect

III. A single scriptural lesson based on well-known biblical verses of hope and encouragement

IV. The sermon: Currier recommends limiting the sermon to five minutes (although some dementia-friendly services allow for a slightly longer timeframe)[30] and informal storytelling rather than a monologue that may provoke boredom and its associated behaviors.

V. The Lord's Prayer

VI. The blessing: Kenneth Carder (*Ministry with the Forgotten,* chapter 4) goes around the room, greeting each person individually by name at the close of the service he regularly provides to a memory care unit.[31]

There are, of course, many variations. Carder always includes the Apostles' Creed in his services because about half of the residents, he says, remember it.[32] The twice-monthly service held at FUMC, following the respite program, has a time for sharing prayer requests and a service of Holy Communion. Whether to offer this sacrament to people with advanced dementia is a source of occasional controversy for reasons ranging from the practical risk of choking on the bread (if swallowing is an issue) to concern about whether it can be properly reverenced by people who have lost the ability to comprehend its meaning. Everman and Wendorf suggest letting the caregiver or partner decide on a loved one's behalf whether joining Communion is appropriate, but hold the position themselves that it's better to err on the side of welcoming everyone to the table. "It's not our table," Wendorf says plainly. "It's the Lord's table."

While a separate service allows for appropriate content and a permissive space where dementia-related behaviors such as wandering and interrupting are easily accepted, some churches cannot add an extra service to the existing schedule and must make the regular service more dementia friendly. Everman describes a small church in which this goal is accomplished by filling the first half of the service with familiar hymns and rituals. The passing-of-the-peace ritual differentiates the initial, dementia-friendly part from the latter half, which contains the sermon and more complex or lengthy components. Caregivers are free to leave unobtrusively with their loved ones while other congregants stand and greet one another. Everman advises (in keeping with this book, as well) educating the congregation, so they are prepared for the possibility that people with dementia may not sit quietly or participate in the expected way.

## COMFORT ROOMS

In an ideal world, all the activities of a church could be made dementia friendly. The reality is that churches will offer services and activities in which certain people with dementia cannot happily participate. There is a wide range of physical, social, and emotional needs among people with dementia, as we've learned, and these needs change from day to day. Difficult behaviors may crop up unexpectedly due to frustration, incomprehension, or an inability to express needs effectively. Remember this adage, mentioned several times throughout this book: If you've seen *one* person with dementia, you've seen *one* person with dementia. Every person's brain is different, so every person reacts differently to the progressive diseases that cause it to fail. We can only plan within broad parameters, hoping that we'll meet *some* of the needs of *many* of the people we are trying to serve.

We've covered ways to address the worship and social needs of people with dementia, within defined limits, as discussed: Respite programs are for those who can still manage their own toileting; caregivers accompany their loved ones to adapted worship services and special meals, and so on. But a caregiver may wish to attend a regular church service, obtain counseling, meet a friend at church for coffee, or take part in a bustling, weeknight dinner that their loved one would not enjoy.

A church can help both caregivers and their loved ones cope with social isolation by providing a quiet, comfortable space,[33] preferably near the sanctuary, and staffed, when in use, by at least two volunteer dementia companions.[34] The person with dementia can enjoy the company of an attentive friend for a reasonable period of time in such a space, so the caregiver can attend an activity. The presence of at least two volunteers, one for each person brought to the room and one, in addition, to summon help from the caregiver should a problem arise, is advisable since church volunteers, as previously mentioned, are not trained to assist with the more challenging physical and emotional aspects of dementia care.

The most important factors in furnishing such a room are safety and comfort. It should be well lit, preferably with natural light or soft, bright artificial light; the color of furniture, while pleasant and calming, should be different from the color of the walls and floor. Avoid throw rugs or large patterned carpets. Remove mirrors. Add objects of comfort: a stuffed animal; a therapy doll;[35] a few books (*The Picture Book of Natural Wonders, The Picture Book of Birds*);[36] a set of "conversation cards" (a deck that includes photos of milkshakes, school desks, and other objects associated with the 1950s accompanied by questions to prompt memories and stories);[37] perhaps a jigsaw puzzle with larger pieces and an adult design,[38] or a rummage bag.[39] Supply bottled water and packaged snacks. Unless a restroom is adjacent, install clear signage leading to it.[40] Some churches have ladies and men's rooms with thumb locks in individual stalls, but no means of locking the main door. These restrooms accommodate several ladies or men at the same time. Caregiving couples are often composed of a man and a woman who need to be in the restroom together, with immediate access to the handicapped stall. If there is not a single-user restroom available, use a method, perhaps a removable sign hung on the door,[41] by which a caregiver can indicate that a restroom with multiple stalls is in private use.

To ease the minds of volunteers and ensure a safe space, here are a few suggested guidelines for caregivers using the comfort room:

1. The comfort room should only be used if the person with dementia can be made comfortable: Those who are prone to behaviors such as wandering, acute agitation, or aggression will probably be unable to use it, for the sake of others. In some people, however, these behaviors may come and go in response to changing environmental factors (lack of sleep, medication effects, caffeine or alcohol intake, pain or discomfort) and whether they'll cope well enough on a given day with unskilled volunteers can be assessed on a situational basis. The caregiver should stay in the room or very close by until her loved one is settled and engaged in an activity.

2. The caregiver must remain in the church with a fully charged cell phone in hand to ensure that she is reachable and can be quickly summoned if needed. She should make sure her loved one has visited the restroom just prior to staying in the comfort room.

3. She must return at the agreed upon time.

While comfort rooms are somewhat similar to nurseries in that they are meant to serve as a sort of waiting room for people who are unable to take part in regular services and activities, be careful not to associate the two in church communications. Avoid, for example, making this statement in a bulletin: "Our Wednesday evening dinners will resume next week, with nursery and dementia care provided." Instead, say this: "Our Wednesday evening dinners will resume next week, with the nursery provided. Caregivers, please contact [the church secretary] if you wish to reserve a space in the comfort room."

## PRACTICAL HELP

Caregivers who tend a loved one in moderate- to late-stage dementia are swamped in every conceivable way, and the chores of daily living can become straws breaking the proverbial camel's back. Think of our friend Michael, trying to keep house with Elaine constantly tagging along, talking in gibberish, and undoing, helpfully, she must have thought, much of his work. Think of Bert, his refrigerator crammed with large pots of plain boiled peas, oatmeal, and rice, because he could warm these rather unappetizing foods quickly, and they are filling. I spoke with a caregiver who reluctantly hired an expensive lawn service to rake her yard at the end of autumn, finally despairing that she'd never get to it herself. Afterward, she left her husband, then with moderate Alzheimer's, alone for a few hours while she ran some errands. When she returned home, she found him standing outside proudly, rake in hand. He had distributed the huge pile of leaves, left at the curb awaiting collection, back across the yard.[42] I spent considerable time with a woman in her seventies, almost birdlike in her fragility, who cared for her husband until she was simply unable to do it any longer. One day, she glanced out of her kitchen window at a yard overrun with weeds. She usually chatted animatedly when we were together, as though for my sake, but that day, she made her hands into tight fists and pressed her knuckles into her forehead. Tears began to slip down her face. "Why can't someone just come over and help me cut the grass sometime?" she asked. "Just one time?" She didn't have the money to hire a laborer or the strength to do it herself.

I can't think of a single caregiver I've interviewed over many years who wouldn't have appreciated help from time to time. Most admit to collapsing exhausted at the end of the day, only to be awakened during the night. Caregiving must continue twenty-four hours a day, seven days a week, and would leave even a young person with little remaining energy.

Christianity is not unique in its emphasis on giving practical help to those in need. In Islam, helping others is an act of purification, meant to enable the highest goal of service to God; Buddhists describe a "noble disciple" as one who delights in sharing and giving that is "free from the stain of stinginess"; in many South Asian religions, salvation itself hinges on charity.[43] A study at the University of California, Berkeley of more than a thousand adults found that atheists were more motivated to help others from a sense of compassion than were the highly religious.[44] Helping through acts of service and generosity thus bridges our differences in belief, culture, education, and economic advantage: We are hard-wired to relieve suffering, it seems, from infancy.[45] Practical help is an activity to which almost everyone relates.

If members—or people the congregation serves—are homebound caregivers, compile a list of tasks church volunteers would be willing to provide, either once or on a regular basis. Family caregivers will likely be grateful for help with non-caregiving chores, such as lawn maintenance, food preparation, house cleaning, minor repairs, and errands. If your church has a weeknight dinner, organize a meals-on-wheels committee to deliver a dinner each week to any caregiver in the community who desires it.

There's no obligation to accept help, should it be unnecessary, but you can make the accepting easier for a proud person by couching the offer as a way *they* are helping *you* (because they are):[46] "We have an eager group of young people starting a summer gardening project called *Cultivating Kindness*. Would you be willing to let a crew work one Saturday this month? They can cut grass, weed, and edge beds. Please consider providing this opportunity. They don't want payment, only the chance to serve," and so on.

As you devise a list of tasks, think of making an impact on stress and isolation for caregivers and their loved ones and the chance such a ministry can give parishioners to share varied skills and interests. Someone who is not comfortable cleaning another person's house or doing outside work, for example, may be a willing prayer partner. We sometimes forget the practicality of prayer. Prayer is comforting. It allays the fight-flight response, mitigates anger, increases the sense of connection with others, and tones down negativity.[47] Long ago, I read about an unfortunate conversation between two Christian women who downplayed the power of prayer.[48] One of them, in miserable circumstances, hung her head and said sadly, "All I can do now is pray," to which the other replied in dismay, "Oh dear, has it come to that?" Sometimes, we're all guilty of failing to see prayer as an answer for which no problem is too great. A prayer partner who listens in confidence, with compassion and prays sincerely gives not only the gift of intercession, which is beyond human understanding,[49] but of consolation. We all have gifts to offer, and some of us aren't willing or able to participate in respite care or help with dementia-friendly worship services. Carving out ways these parishioners can still serve with equal importance acknowledges the unique, different gifts we individually bring to form the body of Christ.[50]

## CONCLUSION

In this chapter we've discussed ways to open the church to people living with dementia, realizing that many who need or want to participate may not be church attenders. They may not be religious at all: When surveyed in 2021, about 30 percent of adult Americans describe themselves as "religious nones," in other words atheists, agnostics or "nothing in particular."[51] Nonbelievers are now the second-largest religious group in North America and Europe, nonbelief being increasingly considered its own religion, since absence of belief affects how people think, particularly about death, how they parent their children, and how they vote.[52]

When we knowingly serve people of different religions (or no religion), we do wish to be sensitive and not alienating, as Daphne Johnston advocates in her role as head of the respite program at FUMC. My friend Kim Newlen may have discovered the best way of handling this dilemma in her ministry, *Sweet Mondays*. Kim and I were housemates when I was in graduate school, and I've never met a person more sincerely committed to Christian evangelism. In the worldwide ministry she established before her death in 2014, she devised a simple formula that succeeded among thousands and thousands of women around the world. "Sweet Monday" socials begin with one minute—literally, a single minute—of devotion and move quickly to the main event, a presentation on a topic in which women are interested; I once spoke at her house on Alzheimer's. In a similar manner, consider having a minute-long devotion, in keeping with your tradition, at dementia-friendly activities (other than worship itself, of course). Leave it at that and trust God with the rest. For meal deliveries and other home-based services, provide a leaflet listing any dementia-friendly activities available at the church along with information on how to participate.

Kim showed true restraint, confining devotions to a brief moment of an entire evening, given her articulate and unfailingly enthusiastic faith. But her mission was to bring the women who attended Sweet Monday socials, whether religious or not, into an environment where they could learn about God indirectly through the loving companionship of others. As testament to the success of the approach, she once set a Guinness World Record by hosting a Sweet Monday tea party at the University of Richmond, attended by no less than 7,250 women.[53] Kim's model is a good one to follow, I believe, and in keeping with Jesus's analogy comparing the kingdom of heaven to yeast, a single celled microorganism that starts the process within a sticky lump of dough eventually resulting in bread.[54]

And that analogy also works as a way of closing this final chapter. I've tried to present many ideas churches can use to become dementia friendly, from ways to prepare and educate congregations to programs that could realistically be implemented. But mainly, I've tried to give an accurate portrayal of dementia: what those who must cope with it may need from a church, as well as the blessings they offer through their presence and participation. By creating a culture in which people struggling with pain and isolation are embraced, the church can have a true impact on the almost indescribable problems dementia causes for millions of individuals and to society as a whole. Think of yeast and start small. Do whatever you can as a church, but do something, understanding that nothing escapes the notice of God[55] and everything, according to his purpose, will work together for good.[56]

# Afterword

Each time I've opened my computer to work on this book, I've thought of my father, to whom it is dedicated. In closing, I must ask your forbearance in allowing me to tell the story of his death because it speaks to the book's purpose—to look at God and the human condition of dementia, acknowledging God's unfailing, unchanging love. I don't use the word *passing*, as so many do, to soften the finality of death. I was standing alone beside my father's bed, with my face not a foot from his. After weeks of having labored for every breath, there was one shallow intake of air, and he was gone. That fast, faster than I can type two words. It felt like dying, not passing. I knew I would never feel his arms around me again, the reassuring familiarity of his body; I would never breathe in the scent of him, of Old Spice, never sweat or dirt, even after he had been riding his tractor in hot summer sun or planting tomatoes in the sandy loam of his North Carolina farm.

But he did "pass away," during the few years before he died, not with the steady downward losses of Alzheimer's disease, but in pieces that seemed to come and go. He had times of lucidity almost to the very end, but he struggled with himself, as though he knew who he was but couldn't get that familiar person to show up consistently. He wept, cried, cursed, ranted, and threatened, in episodic, dementia-induced behaviors I had never witnessed in him before, this stoic man who could have walked through fire without flinching. I almost believed this, once upon a time. During the last years, in his need of help to get dressed, he gave up the dry-cleaned slacks and button-down shirts he had persisted in wearing for most of his retirement and slouched in the ubiquitous sweats of old age, holding a crumpled newspaper a few inches from his eyes in a pretense, every morning, of reading. Helping him buckle his sandals, it was hard for me to think of him as the same father who used to carry me into the ocean, bracing himself against the tides, or myself as that child, whose biggest worry was being knocked from his grip by a rogue wave.

When I was old enough to contemplate faith and had, I felt, some youthful sense of a loving, if enigmatic God, I grew concerned about my father and his disinterest in religion. He delivered babies at all hours, waiting until the final alert from a labor nurse and then bolting from the dining room table, or his chair in the family room, or his bed, so single-minded in his backwards rush from the driveway that on numerous occasions he crashed his car into anything positioned behind it. How could he work so incessantly and not drop dead, I wondered. People are meant to sleep at night; they're meant to rest at least one day of the week. And what if he died? Wasn't heaven the prerogative of believers?

My efforts to persuade my father of the possibility that God could be experienced both at the profound level of soul and within, inexplicably, the least consequential of earthbound circumstances fell flat. I was inarticulate in the face of his dismissiveness, even as his hair grayed and the veins in my hands began to stand out with age. I remember pushing a photo of magnified sand toward him as we sat in the kitchen, exclaiming, "Dad, look! This is sand. How could sand be made so beautiful? Can't you see God in it?"

He glanced briefly at the candylike particles of lace, stars, and vibrant orbs. "So what?" he said flatly. "It's sand." He pushed the picture away. He had always pushed back at any notion that God was more than an abstruse being with a place in consciousness mainly for the purpose of holding personal tragedy at bay. Before dinner, he prayed a simple prayer and attached to it a long list of people he wanted God to protect, zipping through the names as though to skip a single one might result in disaster. He was able, it seemed, to conceive of divine power over events but unable to risk the disruption of his life that might occur should he be confronted by an intimate God—a God who might meet him in every corner of his existence, however real the promise of redemption. I think he was scared, as many of us are, of what might be asked of him. By then, when I showed him the sand, my brother, Greg, had dropped like a stone, dead with not one second's warning, and my father lived with unrelieved grief for the last seven years of his life. God might be real, but God was not good.

One year for his birthday, I bought a set of small blank books that contained a total of 365 pages. On each page, I forced my unruly handwriting into a semblance of calligraphy, and wrote a single Bible verse or short passage, creating, I thought, a distillation of the Bible's most convincing affirmations. After he died, I found the books in his bedside table, the pages still crisp and new. But I also found a family Bible, inscribed to him by his mother on September 19, 1944. On a separate page, he had written, undated, in shaky, almost indecipherable handwriting, *This Bible is to go to Mary, my darling daughter, whom I have loved since before she was born, with all of my love.*

\* \* \*

We may expect in old age to return to a helpless state, not far removed from birth, in our physical capabilities. Our eyes will fail. Flights of stairs will defeat us. We'll need help to walk, and dress, and eat. But stark as these losses, people with dementia are deprived in the end of much more. Approaching death, my father lay motionless in a hospital room. For weeks his existence had consisted only of drawing one breath, and then another, through a painfully constricted throat. He shrieked in protest when he was touched, even gently, unable to comprehend what was happening. He ripped out intravenous lines meant to keep him hydrated and comfortable. I was told his life could end in a matter of hours. I was told this day, after day, after day.

I ordered his casket on one of those days. I'd scrolled with my computer though hundreds of them, made of exotic woods and metals, emblazoned with cherubs, lined in padded silk and linen; the choices and prices were astounding. I was beside his bed, on a faux leather chair that felt like it should have been bolted into a school bus, not placed for a visitor's comfort in a hospital room. The setting, with its unfamiliar accoutrements and sounds, and my father's incomprehension as I made decisions about his death, sitting only a few feet away from him, was unsettling, as though the two of us had somehow become trapped in the last scene of the wrong play. I finally chose a casket from a Trappist monastery in the Midwest. The monks would pray for my father, the website pledged; they'd make the casket by hand, out of wood from a sustainable forest of trees they planted. Finalizing the order form, I encountered an option to have a phrase engraved beneath my father's name. Almost reflexively, I typed in Matthew 28:20, "I am with you always, even to the end of the age."

But I knew he wouldn't have chosen these words for his casket. A few days earlier, afraid he was clinging to life out of fear of death, I had tried to reassure him that he could let go, that he'd be taken into heaven. That Jesus, who had always loved him, would welcome him home, and people he'd loved and lost would be there, too. Greg would be there, I said, waiting for him. To my surprise, when I concluded this speech, he reclaimed a fragment of his mind and expressed himself coherently for the last time.

"That's a bunch of baloney," He mumbled, and turned his head away from me.

Thinking about this, I positioned the cursor and hit the delete key until the verse was erased. In the blank space, I wrote, "Beloved husband, beloved father."

My father died on an afternoon that was no different than the long string of afternoons that had preceded it. I had managed to establish a phone connection with my mother, which I did each day, at least once. This entailed calling her at her home, three hundred miles away, and having the caregiver on duty roust her from bed, make sure the hearing aid she wore in her nondeaf ear was working properly, and adjust the phone so she could hold it and talk to my father, although he mainly remained silent. It took five minutes or more. I had just gotten her on the phone and stood to put the receiver, set to speaker mode, close to my father's ear, when I knew, knew without a doubt, that he was about to die. He didn't change—not his color, not his breathing. I knew it instinctively. And I knew I didn't have time to explain what was happening to my mother.

"Tell him you love him, Mom," I said, urgently. "Tell him right now!"

"Sweetheart, I love you," she said, without hesitating even for an instant. "I have always loved you, and I will love you forever and ever."

"Pray for him, Mom," I said. "Pray right now!" Again without hesitating, my mother prayed for his soul, with words that were so beautifully constructed and pure, the prayer was, it seemed, sacred and deeply spontaneously connected to God. Exactly as she said the word *amen*, my father drew in a short breath that he never exhaled.

"He's gone, Mom," I said. "He's gone." I traced a cross lightly on his forehead with my finger, as though to seal her prayer in some way, using the familiar gesture of Ash Wednesday.

\* \* \*

I concluded chapter 7 with the story of my friendship with Kim Newlen, who began the ministry Sweet Mondays and spread it, quite literally, to the four corners of the world. Before she died of breast cancer, Kim wrote a devotional, entitled *Sweet and Simple Moments with God*, with 101 entries.

Her husband, Mark, sent me an unexpected copy in early 2017. Given my problems then with my father's decline, I was checking my post office box infrequently. I'd find it crammed with bills and advertisements. Sometimes the postal clerk resorted to clearing its contents to a postal locker, no doubt in a state of righteous irritation. One cold, rather dreary day, I found Kim's book in a small package amid the clutter, the bright pink cover so much like Kim that I could not help but smile when I opened it. I didn't realize she had written this book. I left it out in the kitchen, reading a devotion on random mornings and marking my place with a page sleeve provided by the publisher for this purpose, printed with the verse from Psalm 103, "Let all that I am praise the Lord."

The morning after my father's death in May, I was sitting alone in my kitchen, sipping coffee, feeling, to the extent that I understand the term, shell-shocked. Although comforted somewhat by the precise timing of my father's death, in absolute simultaneity with my mother's prayer, I was worried that his face had not relaxed at death into any semblance of peace. He simply died and was gone. I felt the utter emptiness of it within myself, and I contemplated the significance of what we had failed to share, ever, despite the love that ran beneath us like a perennial spring.

My eyes caught the pink cover of Kim's book. I picked it up and flipped with some indifference to the page marker indicating the next devotion. "I am with you always," I read, incredulously, "even to the end of the age," and underneath, the title of the essay for that day: *God Never Exaggerates*. My father, however, did exaggerate, if the situation, he thought, called for it. The habit had always secretly bothered me—I felt a prick of annoyance when he embellished stories, especially about me, as though I didn't quite measure up without the help of his overstatement. Reading those words, and comprehending the complete improbability of such an exquisite coincidence, laid out over years, days, moments, and lives, I felt my emptiness drawn over, as though by a consoling blanket. "I know your father," God seemed to say, not with words I could actually hear; it was more a deep impression of words. "I love your father. I have him. He is safe."

\* \* \*

Among the many griefs of dementia, the ostensible loss of relationship with God is perhaps the most poignant to a person for whom this relationship has been a lifeline, slender thread though it can be when times are bleak, and God seems silent. In this book, we've taken a hard look at dementia, seeing, hopefully, its terrible challenges, as well as the opportunity it provides to give and receive love in the "remaining" way of this unfathomable, intimate God we seek to emulate. We open ourselves, as a church, to all: Nothing should separate a person from seeking companionship and solace in God's house on earth, where God dwells with us, offering the promise that nothing—not the breakdown of our minds, not weariness, not anger, not lost or forgotten faith, not our failures to live up to any standard of love—will ever separate us from his persistent love. I may eventually share my father's plight, genetically tied to him as I am. If I do, I hope I will find in my church a place where I feel valued, accepted, and loved, and where I can continue to worship, in whatever way I can, the God who will be with me, with all of us, holding our times in his hands, until the end of time.

—*Mary Cail*

# *Appendix 1*
## *Books for the Church Library*

The following is a short list of recommended books. It is almost impossible to become familiar with the burgeoning number published on this subject, but each of the books below fits a certain purpose and the list is therefore a good starting point of resources to collect:

### FOR CHILDREN

J. Elizabeth, *Will Grammy Remember Me?* (Purple Scarf Publishing, 2021), 32 pages.
> A loving picture book for very young readers about a granddaughter and her grandmother with early Alzheimer's, told from the perspective of the granddaughter.

Maria Shriver, *What's Happening to Grandpa?* (New York: Little Brown Books for Young Readers, 2004), 45 pages.
> For children ages five through nine, this book tells the story of a young girl and her grandfather as he becomes symptomatic with Alzheimer's. Questions most children would have about dementia (What is Alzheimer's? Will my parents get it, too?) and the answers are sensitively worked into the narrative. Kate finds a way to have the best relationship she can with her grandfather.

### FOR ADULTS

Nancy Andrews, Cary Smith Henderson, and Jackie H. Main, *Partial View: An Alzheimer's Journal* (Dallas: Southern Methodist University, 1998), 120 pages.

Admittedly, this is an older book and may be difficult to obtain at a reasonable price. (I just ordered a copy in "excellent condition" for $5.99, including shipping, so I know it can be done.) I recommend this book because it is poignant and beautiful, and it very quickly, easily leads the reader into an empathetic understanding of mid-stage Alzheimer's disease. Cary Henderson was a college professor whose Alzheimer's disease was confirmed definitively by a brain biopsy, just as his symptoms were emerging. Essentially, it's an adult picture book of artistic photos combined with Henderson's observations of himself, and to my knowledge, there is not a similar book available even after all these years.

Debbie Barr, Edward G. Shaw, and Gary D. Chapman, *Keeping Love Alive as Memories Fade: The Five Languages of Love and the Alzheimer's Journey,* The Five Love Languages Series (New York: Northfield Publishing, 2016), 240 pages.

The authors tackle the fundamental fear experienced by people with Alzheimer's of whether they will continue to be loved when they can no longer recognize family members or engage in the familiar expressions and gestures of love. It provides a hopeful view of the transformative power of love itself and offers guidance about how to stay connected when the common means of connection are lost.

Jolene Brackey, *Creating Moments of Joy Along the Alzheimer's Journey,* 5th ed. (West Lafayette, IN: Purdue University Press, 2017), 376 pages.

With dementia, "moments of joy" in the present are the only ones we can have, and although they will not be remembered, the emotion of joy will stick around longer than the forgotten moment. I heard Brackey speak many years ago at an Alzheimer's conference. She brought dementia care back to simple, guiding thoughts and suggestions, wisely stripped of the interpersonal dynamics and past experiences that can muddy the emotional waters, and this is what she does in her book. She shows caregivers and family members how to have moment-after-moment of joy with their loved one and how to forgive themselves when everything falls apart (which will happen).

Mary Cail, *Alzheimer's: A Crash Course for Friends and Relatives* (Chapel Hill, NC: TrueWind Press, 2014), 203 pages.

I struggled with the idea of including my own book on this list. In fact, I prayed about it, fearing the transgression of self-promotion. But as far as I know, it's the only book available that demonstrates, through stories and conversation guides, to friends, relatives, and others how to communicate empathetically with both caregivers and people who have dementia from early stage through late. Some of the people and stories from it are shared in *Dementia and the Church*, so the two books can be compatibly used together. My website (www.allweatherfriend. org) offers alternative activities from this book if the online resources suggested in chapter 6 are no longer accessible or convenient to use.

Kenneth Carder, *Ministry with the Forgotten* (Nashville: Abingdon Press, 2019), 165 pages.

This book expands on the video series by the same title, which was introduced in chapter 4. Carder examines dementia through the lens of theology and shares the wisdom he learned through caring for his wife, who died with advanced frontotemporal lobe dementia. He discusses the dementia in terms of broad concepts such as personhood, incarnation, salvation, and discipleship.

Daphne Johnston, *Reclaiming Joy Together* (Montgomery, AL: Respite for All Foundation, 2020), 206 pages.

Johnston's book and work on creating respite care at churches are highlighted in chapter 7. This book outlines how and why to begin a respite program. It's a quick, practical starting point for a ministry that could seem, without Johnston's plainly stated advice and encouragement, somewhat formidable.

Jean Lee, *Alzheimer's Daughter* (published by Jean Lee, 2019), 279 pages.

Anyone who has tried to deal with dementia in a parent will be able to relate to this book, and it will help those who haven't understand exactly how challenging the responsibility can be. Both of Lee's parents were diagnosed with Alzheimer's, and this is the touching story of their journey together.

Greg O'Brien, *On Pluto: Inside the Mind of Alzheimer's*, 2nd ed. (Brewster, MA: Codfish Press, 2018), 417 pages.

I once witnessed a keynote speaker at an Alzheimer's Association conference give what I thought was a brilliant address. He paced around the stage, using no notes, and never once did he stumble on a word or pause to think. One of the organizers whispered to me, "He has Alzheimer's." Well, good heavens, I thought. Maybe we all do. I had the same impression of O'Brien's honest and wrenching portrayal of his life with Alzheimer's. An investigative journalist by profession, he helps readers comprehend what it is to experience dementia within one's own mind and consciousness, making obvious the struggles but also the strengths.

**Betsy Peterson, *Voices of Alzheimer's: Courage, Humor, Hope, and Love in the Face of Dementia* (Boston: DaCapo Long Life, 2004), 295 pages.**
This book is a collection of quotes from people who've lived with dementia. Reading it is like sitting in on a support group. It's a wonderful resource for a church to use in bringing many varied "voices" of Alzheimer's into a service or program: The passages can be read aloud by volunteer readers to help parishioners gain an understanding of dementia by listening to the words of people who have dealt with it in their lives. Consider using it to create a "dementia moment" as part of regular services as you begin your church's dementia friendly initiative.

**Gary Small, MD and Gigi Vorgan, *The Alzheimer's Prevention Program*, (New York: Workman Publishing, 2011), 304 pages.**
I haven't seen many books like this one in church libraries, despite the Bible's comparison of our physical bodies to a temple,[1] but I believe two things about dementia (and about Alzheimer's disease, specifically). First, there will never be a cure, not in the sense of a medication or treatment that stops it cold. Second, in some cases, we either slow dementia down or hasten it with our lifestyle choices. We can therefore have hope, and hope is a good thing to find in a church. We've already learned that Alzheimer's and many dementias have a preclinical stage during which the disease is present and progressing but has not yet begun to produce symptoms. To make choices early on that enable natural defenses is to move from fear and helplessness to meaningful action. I like the readability of this guide and the fact that Small recommends changes we can all make in our lives to improve brain function.

**John Swinton, *Living in the Memories of God* (Grand Rapids, MI: William B. Eerdmans Publishing Company, 2012), 308 pages.**

John Swinton is a professor at the School of Divinity, History and Philosophy at King's College in Aberdeen, Scotland. His book is a theological examination of personhood and dementia that will no doubt resonate with clergy, although it may be a little heady for parishioners in search of easily applied information. In this statement, Swinton seems to summarize his premise: "We are not the authors of our own stories. Our calling is to learn to read and interpret the story of God faithfully and well. In this sense people with dementia are reminded and remind us of this fundamental fact about the world. The problem of forgetfulness is not confined to people with dementia. The existence of dementia brings to the fore a broader amnesia that has befallen the world which has caused it to forget where and what it is: *creation*" (chapter 7, *Personhood and Humanness: The Importance of Being a Creature*).

**David Wolpe, *Making Loss Matter: Creating Meaning in Difficult Times* (New York: Riverhead Books, 2000), 240 pages.**

I read this book when it was first published shortly after my husband's death by suicide, and I must agree with the Publishers Weekly review of it:[2] "Wolpe's easy manner and eloquent storytelling will help readers suffering from loss feel as if they have found a companion on their journeys." This is how I felt, that in reading Rabbi Wolpe's profound treatise, I had found a companion for the most difficult journey of my life. It is one of the best books I have ever read on grief.

# *Appendix 2*

## *Supplementary Activities: Educating the Congregation*

### FACTS ABOUT ALZHEIMER'S DISEASE

<u>Objective</u>: To increase general knowledge about Alzheimer's disease

<u>Materials</u>:

- Pen and quiz (see below) for each participant
- Handouts of *either* the long quiz answers and further reading links (see "The Answers" below) *or* the downloadable publication, "Alzheimer's Disease," (available for free distribution on the Alzheimer's Association website https://www.alz.org/media/Documents/alzheimers-dementia-about-alzheimers-disease-ts.pdf), whichever you think the group would find most helpful

<u>Time Required</u>: About 20 minutes

<u>Process</u>:
Introduce the topic, Alzheimer's disease, and the reason for learning specifically about this form of dementia: The majority of people with dementia have Alzheimer's or a mixed dementia that includes Alzheimer's, and its symptoms are common to many dementias. The purpose of the activity is to review some of the facts about Alzheimer's presented in the Kenneth Carder videos (see chapter 4).

1. Distribute the tests (see below) and allow a few minutes to complete. Do not collect.
2. Share the "short" answers (below the test). The "long" answers contain background information if the group wants additional information or you wish to enlarge on the shorter answer. You can make the

activity more engaging by having participants raise hands to reveal their answers, before reading the answer, to each question, "How many chose *true* [for number one]? How many chose *false*?" After the answers have all been read, ask if there was new or surprising information.

\* \* \*

### *The Test*

This is not a real test, as you'll see, but . . .

### How Much Do You Know about Alzheimer's?

Maybe more than you think. Mark each statement *True* or *False*.

1. **TRUE or FALSE**: The majority of people with dementia have Alzheimer's disease (up to 80%, according to the Alzheimer's Association); most of the rest have vascular dementia.

2. **TRUE or FALSE**: The single biggest risk factor for Alzheimer's disease (AD) is increasing age.

3. **TRUE or FALSE**: Alzheimer's disease can stabilize in some people— meaning that it reaches a certain point and does not get worse.

4. **TRUE or FALSE**: Alzheimer's disease is always fatal.

5. **TRUE or FALSE**: As many people in the United States have AD as live in New York City.

6. **TRUE or FALSE**: There are steps we can take to prevent AD.

7. **TRUE or FALSE**: People with AD can live with the disease for twenty years *after* it becomes symptomatic.

8. **TRUE or FALSE**: Medications for AD increase the patient's lifespan.

9. **TRUE or FALSE**: Alzheimer's disease can be contagious under certain circumstances.

10. **TRUE or FALSE**: Alzheimer's disease is different in every person.

*The Answers*

1. **TRUE or FALSE**: The majority of people with dementia have Alzheimer's disease (up to 80%, according to the Alzheimer's Association); most of the rest have vascular dementia.

   **The short answer—TRUE**: Dementia is an umbrella term that refers to all of the many diseases and conditions that cause it. There are over one hundred types of dementia, according to Alzheimer's Disease International (https://www.alzint.org/about-us/), a federation of dementia organizations around the world.

   **The long answer**—It is believed that 60 to 80 percent of people with dementia have Alzheimer's disease. The Center for Disease Control estimates that 10 percent have vascular dementia. These figures may vary somewhat depending on the source, but AD and vascular dementia are frequently described as the two main types, accounting for up to 90 percent of cases. Lewy body dementia, which affects over a million people (in the United States), is third in line, and some experts think it is more common than generally assumed. *Further reading*—Alzheimer's Society of the United Kingdom: https://www.alzheimers.org.uk/about-dementia/types-dementia.

2. **TRUE or FALSE**: The single biggest risk factor for Alzheimer's disease (AD) is increasing age.

   **The short answer—TRUE**: The risk of AD inevitably increases with age: 5.3 percent of people from ages 65–74 have AD compared to 34.6 percent at age 85 and older.[1]

   **The long answer**—While there are many risk factors for AD (among them gender, the same lifestyle factors that contribute to heart disease and diabetes, previous head injuries, genetic traits, lack of exercise, and lower educational level), the main risk factor is age, which explains why it is increasing: We are living longer. By 2050, it is estimated that 153 million people worldwide will have AD.[2] *Further reading on modifiable risk factors*—Alzheimer's Association International Conference (July 2020): https://www.neurologylive.com/view/12-modifiable-risk-factors-to-reduce-dementia-risk.

3. **TRUE or FALSE**: Alzheimer's disease can stabilize in some people—meaning that it reaches a certain point and does not get worse.

**The short answer—FALSE**

**The long answer**—There is not an intervention or treatment that stops the disease process, and AD is progressive. However, it develops at different rates in different people. It may seem to plateau for a while, encouraging hope that it has stabilized, but unless the person dies by another cause, the disease eventually reaches an advanced stage when the brain effectively shuts down. *Further reading*—National Institute on Aging: https://www.nia.nih.gov/health/alzheimers-disease-fact-sheet.

4. **TRUE or FALSE**: Alzheimer's disease is always fatal.

**The short answer—TRUE**: Alzheimer's is a fatal disease that ultimately ends in death.

**The long answer**—AD can also be the main factor in death from other causes, such as infection, falls and injuries, and aspiration pneumonia. People with moderate to severe AD are unable to participate in their own care by reporting symptoms, and they eventually become bedridden. Auguste Deter, the patient studied extensively by Alois Alzheimer died of sepsis from infected bedsores.[3] It is considered the sixth leading cause of death in the United States. *Further reading*—2020 Alzheimer's Association Report (March 2020), https://alz-journals.onlinelibrary.wiley.com/doi/full/10.1002/alz.12068. [*Note*: This is an excellent comprehensive overview of Alzheimer's disease, encompassing much of the material in these answers. To find information related specifically to this item, scroll to section 4.1, "Deaths from Alzheimer's Disease."]

5. **TRUE or FALSE**: As many people in the United States have Alzheimer's disease as live in New York City.

**The short answer—FALSE**: According to the latest census data, NYC had a population of 8,623,577. An estimated six million people in the United States have AD. This is roughly the combined population of Los Angeles and Chicago. Barring an effective treatment, the figure is expected to more than double by the year 2050.

6. **TRUE or FALSE**: There are steps we can take to prevent AD.

   **The short answer**—Possibly **TRUE** (to some extent, in some people) **FALSE** in others. In rare cases (less than 1 percent), Alzheimer's is *caused* by genes. In most people, the risk of Alzheimer's is *increased* by certain genes. The degree of risk might be affected by lifestyle choices.[4]

   **The long answer**—Rarely, deterministic genes (like the genes that cause eye color) cause AD. More commonly, a genetic predisposition increases the risk, but the disease likely results from an interaction between these susceptibility genes and the environment. Certain controllable factors, such as diet and exercise, may influence the expression of genes linked to AD. *Further reading*: US National Library of Medicine (May, 2021), https://medlineplus.gov/genetics/understanding/mutationsanddisorders/predisposition/. See also answer 2 above.

7. **TRUE or FALSE**: People with Alzheimer's can live with the disease for twenty years after it becomes symptomatic.

   **The short answer—TRUE**: When AD is diagnosed during the first symptomatic stage, mild or early Alzheimer's, a person can live for about twenty years, as the disease progresses from mild, to moderate, to severe, but, as previously stated, the rate of decline varies between people. For some, the disease advances more quickly. *Further reading*—Penn Medicine Neuroscience Blog: https://www.pennmedicine.org/updates/blogs/neuroscience-blog/2019/november/stages-of-alzheimers.

8. **TRUE or FALSE**: Medications for Alzheimer's increase the patient's lifespan.

   **The short answer—MAINLY FALSE:** Most of the drugs reduce symptoms. They may improve short-term memory for a limited time but they do not slow the disease.

   **The long answer**—Only one drug at present, aducanumab (ad-duh-KA-nuh-mab), which is not without risks and a prohibitive price tag—at the time of this writing $56,000 per year, addresses the underlying pathology of AD. By reducing amyloid plaques in the brains of people with early-stage Alzheimer's or mild cognitive impairment (MCI), it is aimed at slowing clinical decline. While not a cure, it can in some people forestall a transition from MCI to Alzheimer's.[5] Other drugs increase the bioavailability of certain chemicals in the brain that facilitate attention and memory. The goal of these treatments is symptomatic relief. They may (again, only in some people) extend independent functioning, but they do not increase lifespan. *Further reading*—For a refreshingly approachable scientific article, which plainly makes the point that despite the considerable body of related knowledge, Alzheimer's is a complicated, in most cases idiopathic disease, and treatments are limited in effectiveness, see "Challenges for Alzheimer's Disease Therapy: Insights for Novel Mechanisms Beyond Memory Defects."[6] [*Note*: This article was published before approval of aducanumab. The conclusions are still accurate.]

9. **TRUE or FALSE**: Alzheimer's disease can be contagious under certain circumstances.

**The short answer—FALSE**

**The long answer**—Contagious and possibly transmissible under extraordinary circumstances are two different things. Creutzfeldt-Jakob (kruts-felt-ya-cob) disease (CDJ), a form of dementia which afflicts one in a million people worldwide, was observed decades ago in patients treated daily for a period of years with injections of a hormone extract derived from the pituitary glands of cadavers.[7] Researchers speculate that these unfortunate patients were probably also subjected to the medical transmission of AD. It has been demonstrated that characteristic AD pathologies can, in fact, be imparted to mice through intracerebral inoculation of the same growth hormone to which these patients were exposed.[8] Also, there are a few reported cases in which transmission of CDJ has been associated with neurosurgical procedures. But obviously, these extremely rare events, some long past, are not related to any activity we engage in during daily life. Alzheimer's is not transmittable through blood transfusion, for example—not that blood transfusion is an activity of daily life. It is, however, a relatively common medical procedure. *Further reading*—An article which summarizes the research described above: "Transmissible Alzheimer's Theory Gains Traction."[9]

10. **TRUE OR FALSE:** Alzheimer's disease is different in every person.

**The answer—TRUE**, and this truth is the basis of the common saying, "If you've seen one person with Alzheimer's, you've seen one person with Alzheimer's (or the term *dementia* can be substituted)." The disease unfolds in stages, in which life skills are lost in a somewhat predictable order, but because every person's brain is unique, the manifestations of the disease can be strikingly different from person to person. *Further reading*—Social Care Institute for Excellence, London, UK, "Understanding Dementia." [*Note*: This article contains Carey Mulligan's YouTube video (below) and in it, she discusses the inconsistencies in her grandmother from day to day and also between people with dementia.]

## VIDEO WITH AN IMPORTANT MESSAGE

Objective: To learn about the inconsistency and variability of dementia; to observe a setting that shows positive interactions between people with dementia and their caregivers.

Materials:

- Equipment to show Carey Mulligan's 2012 YouTube video about her grandmother: https://www.youtube.com/watch?v=HqDCdgJ-gTU[10] (*Note*: Carey Mulligan is an English actress who has won, among other awards, two Oscars, two Golden Globe Awards, and a Tony Award. Her grandmother died in 2017, after 17 years with Alzheimer's disease.)

Time Required: 15–20 minutes

Process:

1. View and discuss the Carey Mulligan video. (1) How does Carey feel about her grandmother, as she was earlier in life and as she is portrayed in this video? What are some of the symptoms of her grandmother's Alzheimer's? (2) Carey's main message to us is to care and show respect. What are the best ways to show respect *to anyone* and is it different, essentially, with people who have dementia? [Listen with an open mind; be courteous; don't contradict and dispute; avoid scoffing, eye

rolling and other dismissive gestures; make affirming eye contact.] *Note*: Bracketed material is for the leader's use in facilitating discussion.

2. How do we continue in our love for a person when they've changed so radically? Carey's grandmother and others in this video seem content, but that is not always the case. People with dementia can be exasperating in their demands and needs. As months and years go by, and things are only getting worse, it's hard to keep loving in the same way. The experience of love changes with dementia. What is it about Carey's situation with her grandmother that helps her remain loving and positive? What can Carey and her grandmother teach us about love? [Carey is not her grandmother's primary caregiver; her grandmother lives in a facility that is meeting her needs. Carey is educated about Alzheimer's and is keeping her expectations consistent with her grandmother's capabilities.]

# *Appendix 3*
## *Support Group Leader Training Guide*

This guide provides training suggestions for caregiver support group leaders. It assumes prospective leaders have either already completed the educational activities in chapters 4–6 or that they are experienced dementia caregivers. If not, begin the training with the activities in these chapters. Use the material below to develop a group leader training seminar.

### Objectives

To help prospective caregiver support group leaders:

1. Understand the purpose of support groups and the difference between support groups and therapy groups
2. Formulate effective support group guidelines
3. Plan and follow an agenda
4. Respond to problematic behaviors
5. Know when and how to make referrals if necessary.

## The difference between support groups and therapy groups

*Background information*

I once attended a conference in which a woman with no experience as a therapist (or so it seemed) tried to demonstrate to us the power of group sharing. She summoned a volunteer to the front of the room, had him sit in a chair, and picked away at him with questions about his life and childhood until the poor man was weeping inconsolably, having just confessed to a roomful of strangers his father's brutality and his mother's inability to protect him from it. The presenter crept up to him, took his hand in hers, and gave the audience a weak smile. I was appalled. This woman had inadvertently tapped into a huge well of childhood trauma, and she apparently had no idea how to help the man regain control of his emotions. More significantly, she could not predict how he might react later on when she was not present to hold his hand, and she was not in a position to offer him any follow-up. I tell this story to illustrate the danger of straying into therapeutic waters when the intention is only to provide comfort and connection. It underscores the importance of having support group leaders who know their limits: They facilitate support, and support is not the same as therapy. Therapy groups are meant to explore the experiences, thoughts, and beliefs that underpin emotional response and behavior—for the purpose of bringing about adaptive change. Support groups are meant to offer comfort, affirmation, empathy, and useful information to people coping with a common adversity and to suggest practical solutions to practical problems.

### *Activity*

1. Watch the YouTube video "Conversations with Caregivers," produced by the University of California, San Francisco Memory and Aging Center, for an example of how support groups should ideally function: https://www.youtube.com/watch?v=X_RRbVfM0ck. This 13-minute video of a frontotemporal lobe caregiver support group shows each of the qualities mentioned above: comfort, affirmation, empathy, and education between members.

2. Watch therapist Nate Page's 11–minute YouTube video, "The Difference Between Therapy Groups and Support Groups," https://www.youtube.com/watch?v=3XB7V5n6PWk. *Again, please note*: As with other online resources, these videos were available at the time of publication. If they've been taken down, however, there are many sources of similar information. Visit the book page on my website (www.allweatherfriend.org) for suggestions.

3. Using a handout or dry erase board, go over the following suggestions for appropriate leader behavior in a support group:

   - *Refrain from asking leading, intrusive, or prying questions.* Think of yourself as a sympathetic friend at a coffee shop. If a group member says, "I always hated my father growing up, and now I have to bathe and dress him. I can't stand it," a supportive response would be, "Your past relationship makes the caregiving more difficult." A therapeutic response might be, "Why did you hate your father when you were a child?"

- *Refrain from interpretation and judgment.* Attach universal emotional terms to general observations: "I can hear your [frustration, sadness, sense of loss, fear, discomfort, anger]." Instead of: "Your father abused you, Tim, when you needed *him* to care for *you*. He's forgotten about that, and now you're having to care for his most intimate needs. You're angry."

- *Shift the focus to another person.* If you sense that a member may be revealing too much information or is struggling with problems beyond a loved one's dementia, shift the discussion to the group: "I had problems with my parents when I was growing up, Tim, but not the same as yours. I wonder if anyone else in the group struggles with feelings of anger? What helps you deal with these feelings?" Take Tim aside privately after the meeting and suggest that he speak with a minister. Ask if you can brief the minister on the trouble he's having with his father.

- *Or bring the focus back to the group objectives.* "You surely have a heavy load to carry. Can the rest of us help Tim with making his father's bath time easier? Tim, would you like some suggestions?" Again, take Tim aside after the meeting and encourage him to speak with a minister who can give him more time and freedom to express himself and help him to engage the supportive community services that might be available to him.

## Support Group Guidelines

*Background information*

Having rules or guidelines for the support group will help it stay on track. Without such direction, the discussion can too easily veer into subjects that aren't productive, or the meeting may lapse into a social occasion in which people are simply chatting among themselves. I've had both happen. Guidelines help group members feel safe by controlling the discussion and ensuring certain emotional safeguards, such as confidentiality. For example, in a support group with community members of different faiths and beliefs, a part of feeling safe may be the reassurance that biblical talk will be limited, and the group will not turn into a Bible study or a prayer meeting. Guidelines should be couched in encouraging language and aimed at both time management and at directing member behavior within the group. Despite the temptation as a leader to decide the rules before beginning the group, it is widely accepted that guidelines are most effective when the members themselves formulate them.

Some groups function well enough without any guidelines, but I think it's best to create a few at the outset. I've witnessed a group with more than twenty regular members go along beautifully, time after time, without guidelines. But I've led a group of six or seven that were too often booted off-course by a petite lady with cat-eye glasses and a thick gray bob who would give me a wicked little smile and say something like, "I really couldn't believe the wilted lettuce at last night's dinner. Absolutely brown. I heard the social director is doing the cooking now." The functionality of the group depends not only on effective leadership but on member dynamics, which, in this case, seemed driven by preexisting friendships among certain of the group members. Guidelines are a way of establishing a precedent that members, not just the group leader, share the responsibility of keeping the discussion focused.

Confidentiality is one of the most important guidelines to establish. Members need to feel free to share without fear that their divulgences will be discussed outside the group or privately among other group members after the group has disbanded. As a rule of thumb, what is said in the group must stay in the group. An exception occurs when a person's physical safety is threatened, as explained in chapter 3 and in section 5 below. A volunteer leading a support group cannot be expected to *ensure* confidentiality, only to encourage it. But she should set an example. The way in which confidentiality will be handled by the group leader can be explained in a written statement provided prior to the first meeting or after the group guidelines have been established, as mentioned in chapter 7.

## *Activity*

1.  Ask the group to think of qualities that they believe a support group leader needs in order to lead a successful group. Note these on a dry-erase board (or other large writing surface) and discuss the reasons for each one. Try to steer the discussion toward these essential items:

    *   Listening with compassion and patience
    *   Being informed about dementia and the resources at church and within the community
    *   Friendliness
    *   Ability to keep group conversation flowing

2.  Ask: Why would the fourth leadership quality be easier to carry out if guidelines have been established by the group? [Because these guidelines provide structure and are a means of gently bringing the attention back to a mutually determined purpose if necessary: "I completely sympathize with the excessive cost of toiletries in care facilities. Let's remember, though, that we all wanted to keep this time special, for sharing our caregiving experiences and problems. Tim, how is your father settling in at Rivermont?"]

3.  Think of four or five guidelines that would be important to help group members feel safe, valued, and encouraged to participate. As an ice-breaking activity that may be used during a first session if things are a bit slow to start, think of an acronym to represent the guidelines. An acronym makes lists easier to keep in mind and can provide a nonthreatening way of reminding members of group expectations, if needed: "Let's be reminded of the 'a' in 'grace.'" Instead of: "Carol Ann, thanks for your idea, but that advice would be hard to follow. Tim, are you looking for suggestions or mainly wanting to express your frustration?" You can use any word, but here is an example using the word *grace*:

    *   **G** — Give comfort and support, not criticism.
    *   **R** — Respect different beliefs and lifestyles.
    *   **A** — Advice is okay, but only if it's requested.
    *   **C** — Confidentiality is a priority. What we say in the group stays in the group.
    *   **E** — Each person needs equal time to talk, so let's stay on track.

# The Agenda

*Background Information*

An agenda is like a recipe for group success. You don't need one if you're a really good cook and everything in the kitchen is working, but when more than a few people with different personalities are trying to connect constructively around a difficult life circumstance, loosely following an agenda helps: It can guide expectations, motivate members to take part, and ensure that everyone is heard. You don't need to pass around a written agenda at every meeting as though you're at a corporate board meeting, but do have a plan in mind and try to stick to it.

Below is the sample agenda outlined on page 144 of this book, along with suggestions for how the leader can help the group follow it from week to week:

- Arrival (about 10–15 minutes): greetings, refreshments

Use this time to greet newcomers individually.

- Opening (3–5 minutes): welcome, prayer or devotion

Whether to include prayer or devotion in the opening will depend on the group's composition. If the group is made up of church members, this will likely be welcome and expected. If it's a mix of church and community members, you may want just to extend a general greeting. Thank everyone for coming; if new members from the last meeting have returned, acknowledge their presence: "Sam, we're glad to see you again this week! And you, too, Lydia." If a regular attender has been absent, welcome them back: "Howard, you must be feeling better. It's good to have you here." When there are new members (or occasionally) restate the purpose of the group: "Dementia is hard. It's easier when we can get together and talk about it. That's the main reason for our group—to offer each other support and friendship. And please remember that we keep things we say here confidential."

- Introduce new members (about 5 minutes)

Give the person's name and caregiving relationship, but let them share details. "Today we're happy to welcome a new member, Laura Wilder. Laura is a caregiver to her husband, Charles. Laura, would you like to take a few minutes to tell us about yourself and Charles?" At any hint of resistance, reassure: "It's okay if you'd rather wait. There's no pressure in this group. We all have enough stress in our lives. We're just glad you're here."

- <u>Checking in</u> (about 45 minutes):

Each person is given the opportunity to share what has happened since the last group. Going around a circle ensures everyone has a chance to speak even if they opt to pass. Since people tend to sit in the same place from one meeting to the next, begin the circle with a different person at each meeting. Ask, but don't call on members to participate: "Howard, is it okay if we start with you today? How are you, and how are things going with Stella?"

- <u>Review and focus</u> (optional depending on how long "checking in" takes; probably about 15 to 20 minutes):

Ask about past concerns, direct more attention to individuals who may need it, or encourage discussion around a common theme or problem:

- o "Carol Ann, you seem very worried about Edward and his unwillingness to give up driving. Can we try to help you a little more with that?"
- o "Tim, last time we met you were tired because your dad was up and down all night. Has it gotten any better?"
- o "A common theme in our conversation is the decision looming for most of us about whether and when to place our husband, mother, or father in a facility when caregiving gets too hard to continue at home. Let's talk about it during the time that remains."
- o "Would you like to have a guest speaker at support group occasionally? What kind of information would be helpful to you?"

- <u>Closing</u> (5 minutes): prayer requests, affirmations

If prayer requests are part of the agenda, asking for these at the finish of the meeting establishes continuity of care between members: "We can't fix each other's problems, but we can pray for each other. Does anyone have a specific request?" Also consider having members take turns closing with a positive affirmation: "I'll end this evening with an anonymous saying that

I think to myself whenever I feel overwhelmed: 'So far you've survived 100 percent of your worst days. You're doing great!'" Thank everyone for coming, encourage them to come back, and give the date and time of the next meeting.

## Problem Behaviors

*Background Information*

Problem behaviors are usually a result of unmet needs, insecurities, defensiveness, and pain. We've already addressed some of the differences between therapy and support groups. In therapy groups, it is appropriate to confront these behaviors to create a context in which change can be practiced in a controlled setting. Confrontation can be unpleasant no matter how tactful, however, and participation in therapy groups is often contingent on members' commitment to attend despite such discomfort. In support groups the goal is to keep everyone feeling safe and valued at all times by cultivating an attitude of mutual respect. The intention is only to influence the behavior for the sake of the group's productivity. Think of these options to address problem behaviors:

1. Ignore the behavior if you can and it isn't habitual.
2. Demonstrate the respect you want to achieve. Refrain from embarrassing or humiliating a member by calling attention to a specific behavior. Instead call attention to the *result* of the behavior without directly naming the person involved.
3. Find something positive in the intention behind the behavior while redirecting the group's focus.
4. Use humor and gestures—gently.
5. If all else fails, speak with the member in private after the group. Be compassionate and diplomatic.

### Activity

Consider the responses below to behaviors of monopolizing, interrupting, criticizing, inappropriate laughter or scoffing, carrying on a side conversation, and never or seldom participating. Which of the above options does each illustrate? Try to think of other constructive responses.

- Monopolizing is only a problem if it happens frequently enough to be obvious and irritating. Everyone—at times—needs more time from the group due to a particularly hard week, a new or worsening problem, a crisis, or an impending decision. Monopolizing happens when one member *consistently* takes a lion's share of the available time and others feel left out or rushed. People habitually monopolize for different reasons: They're nervous, they don't realize they're doing it, they feel self-important, or they just enjoy being the center of attention:

    o Smile and make a timeout hand signal while summarizing to help the person focus: "Hold on Howard, I'm losing track. Is the main problem your wife's frustration at not being able to go places by herself, or is it that you feel trapped at home?"

    o When the monopolizing person pauses to draw breath (which they'll have to do eventually) praise the first or main thing they've said, and then shift the focus back to the group: "I really like that Howard has brought up a problem we all face—the issue for us, as caregivers, of feeling trapped. Howard, I know we've all felt the way you do. How do the rest of us cope with being stuck at home for such long hours?"

- Interrupting is a gaffe most of us commit occasionally. Ignore unless it happens often enough to be noticeable:

    o Without calling out the interrupter, elevate a hand briefly, slightly (meaning not like a traffic cop) and bring the attention back to the member who was speaking: "Wait a second. Carol Ann, you were saying your mother ate some soap, and you weren't able to get in touch with her doctor. What happened then?" When Carol Ann finishes, check in with the person who interrupted her: "Howard, have you had problems like that, too?"

- Criticism is harder to ignore than some of the other behaviors in this list because it can cause a person to shut down, unless it is both fair and justified, as in the context of a productive work review. It has no place in a support group in which people are struggling with a complex, physically challenging, emotionally taxing situation with little chance for relief:

- Again, don't respond to the criticism. Use the acronym or another way of reminding all of the members, not singling out the critical one, of the group guidelines: "I'm going to remind us all of the need for the "G" in "GRACE" while we're here. When you're in the moment, it's hard not to react. Carol Ann, we've all lost control. It's okay to talk about it."

- Laughing is good, unless it is contemptuous or ridiculing. Stories about dementia can be genuinely funny, and being able to laugh *with* each other is healing. But I once had a friend who'd roll her eyes and snort in derision whenever another person said something a bit stupid or with which she disagreed. As with interrupting, quickly affirm the other member. No one likes to be laughed at or snorted at:

  - "Wow, Tim. What you're telling us is something I surely faced as a caregiver. People with dementia sometimes can't express discomfort, can they? Were you able to help your father with his broken toenail? I bet it was hurting him. With dementia, the smallest things can cause huge problems."

- Side conversations are distracting for everyone and almost beg to be stopped with that old grammar-school teacher quip, "If you can't say it to everyone, please don't say it at all." However, in a support group of adults, particularly a group of adults who may have little chance otherwise to socialize, a certain amount of side talking can be forgiven. If it goes on for too long or is too bothersome:

  - "Sorry, I'm having a hard time hearing." Should the extraneous talking continue (hard to believe it would), repeat, "Again, *I'm* so sorry for *my* distractibility, but I'm not able to focus on what Tim is saying, and I think we'd all like to be able to help him."

- Never or seldom participating is a personal right. Perhaps a quiet member benefits from the chance to socialize before or after the meeting or enjoys listening to others more than talking. But it could be that she needs some encouragement and reassurance that it's safe:

o "Lydia, I appreciate how well you listen to everyone. I want to be sure you have the chance to talk, too, though. Is there anything you need help with today?" If the answer is "No, not really," respond, "Just know we're here for you, and we care about you. We're all in this boat together."

## *Activity*

Take turns practicing with problem behaviors. Assign different members different problem roles to act out (one at a time, not all at once, rotating leaders as the behaviors change). Begin a discussion on any topic with which all members are familiar (dealing with rude or unhelpful company representatives, bad or dangerous experiences while traveling, household disasters[1]). When the "problem" member exhibits the problem behavior, the current leader tries to intervene using one of the methods we've discussed. Give feedback: How did the leader's effort to stop the behavior affect the rest of the group? Could he or she have done it differently?

### WHEN TO MAKE A REFERRAL

In my years as a support group leader, I never needed to refer anyone for further help for reasons of safety, so I must assume it's a rather rare event. Breaking confidentiality to make a referral is justified by a legitimate threat to a person's safety, meaning that a group member expresses, either overtly or suggestively, the intention to hurt herself or her loved one, or she fears being hurt by a person who has lost control due to brain dysfunction. While a support group volunteer isn't in the same reporting category as a minister, who may have a mandated responsibility to refer certain concerns to an appropriate authority, it's generally wise, I think, to be conservative. I offer this caution based on an experience I had as a beginning counselor, in which a woman told me (not in a counseling session but nonetheless in my office), that she wanted to kill her husband. Her frustration seemed typical of most marriages to me, at least *most* marriages *some* of the time, and I failed to perceive her desperation or attach proper meaning to her choice of words—we often use the word "kill" in a nonliteral, hyperbolic way. But that night, she went home and shot at the man with a loaded gun, causing a domestic incident to which the police were summoned. While we do not want to become hypervigilant, imagining risk where none exists, support group leaders do need to be free to obtain appropriate help by referring matters to a minister or church leader if they are worried about a member's disclosures, emotional state, or worrisome behavior.

Safety isn't the only reason for referral. Support group leaders are sometimes asked by members for referrals to outside services, and it is within the leader's responsibility to know generally where to go for help—perhaps to the minister or another staff member involved in pastoral care, the local chapter of the Alzheimer's Association, the board of aging, and certain national alliances and groups that maintain databases of resources.

## CONCLUSION

This information is meant to form the core of a support group leader training session that lasts approximately two hours. Consider adding roleplaying and other activities for extended practice with beginning and ending the group, following an agenda, leading a session on setting group guidelines, and general group leader skills. The more practice provided ahead of time, the more comfortable the group leader and thus the group.

# *Notes*

## CHAPTER 1

1   E. L. Cunningham et al., "Dementia," *The Ulster Medical Journal* 84, no. 2 (May, 2015): 79–87, https://tinyurl.com/2y3du5fk.

2   The simpler term "person with dementia" may make more sense in a given context (see *Sermons*, chapter 3). Dogmatic insistence on a phrase or word, particularly one that is not in common use, can be annoying, and this may defeat the effort to be inclusive.

3   Maurer, Konrad, Stephen Wolk, and Hector Gerbaldo, "Auguste D and Alzheimer's Disease," *The Lancet* 349, no. 9064 (May 1997), 1546–1549.

4   It has been suggested that Auguste Deter may also have had arteriosclerosis of the brain in addition to AD. See Claire O'Brien, "Auguste D. and Alzheimer's Disease," Abstract, *Science* 273, No. 5271 (July 5, 1996), https://tinyurl.com/2nmd35uv.

5   One of the books I recommend for church libraries is *Partial View: An Alzheimer's Journal*, by Cary Smith Henderson (Southern Methodist University, 1988). Henderson was definitively diagnosed with AD following a brain biopsy performed during a procedure for the treatment of suspected hydrocephalus.

6   These portraits can be accessed from a number of sources. At present, this is the best: https://tinyurl.com/ysauk3am.

7   Alzheimer's Association, "2022 Alzheimer's Disease Facts and Figures," (Chicago: Alzheimer's Association, 2022): 19, https://tinyurl.com/2p9ex25d.

8   Brookmeyer, R, et al., cited in GBD Dementia Forecasting Collaborators, "Estimation of the Global Prevalence of Dementia in 2019 and Forecasted Prevalence in 2050: An Analysis for the Global Burden of Disease Study," *The Lancet* 7 (February 2022): e112, https://tinyurl.com/25fcee7k.

9   For a readable but not overly simplistic "tour" of the brain, explaining the location and function of its major structures, see the National Institute of Neurological Disorders and Stroke online publication, "Brain Basics: Know Your Brain," https://www.ninds.nih.gov/health-information/public-education/brain-basics/brain-basics-know-your-brain.

10   Columbia University Irving Medical Center, "Study Shows Where Alzheimer's Starts and How It Spreads (New York: Columbia University Irving Medical Center, December 22, 2013), https://tinyurl.com/52vrk42z.

11   Khalid H. Jawabri and Sandeep Sharma, "Physiology, Cerebral Cortex Functions," (Bethesda, Maryland: National Library of Medicine, April 22, 2022), https://www.ncbi.nlm.nih.gov/books/NBK538496/.

12 Kris Bakowski, "Thanksgiving," *Dealing with Alzheimer's* (blog), November 18, 2004, https://tinyurl.com/5fexjdma. [*Note:* This URL is associated with Kris's earlier blogs. For her current website and blog, see https://creatingmemories.home. blog].

13 Bakowski, "Loneliness," June 13, 2004.

14 For an explanation of amyloid plaques and neurofibrillary tangles, as well as other basic information on Alzheimer's disease, see the National Institute on Aging online publication, "What Happens to the Brain in Alzheimer's Disease?" at https://www. nia.nih.gov/health/what-happens-brain-alzheimers-disease.

15 "Spread" may seem like a strange word to use, suggesting a viral-like process, but it has, in fact, been demonstrated that tau pathology can be transmitted along synaptic tracts in the brain. For more information, see Karen E. Duff, Colombia University Department of Pathology and Cell Biology, "Research," (2022): https://www.vagelos. columbia.edu/profile/karen-e-duff-phd.

16 Howard H. Feldman et al., "Alzheimer's Disease Research and Development: A Call for a New Research Roadmap," *Annals of the New York Academy of Sciences* (April 22, 2014): 1–16, https://tinyurl.com/2c3e3bky.

17 "This Experimental Drug Could Change the Field of Cancer Research," presented by Sacha Pfeiffer and Jonaki Mehta, aired on June 7, 2022, on NPR Radio IQ. https:// tinyurl.com/8876ztes.

18 Dilys Ngu and Antonia Phillip, "A Possible Case of Limbic-Predominate Age-Related TDP-43 Encephalopathy (LATE) in Black Female with Caregiver Burden and Limited Resources: A Novel Presentation with Symptoms Similar to Alzheimer's Disease [Poster Number: LB-5]," *The American Journal of Geriatric Psychiatry* 30 no.4 (April 2022): S118–119, https://tinyurl.com/2rzntrpw.

19 Peter T. Nelson et al., "Limbic Predominate Age-Related TDP-43 Encephalopathy (LATE): Consensus Working Report," *Brain* 142 no. 6 (April 30, 2019): 1503–1527, https://tinyurl.com/yck2fu8a.

20 Nelson et al., "Limbic Predominate Age-Related TDP-43 Encephalopathy (LATE): Consensus Working Report."

21 Antonia Culebras and Sanam Anwar, "Sleep Apnea Is a Risk Factor for Stroke and Vascular Dementia," Abstract, *Current Neurology and Neuroscience Reports* 18, no.53 (June 2018), https://tinyurl.com/2pfmyt5r.

22 Andreia Andrade et al., "The Relationship Between Obstructive Sleep Apnea and Alzheimer's Disease," *Journal of Alzheimer's Disease* 64, Suppl 1(May 2019): S255–270, https://doi.org/10.3233/JAD-179936, https://tinyurl.com/bddhrpms.

23 Alifiya Kapasi, Charles DeCarli, and Julie A. Schneider, "Impact of Multiple Pathologies on the Threshold for Clinically Overt Dementia," *Acta Neuropathologica* 134, no.2 (May 2017): 171–186, https://doi.org/10.1007/s00401-017-1717-7, https:// tinyurl.com/2vht5pfr.

24 Juan Joseph Young et al., "Frontotemporal Lobe Dementia: Latest Evidence and Clinical Implications," *Therapeutic Advances in Psychopharmacology* 8, no.1 (January 2018): 33–48, https://doi.org/10.1177/2045125317739818.

25 David B. Hogan et al., "The Prevalence and Incidence of Frontotemporal Lobe Dementia," *The Canadian Journal of Neurological Sciences* 43, Suppl 1(April 2016): S96–S109, https://doi.org/10.1017/cjn.2016.25.

26  Brooke Arterberry et al., "Application of Generalizability Theory to the Big Five Inventory," *Personality and Individual Differences* 69 (October 2015): 98–103, https://doi.org/10.1016/j.paid.2014.05.015, https://tinyurl.com/yv4xk5zn.

27  Colin J. Mahoney et at., "Neuroanatomical Profiles of Personality Change in Frontotemporal Lobar Degeneration," *The British Journal of Psychiatry* 198, no. 5 (January 2018), https://tinyurl.com/2p8wk8hh.

28  Malcolm MacMillan, "Phineas Gage: Unravelling the Myth," *The Psychologist* 21(September 2008): 828–831, https://tinyurl.com/mr38mfsd.

29  Young, et al., "Frontotemporal Lobe Dementia."

30  Young, et al., "Frontotemporal Lobe Dementia."

31  M. L. Henry and M. L. Gorno-Tempeni, "The Logopenic Variant of Primary Progressive Aphasia," *Current Opinion in Neurology* 23, no.6 (December 2010): 633–637, https://doi.org/10.1097/WCO.0b013e32833fb93e, https://tinyurl.com/2p956nwf.

32  Marsel Mesulam et al., "Alzheimer's and Frontotemporal Pathology in Subsets of Primary Progressive Aphasia," *Annals of Neurology* 63, no.6 (June 2008): 709–719, https://doi.org/10.1002/ana.21388. https://tinyurl.com/yv334t22.

33  Young, et al., "Frontotemporal Lobe Dementia."

34  Young, et al., "Frontotemporal Lobe Dementia."

35  Robin Williams (1951–2014) was a Julliard-educated actor and comedian, known for his funny improvisations in movies like *Mrs. Doubtfire*, although he played serious roles equally as brilliantly. He won numerous awards, including five Grammys, four Golden Globes, two Emmys, and an Oscar. Williams was almost as well-known for his humanitarian work. He toured war zones to lift the morale of troops, visited children in hospitals, and donated to earthquake victims in a long, long list of charitable acts aimed at many causes.

36  Susan Schneider Williams, "The Terrorist Inside My Husband's Brain," *Neurology* 87, no.13 (September 2016): 1308–1311, https://doi.org/10.1212/WNL.0000000000003162, https://n.neurology.org/content/87/13/1308.

37  The preferred term at present is "dementia with Lewy bodies," rather than "Lewy body dementia," although the latter is still in frequent use.

38  Samuel E. Marsh and Matthew Blurton-Jones, "Examining the Mechanisms of B-amyloid and A-synuclein Pathologies," *Alzheimer's Research Theory* 4, no. 2 (April 2012): https://doi.org/10.1186/alzrt109.

39  Stephen N. Gomperts, "Lewy Body Dementia: Dementia with Lewy Bodies and Parkinson Disease Dementia," *Continuum (Minneapolis, Minnesota)* (April 2016): 435–463, https://doi.org/10.1212/CON.0000000000000309, https://tinyurl.com/5cpyc5u3.

40  Mohsen Khosravi, "Lewy Body Dementia: Ursodeoxycholic Acid as a Putative Treatment for Gastrointestinal Dysfunction," *European Journal of Translational Myology* 31, no. 2 (July 2021): 9876, https://doi.org/10.4081/ejtm.2021.9876, https://tinyurl.com/bdccdnmr.

41  Olfactory dysfunction can be a symptom of many dementias, including each of the types we discuss in this chapter, due to its location relative to the initial pathways of these diseases. See Yong-Ming Zou et al., "Olfactory Dysfunction in Alzheimer's Disease," *Neuropsychiatric Disease and Treatment* 12 (April 2016): 869–875, https://doi.org/10.2147/NDT.S104886.

42  Lewy body dementia is closely related to Parkinson's disease, and motor symptoms are frequently observed.

43  Williams, "The Terrorist Inside My Husband's Brain."

44  Gomperts, "Lewy Body Dementia."

45  Susan Williams does mention delusions and paranoia in her 2016 essay for *Neurology*, as well as the suspicion that Williams had hallucinations but hid them from others.

46  R. C. Hamdy et al., "Hallucinations Are Real to Patients with Dementia," *Gerontology and Geriatric Medicine* 3 (January–December 2017): https://journals.sagepub.com/doi/10.1177/2333721417721108.

47  Hamdy et al., "Hallucinations Are Real to Patients with Dementia."

48  Williams, "The Terrorist Inside My Husband's Brain."

49  Melissa Armstrong, et al., "End of Life Experience in Dementia with Lewy Bodies: Qualitative Interviews with Former Caregivers," *PloS One* 14, 15 (May 2019): e0217039, https://doi.org/10.1371/journal.pone.0217039.

50  Michael H. Conners et al., "Non-pharmacological Interventions for Lewy Body Dementia: A Systematic Review," *Psychological Medicine* 48, no. 11 (August 2018): 1749–1758. https://doi.org/10.1017/S0033291717003257.

51  Conners et al., "Non-pharmacological Interventions for Lewy Body Dementia."

## CHAPTER 2

1  Els Van Wijngaarden et al., "Entangled in Uncertainty: The Experience of Living with Dementia from the Perspective of Family Caregivers," *Plos One* (June 13, 2018), https://doi.org/10.1371/journal.pone.0198034.

2  Psalm 46:3.

3  See Richard Taylor, "Alzheimer's from the Inside Out." YouTube video, 23:48, April 6, 2016. https://tinyurl.com/5x93mmer. Taylor was diagnosed with Alzheimer's at sixty-one, while still working as a psychologist. About five years into his diagnosis, he wrote a memoir of short essays, also entitled *Alzheimer's from the Inside Out* (Health Professions Press, 2007).

4  For some dementia patients, the changes in cognition are so gradual that passage from preclinical to clearly symptomatic disease happens without conscious awareness of the process. *Anosognosia* refers to an inability, due to brain dysfunction, to perceive one's deficits. For more information, see Howard J. Rosen, "Anosognosia in Neurodegenerative Disease," *Behavior, Cognition and Neuroscience* 17, no. 3 (June 2011): 231–241, https://doi.org/10.1080/13554794.2010.522588, https://tinyurl.com/5n7ewsnt.

5  Jim Garner died in 2016 at the age of 52. I met Karen before his death at a national press conference on Alzheimer's in 2013. In a show of resilience and compassion, she has since become an advocacy manager for the Alzheimer's Association, serving Virginia, Maryland and Washington, DC. Karen says she'll talk to anyone who will listen about Alzheimer's and the toll it takes on families.

6  According to the AARP Public Policy Institute report, *Valuing the Invaluable: 2019 Update, Charting a Path Forward* (AARP.org, November 2019), during the single year of 2017, forty-one million family caregivers provided thirty-four billion hours of

unpaid care to adults with dementia or another disabling condition, at an economic value of $470 billion.

7 The average cost of a shared nursing home room in the United States in 2021 was $94,900 (American Council on Aging: https://www.medicaidplanningassistance.org/nursing-home-costs/). The national median family income in 2021 was $79,900 (US Department of Housing and Urban Development: https://www.huduser.gov/portal/datasets/il/il21/Medians2021.pdf).

8 Matthew 6:28, 10:29.

9 Deuteronomy 34:7.

10 Drs. John M. O'Keefe, May-Britt Moser, and Edvard I. Moser won a Nobel Prize for discovering that cells in the hippocampus, where Alzheimer's initially affects the brain, are responsible for proper orientation in space and time. For more information, see Carmen Drahl, "John O'Keefe, May-Britt Moser, and Edvard Moser win 2014 Nobel Prize in Physiology or Medicine, *Chemical and Engineering News*, October 6, 2014, https://tinyurl.com/yytp3522.

11 Philippians 4:5.

12 Ephesians 4:15.

13 For an excellent article employers can use as a guide, see Carole Fleck, "Coping with Cognitive Declines at Work," *SHRM Foundation, HR Magazine* (September 3, 2015), https://tinyurl.com/36h2b4ke.

## CHAPTER 3

1 "Why Americans Do (and Don't) Go to Religious Services," *Pew Research Center* (August 1, 2018), Accessed August 1, 2022, https://tinyurl.com/ycks367x.

2 Mark A. Lumley et.al., "Pain and Emotion: A Biopsychosocial Review of the Recent Research," *Journal of Clinical Psychology* 67, no. 9 (September 2011): 942–968, https://doi.org/10.1002/jclp.20816, https://tinyurl.com/2ysybfrh.

3 Alys Wyn Griffiths, "Relational Counselling as a Psychosocial Intervention for Dementia: Qualitative Evidence from People Living with Dementia and Family Members," *Dementia (London)* 20, no. 6 (August 2021): 2091–2018, https://doi.org/10.1177/1471301220984912.

4 Sylvia A. Morelli et.al, "The Neural Bases of Feeling Understood and Not Understood," *Social Cognitive and Affective Neuroscience* 9 no. 12 (December 2014):1890–1896, https://doi.org/10.1093/scan/nst191.

5 Constance Frisby Fain, "Minimizing Liability for Church-Related Counseling Services: Clergy Malpractice and First Amendment Religion Clauses," *Akron Law Review* (July 2015): 221–258, https://tinyurl.com/6jchsrus.

6 Constance Frisby Fain, "Minimizing Liability," 221–258.

7 For a well-organized, accessible article comparing the four main modes of pastoral counseling to a secular approach, see Timothy Keller, "Four Models of Counseling in Pastoral Ministry," *Redeemer City to City* (2010): 1–10, https://tinyurl.com/9excjux4.

8 Carl R. Rogers, "Significant Aspects of Client Centered Therapy," *American Psychologist, 1* no. 10 (1946): 415–422, posted online by Christopher D. Green, York University, https://tinyurl.com/2p8vy6bz.

9  Sun Kyung Kim and Myonghwa Park, "Effectiveness of Person-Centered Care on People with Dementia: A Systematic Review and Meta-Analysis," *Clinical Interventions in Aging* 12 (February 2017): 381–397, https://doi.org/10.2147/CIA.S117637.

10  C. H. Patterson, "A Current View of Client-Centered or Relationship Therapy," *Sage Social Science Collections* (first published June 1, 1969), https://tinyurl.com/2p8ukhxt.

11  C. H. Patterson, "Some Misconceptions of and Questions about Client-Centered Therapy," in *The Therapeutic Relationship* (Monterey: Brooks Cole Publishing Company, 1985), 215, published online by *Sage of Ashville*, https://tinyurl.com/yckeucrv.

12  Ephesians 5:2.

13  Saybrook University, "A Conversation with Carl Rogers: The Job of a Therapist," *YouTube* video, 28:14, June 26, 2012, https://tinyurl.com/34fab8w3. [*Note*: Do watch this video for a concise explanation from Rogers, himself, of the ideal attitude toward the client in the person-centered model.]

14  Jacob Nacht, "The Symbolism of the Shoe with Special Reference to Jewish Sources," *The Jewish Quarterly Review* 6, no. 1 (July 1915): 1–22, Published online by the University of Pennsylvania Press, https://tinyurl.com/4b5ypwhe. [I recommend this fascinating, exhaustive article, which surely must cover everything of importance that can be said on the subject. Having often struggled in my work to find precise sources, I smiled especially over one sentence, although I also disagreed with it: "'Civilized people lose easily their religion but rarely their superstitions,' says Karl Goldmark somewhere" p. 21.]

15  Jeremiah 17:10.

16  Psalm 56: 8.

17  Galatians 6:2.

18  Matthew 19:14.

19  One of the best all-encompassing, unapologetic (admittedly untherapeutic) answers to suffering may be in C. S. Lewis's *The Problem of Pain* (New York: Touchstone, 1996), 42: "You asked for a God of love: you have one. The great spirit you so lightly invoked, the 'lord of terrible aspect,' is present: not a senile benevolence that drowsily wishes you to be happy in your own way, not the cold philanthropy of a conscientious magistrate, nor a host who feels responsible for the comfort of his guests, but the consuming fire Himself, the love that made the worlds, persistent as the artist's love for his work and despotic as a man's love for a dog, provident and venerable as a father's love for a child, jealous, inexorable, exacting as love between the sexes."

20  Job 42:3–6.

21  Ezra E. H. Griffith and John L. Young, "Clergy Counselors and Confidentiality: A Case for Scrutiny 32 (2004): 43–50, http://jaapl.org/content/jaapl/32/1/43.full.pdf.

22  Richard Hammar, "Understanding Pastoral Liability," *Christianity Today, Church Law & Tax*, 9, https://tinyurl.com/yc4vcnff.

23  Memorandum, "HIPPA Privacy Rule and Local Churches," General Council of Finance and Administration of the United Methodist Church (February 2004), http://s3.amazonaws.com/Website_GCFA/HIPAA_Privacy_Rule_and_Local_Churches.pdf. [This is an informative article for a discussion on the limited application of HIPPA to churches, as well as unrelated issues of privacy. *Note*: In the case of *Mitnaul vs Fairmont Presbyterian Church* a Director of Music Ministries sued for invasion of privacy over the following notice, posted on the church's website: "We have good news for you. [Plaintiff] is returning to Fairmont after a long medical leave of absence.

Since the summer of last year, [Plaintiff] has been treated for bi-polar illness, a condition which at times has resulted in serious depression for him. Various therapies and medications have been tried, and after much experimentation, his health has improved considerably. For this, we are all very happy!" The music director prevailed in the case, as might be expected (p. 9).]

24  David O. Middlebrook, "Pastor Confidentiality: An Ethical and Legal Responsibility," Assemblies of God, February 2, 2010, https://tinyurl.com/2ejebten.

25  See this brief statement, adapted from *The Deacon's Bench* 16 no. 3 (Summer 2005): "Prayer Lists: How to Protect Privacy," https://tinyurl.com/mry74k7k.

26  State Elder Abuse Statutes, *The United States Department of Justice*, https://tinyurl.com/5ekmr5en.

27  Cail, *Alzheimer's: A Crash Course for Friends and* Relatives, p. 63.

28  Keep in mind, this figure means the majority of people with dementia are *not* aggressive. Aggression is often related to an unmet need. UCLA Health provides a set of caregiver training videos to help with the management of many difficult behaviors. Here's a link to the video on aggression: https://www.uclahealth.org/medical-services/geriatrics/dementia/caregiver-education/caregiver-training-videos, *UCLA Alzheimer's and Dementia Care Program*.

29  Tracey Wharton and Bryan K. Ford, "What is Known about Dementia Recipient Violence and Aggression against Caregivers?" *Journal of Gerontology Social Work* 57, no. 5 (June 2014): 460–477, https://doi.org/10.1080/01634372.2014.882466, https://tinyurl.com/bddav4yu.

30  For a wrenching but revealing article, see Rob Stein, "Legal System Struggles with Dementia Patients," *Washington Post* (July 28, 2003), https://tinyurl.com/mr3a9x7t. See also Madeline Liljegren, et al., "Criminal Behavior in Frontotemporal Dementia and Alzheimer Disease," *Jama Neurology* 72 no. 3 (March 2015), p. 295–300. https://doi.org/10.1001/jamaneurol.2014.3781.

31  For more information: "Types of Abuse Defined in Adult Protective Services Statutes," American Bar Association Commission on Aging (June 2021), https://www.americanbar.org/content/dam/aba/administrative/law_aging/2020-abuse-definitions.pdf.

32  Carol J. Whitlatch and Silvia Orsulic-Jeras, "Meeting the Informational, Educational, and Psychosocial Needs of Persons Living with Dementia and Their Family Caregivers," *The Gerontologist* 58, no. 1 (February 2018): S58–73, https://academic.oup.com/gerontologist/article/58/suppl_1/S58/4816739. [*Note*: This article contains a well-organized list of needed community supports, and churches could provide some of them. Some are included in this book.]

33  Jeffery M. Girard et al., "Nonverbal Social Withdrawal in Depression: Evidence from Manual and Automatic Analysis," *Image and Vision Computing* 32, no. 10 (October 2014): 641–647, https://doi.org/10.1016/j.imavis.2013.12.007, https://www.ncbi.nlm.nih.gov/pmc/articles/PMC4217695/.

34  "Pastors' Long Work Hours Come at the Expense of Ministry, People," Lifeway Research, January 5, 2010, https://tinyurl.com/4435c2fw.

35  Richard Weissbourd, Melina Batanova, Virginia Lovison, and Eric Torres, "Loneliness in America: How the Pandemic Has Deepened an Epidemic of Loneliness and What We Can Do About It," Harvard University School of Education, PDF accessed December 16, 2021, 1–15, https://tinyurl.com/2p854m2v.

36  Luke 15:4.

37  Luke 18:1–8.

38  1 Peter 5:7.

39  Angela Ghesquiere, "I Was Just Trying to Stick it Out Until I Realized I Couldn't: A Phenomenological Investigation of Support Seeking Among Older Adults with Complicated Grief," *Omega (Westport)* 68, no. 1 (May 2013):1–22, https://tinyurl.com/4d9se3f6, https://doi.org/10.2190/om.68.1.a.

40  Weissbourd, "Loneliness in America," 5.

41  For the blog describing this unfortunate incident, see https://tinyurl.com/3hxy3new.

42  Marilyn Truscott, "Looks Can Be Deceiving: Dementia, the Invisible Disease," Presented at the A.I.D Conference, Kyoto, Japan, October 15, 2004, https://studylib.net/doc/8066668/looks-can-be-deceiving.

43  Dilip V. Jeste, Brent Mausbach, and Ellen E. Lee, "Caring for Caregivers / Care Partners of Persons with Dementia," *International Psychogeriatrics* 33, no. 4 (April 2021): 307–310, https://doi.org/10.1017/S1041610221000557.

44  For helpful suggestions on confronting suspected dementia at work, see Carole Fleck's article, "Coping with Cognitive Declines at Work," also noted in chapter 2: https://tinyurl.com/36h2b4ke.

45  Sister Pat was clear about the limits of her confidentiality. I knew she would break it if I discussed suicide, so I didn't. I learned though, or relearned, that there was nothing I could not tell God.

46  Romans 8:28.

47  Psalm 46:10.

48  Angela L. Smith, "The Stages of Caregiving: The Spiritual Connection for the Journey with Alzheimer's," *American Journal of Pastoral Counseling* 4 no. 3 (July 2010): 30, https://doi.org/10.1300/J062v04n03_03.

49  Smith, "The Stages of Caregiving," 30.

50  Psalm 121:5–6.

51  Psalm 56:8.

52  Obviously, I don't recommend this as a technique, because it could too easily be misconstrued or misused. It was a unique situation between two people who came together at a certain point in time, I believe, by the grace and provision of God.

53  Kesstan Blandin and Renee Pepin, "Dementia Grief: A Theoretical Model of a Unique Grief Experience," *Dementia (London)* 16 no.1(January 2017): 67–78, https://doi.org/10.1177/1471301215581081, https://tinyurl.com/yc7b8vbk.

54  Ad J. J. M. Vingerhoets and Lauren M. Blysma, "The Riddle of Human Emotional Crying: A Challenge for Emotion Researchers," *Emotion Review* 8 no. 3 (July 2016): 207–217, https://tinyurl.com/2p83krse.

55  Here is an article worth posting in the counseling office, which summarizes this information in readable, reassuring style by the author of *The Empath's Survival Guide*: Judith Orloff, "The Health Benefits of Tears," *Psychology Today* (July 27, 2010), https://tinyurl.com/3uct9xr6. [*Note*: Blandin & Pepin (see note 53) extensively cite conflicting studies on the function and composition of emotional tears, eventually concluding that while these tears are, with little question, beneficial to the individual and to society at large, there is still "much to discover."]

56  Benedict Cary, "The Muddled Tracks of All Those Tears," *The New York Times*, February 2, 2009, https://tinyurl.com/5yvmshsu.

57 Jay Efran, "What to Do if Your Client Cries: If It's Not Broken, Don't Fix It," (blog), Psychotherapy Networker, May/June 2012, https://tinyurl.com/484kc6hu.

58 Ad J. J. M. Vingerhoets, Lauren M. Blysma, and Jonathan Rottenberg, "Crying: A Biopsychosocial Phenomenon," In T. Fogen ed., *Tears in the Graeco-Roman World* (2009): p. 439, https://tinyurl.com/3nwmm9y3.

59 Charles Dickens, *Great Expectations: A Norton Critical Edition*, ed. Edgar Rosenberg (New York: Norton and Company, 1999), p. 116.

60 Informed prayer is like informed compassion, defined in the introduction. When you have talked with a person confidentially, you've been entrusted with a deeper knowledge of them, and to bring their needs to God honors this trust and the expectation behind it. Think of Jesus asking blind men to tell him what they wanted (Matthew: 20:32), although he already knew. The understanding that you will pray more specifically is a comfort.

61 John R. Finney and H. Newton Maloney Jr., "Empirical Studies of Christian Prayer: A Review of the Literature," *Journal of Psychology and Theology* 13, no. 2 (1985): 104–115, https://journals.sagepub.com/doi/10.1177/009164718501300203.

62 Job 42:7.

63 Frederick Buechner, "Theodicy," *Sermon Illustrations* (Blog), November 19, 2018, https://tinyurl.com/ye27f6f9.

64 "When two or three are gathered in my name, I am there" (Matthew 18:20, NIV).

65 Matthew 17:20.

66 Psalm 139.

67 Matthew 26:39.

68 1 Corinthians 13:12.

69 For a short, interesting discussion on early mirrors, see John DeLancey, "Ancient Mirrors," *Biblical Israel Ministries and Tours* (Blog), December 1, 2016, https://tinyurl.com/3bvwzxdr.

70 Romans 8:26.

71 Psalm 139.

72 For an article on the photos of Gary Greenberg with a link to his online gallery, see Diane Spector, "What Sand Grains Look Like Through a Microscope," BusinessInsider.com, January 27, 2014, https://tinyurl.com/3hk8jz94.

73 Anna Dina L. Joaquin and Andrea W. Mates, "'I don't know what to do. Pray I guess.': Faith and coping with Frontotemporal Dementia," *Journal of Religion, Spirituality & Aging* 30, no. 3 (April, 2018): 251–267, https://tinyurl.com/3xyjevp9.

74 Joaquin and Mates, "'I don't know what to do. Pray I guess.'" p. 254.

75 Francis, "Why Does It Seem Like God Doesn't Answer Our Prayers Sometimes?" Weekly Wednesday audience, delivered on May 26, 2021 at the feast of St. Philip Neri, *America, the Jesuit Review*, https://tinyurl.com/524ecb6b.

76 Joaquin and Mates, "'I don't know what to do. Pray I guess.'" p. 258. (*Note*: The entire prayer is reproduced in Joaquin and Mates's article on this page.)

77 "This is my body, which will be given for you. Do this in memory of me" (Luke 22:19).

78 Hide, Kerrie, "Symbol Ritual and Dementia," *Journal of Religious Gerontology* 13 no. 3–4 (2002): 77–90. https://tinyurl.com/munfhczu.

79 Hide, Kerrie, "Symbol Ritual and Dementia," p. 89. [Note: For an amazing example, watch Naomi Feil, a Jewish social worker who developed an approach known as validation therapy, work with a woman in advanced dementia by singing hymns with her: "This is Love! Lady Touches Soul of Alzheimer's Sufferer with Christian Hymns,"

https://tinyurl.com/ycktew9p. See also: Feil, Naomi, *The Validation Breakthrough: Simple Techniques for Communicating with People with Alzheimer's and Other Dementias,* 3rd ed. (Baltimore: Health Professions Press, 2012).]

## CHAPTER 4

1  Stephen J. Cutler, "Worries About Getting Alzheimer's: Who's Concerned?" *American Journal of Alzheimer's Disease and Other Dementias* 30, no. 6 (September 2015): 591–598. https://doi.org/10.1177/1533317514568889.

2  Rosabeth Moss Kantor, "Ten Reasons People Resist Change." *Harvard Business Review,* September 25, 2012, https://tinyurl.com/yck8326z.

3  Dale S. Ryan in "The Promises and Pitfalls of Congregation Support Groups," *The National Association for Christian Recovery* (undated): https://tinyurl.com/2p8vbwmv. [*Note*: Ryan is referring in his article specifically to support group ministries for addiction recovery.]

4  1 Corinthians 13:12.

5  Chris Musser and Scott DeKoster, "Don't Let Good Data Go to Waste," Gallup Workplace, September 30, 2020, https://tinyurl.com/33pyetkm.

6  The use of receptacles provides greater anonymity, which contributes to accuracy of data. See Ann Bowing, "Mode of Questionnaire Administration Can have Serious Effects on Data Quality," *Journal of Public Health* 27, no. 3 (September 2005): 281–291, https://doi.org/10.1093/pubmed/fdi031.

7  SurveyMonkey.com provides suggestions and methods for analyzing unstructured data. See https://tinyurl.com/2p9ajkyu.

8  Age and gender are mainly relevant if these demographics are used to form regular groups in the congregation. If the data shows, for example, that younger members have little experience with dementia, education can be provided to the young adult groups they attend. If a number of women express an interest in helping with a respite program, church leaders could meet with women's groups to explain what it entails. For some congregations, other demographics pertaining to education, activities, and service options may be appropriate.

9  Depending on the makeup of your congregation, *Other* or *Prefer-Not-to-Answer* may also be provided as choices.

10 Kantor, "Ten Reasons People Resist Change."

11 Imran Muhammad and Saqib Mahmood, "An Overview of Human Prion Diseases," *Virology Journal* 8, no. 559 (December 2011), https://virologyj.biomedcentral.com/articles/10.1186/1743-422X-8-559.

12 Jill U. Adams, "Do Microbes Trigger Alzheimer's?" *The Scientist,* September 1, 2017, https://tinyurl.com/3967urbn.

13 Sara B. Algoe, Patrick C. Dwyer, Ayana Younge, and Christopher Oveis, "A New Perspective on the Social Functions of Emotions: Gratitude and the Witnessing Effect," Abstract, *Journal of Personality and Social Psychology* 119 (July 2020), https://doi.apa.org/doi/10.1037/pspi0000202.

14 Adam M. Grant and Francesca Gino, "A Little Thanks Goes a Long Way: Explaining Why Gratitude Expressions Motivate Prosocial Behavior," *Journal of Personality and Social Psychology* 98, no. 6 (2010): 946–955, https://doi.org/10.1037/a0017935, https://tinyurl.com/4cwp5ejf.

15 Statistically, this number of randomly selected surveys (from a thousand) would enable a researcher to state with certainty 95 percent of the time that the results reflect the true mean of the population.

16 Angela M. Pazzaglia, Erin T. Stafford, and Sheila M. Rodriguez, "Survey Methods for Educators: Selecting Samples and Administering Surveys," (Part 2 of 3, REL 2016–160), Washington, DC: US Department of Education, Institute of Education Sciences, National Center for Education Evaluation and Regional Assistance, Regional Educational Laboratory Northeast & Islands (August 2016), https://eric.ed.gov/?id=ED567752.

17 Bob Smietana, "Most Churches Offer WiFi but Skip Twitter." Lifeway Research, January 8, 2018, https://tinyurl.com/mr2rxucm.

18 Daniel Cox, "Churches Face Challenges in Upgrading to Religion 2.0," PPRI, August 6, 2012, https://tinyurl.com/3vnpcue5.

19 Lori Harper et al., "Stigma in Dementia: It's Time to Talk About It," *Current Psychiatry* 18, no.7 (July 2019): 16–23. https://tinyurl.com/yckzuhcd.

20 For a large church, this may be the only workable method. Practicality matters. Google Workspace offers methods to create online survey forms and analyze the results, as does SurveyMonkey. See https://tinyurl.com/26r8swj8 and https://tinyurl.com/bdhj3udz. (The second link is a video on how to use SurveyMonkey to conduct a survey.)

21 Roderick M. Krammer, "Rethinking Trust," *Harvard Business Review*, June 2009, https://hbr.org/2009/06/rethinking-trust.

22 Charles E. Naquin, Terri R. Kurtzberg, and Liuba Y. Belkin, "The Finer Points of Lying Online: Email Versus Pen and Paper," *Journal of Applied Psychology* 95, no. 2 (March 2010): 387–394. https://doi.org/10.1037/a0018627, https://www.researchgate.net/publication/41967730_The_Finer_Points_of_Lying_Online_E-Mail_Versus_Pen_and_Paper.

23 For a copy of "Terminus," see https://tinyurl.com/2tvzaham.

24 Henri Nouwen, *Adam: God's Beloved*, Anniversary Edition, (Ossining, New York: Orbis Books, 2012), 16–17.

25 Kenneth L. Carder, *Ministry with the Forgotten: Dementia through a Spiritual Lens* (Nashville: Abington Press, 2019), back cover.

26 Kenneth Carder, interview with the author, September 21, 2021.

27 Cindy Solomon, "Free Resource Helps Congregations Care for People with Dementia Diseases and Their Loved Ones," Encore Ministry, Accessed September 21, 2022, https://encoreministry.org (see related comment in the chapter).

28 CBC News, "Bishop Michael Curry's FULL Royal Wedding Sermon," *YouTube* video, May 19, 2018, https://tinyurl.com/mtdm4mdp.

29 Alzheimer's Disease International, *World Alzheimer's Report*, accessed July 26, 2021, https://tinyurl.com/2p82f7vy.

30 Michael Rosato et al., "Factors Associated with Public Knowledge of and Attitudes to Dementia: A Cross-Sectional Study," *PLoS One* 14, no. 2 (February 2019), https://doi.org/10.1371/journal.pone.0210543.

31 Prentice, D. A., & Carlsmith, K. M. (2000). "Opinions and Personality: On the Psychological Functions of Attitudes and Other Valued Possessions." In eds. G. R. Maio & J. M. Olson, *Why We Evaluate: Functions of Attitudes* (New Jersey: Lawrence Erlbaum Associates Publishers, 2000), 223–248.

32 Matthew 10:34.

33  Merlin, Venus, Daan Stam, and Daan van Knippenberg, "Visions of Change as Visions of Continuity," Abstract, *Academy of Management Journal* 62 (June 14, 2019), https://doi.org/10.5465/amj.2015.1196, https://tinyurl.com/ef5sep4y.

34  Interestingly (or depressingly, as the case may be), three-quarters of churchgoers, questioned a day after hearing a sermon reported that it was "good" or "very good," but two-thirds of these same respondents could not remember what the sermon was about. See William D. Howden, "'Good Sermon, Preacher': The Effects of Age, Sex, and Education on Hearer Response to Preaching," *Review of Religious Research* 31, no. 2 (December 1989): 204.

35  Henk Stoorvogel, "Moving Sermons: Studies into the Persuasive Effects of Preaching" PhD diss., University of Twente, 2019, 77, https://tinyurl.com/de3e2ate.

36  Stoorvogel, "Moving Sermons," 172.

37  For an abysmal description of old age, if not dementia per se, see Ecclesiastes 12:1–8.

38  Revelation 21:5.

39  2 Peter 3:8.

40  2 Timothy 1:12.

41  Merlijn Venus, Daan Stam, and Daam Van Knippinberg, "Research: To Get People to Embrace Change, Emphasize What Will Stay the Same," *Harvard Business Review* (August 15, 2018), https://tinyurl.com/yhn3ejny.

42  Use of this ritualistic beginning should be the prerogative of ministers, I suspect, but to me, these words are a simple, necessary prayer to honor God and convey truth; I could say them silently to myself. For a related sermon, delivered more than a decade ago but never more relevant than now, read Reverend Sam Chandler's, "In the Name of God: Father, Son, and Holy Spirit," The Cathedral of St. Philip, Atlanta, Georgia, May 18, 2008: https://tinyurl.com/9e7cxdjv.

43  Romans 2:1–3.

44  1 Samuel 16:7.

45  Matthew 7:1–5.

46  Fleming Rutledge, *The Crucifixion: Understanding the Death of Jesus Christ* (Grand Rapids, MI: William B. Eerdmans Publishing Company, 2015), 92, 95.

47  Matthew 6:3.

48  Tyler Brown, "Exegesis of Matthew 25:31–46 with an Emphasis on the Identity of 'All the Nations' and 'The Least of These,'" ONT508 Gospels, 2016–2017, https://www.academia.edu/34353125/Exegesis_of_Matthew_25_31_46_with_an_Emphasis_on_the_Identity_of_All_the_Nations_and_the_Least_of_These_.

49  Ian Paul, "What Did Jesus Have Against Goats?" (blog), September 13, 2018, https://www.psephizo.com/biblical-studies/what-did-jesus-have-against-goats/.

50  Matthew 25:41.

51  Mark 4:35–37.

## CHAPTER 5

1  Amelia Gentleman, "The Raw Horror of Alzheimer's," *The Guardian*, June 1, 2010, https://tinyurl.com/2ccjw5vb.

2  According to the Alzheimer's Association, one in three seniors dies with Alzheimer's or another type of dementia (https://tinyurl.com/mmnpvrsr). Alzheimer's begins to

affect the brain years, even decades, before it becomes symptomatic, meaning almost any person, from middle-aged on, has a legitimate reason for concern.

3   Alexandra Hillman and Joanna Latimer, "Cultural Representations of Dementia," *PLOS* Medicine 14, no. 3 (March 2017): https://tinyurl.com/4pct7tsz.

4   Hillman and Latimer, "Cultural Representations of Dementia."

5   The movies *Still Alice* (2015) and *Iris* (2001) are among these exceptions. Both tell the story of dementia in a way that leaves the audience with a stronger impression of transformation than deterioration.

6   Hillman and Latimer, "Cultural Representations of Dementia." For a review of the media's influence on perceptions of dementia, see Lee-Fay Low and Farah Purwaningrum, "Negative Stereotypes, Fear and Social Distance: a Systematic Review of Depictions of Dementia in Popular Culture in the Context of Stigma," *BMC Geriatrics* 20, no. 477 (November 2020), https://doi.org/10.1186/s12877-020-01754-x.

7   Alzheimer's disease is the form of dementia mainly covered in this and later chapters, because it is by a longshot the most common, and the three stages provide a way of understanding the progression of dementia from barely noticeable to severe. Even people who show little evidence of cognitive decline at death have been shown on autopsy to have significant AD pathology in the brain, masked, it seems by cognitive reserve. See D. A. Bennett, et al., "Neuropathology of Older Persons Without Cognitive Impairment from Two Community Based Studies," *Neurology* 66 (June 2006): 1842, https://tinyurl.com/4c3h2bmf.

8   Rebecca Carlson McCall, Kristy Padron, and Carl Andrews, "Evidence Based Instructional Strategies for Adult Learners: A Review of the Literature." CUNY Academic Works, Spring 2018, 39–40, https://academicworks.cuny.edu/bx_pubs/43/.

9   Philippians 4:8.

10   James 3:3–4.

11   Lynn K. Herrmann et al., "A Systematic Review of Dementia-related Stigma Research: Can We Move the Stigma Dial?" *The American Journal of Geriatric Psychiatry* 26, no. 3 (March 2018): 316–331. https://doi.org/10.1016/j.jagp.2017.09.006.

12   Ephesians 2:10.

13   Avraham Z. Cooper and Jeremy B. Richards, "Lectures for Adult Learners: Breaking Old Habits in Medical Education," *The American Journal of Medicine* 130, No 3 (March 2017): 376–381. http://dx.doi.org/10.1016/j.amjmed.2016.11.009.

14   For a relevant article on ostracism, see Daryl Austin, "What You're Saying When You Give Someone the Silent Treatment," *The Atlantic* (March 26, 2021). https://www.theatlantic.com/family/archive/2021/03/psychology-of-silent-treatment-abuse/618411/.

15   See Ernst, J, et al, "Perceived Stigmatization and Its Impact on Quality of Life—Results from a Large Register-Based Study Including Breast, Colon, Prostate, and Lung Cancer Patients," *BMC Cancer* (November 9, 2017), https://doi.org/10.1186/s12885-017-3742-2.

16   The answer to this question is apparently *yes*. For an exhaustive, informative review of research, worth reading, see Roy F. Baumeister, Ellen Bratslavsky, and Catrin Finkenhaur, "Bad is Stronger than Good," *Review of General Psychology* 5, no. 4 (2001): 323–370. https://assets.csom.umn.edu/assets/71516.pdf.

17   Adam Wang Deming, Martin S. Hagger, and Nikos L. D. Chatzisarantis, "Ironic Effects of Thought Suppression: A Meta-Analysis," Abstract, *Perspectives on Psychological Science* (April 14, 2020), https://doi.org/10.1177/1745691619898795.

18   Scientific research is yielding more precise diagnostic methods, which can detect some of the conditions that cause dementia before symptoms have emerged. During

the preclinical stage of Alzheimer's, the characteristic cellular changes are occurring steadily in the brain—the disease is present—but there are no outward symptoms of it.

19 Consider the implications of the preclinical stage: If more than one in nine people from age 65 on have symptomatic Alzheimer's, the disease began for many when they were in their mid-fifties or earlier, still working, living unsuspecting lives.

20 Mary McDaniel Cail, *Alzheimer's: A Crash Course for Friends and Relatives*. (Chapel Hill, NC: TrueWind Press, 2014).

21 A very simple playbill template you can use: https://tinyurl.com/5dr3e9jt.

22 I've mentioned that I use this term as a way of describing my work. See www.allweatherfriend.org.

23 Christine Bryden's work is a remarkable testimony to determination and accomplishment despite advanced dementia. Look at the photos of her brain scan on the website page entitled "Christine Now." But should her website be unavailable, there are many comparable YouTube videos you can substitute to make the same point. Consider this interview with Don Hayden, MD: https://tinyurl.com/ykfxbprb. (Please note: The video was produced in 2008, so Hayden's remarks about diagnosis are no longer accurate. Alzheimer's can now be diagnosed earlier.)

24 For a brief discussion, see Joseph Hartropp, "Why Names Are So Important in the Bible, and So Is Yours," *Christianity Today* (November 17, 2016), https://www.christiantoday.com/article/why-names-are-so-important-in-the-bible-and-so-is-yours/101095.htm.

## CHAPTER 6

1 According to a 2014 US Religious Landscape Study, the median age of people who claimed no religious affiliation was thirty-eight. The median age for agnostics and atheists was a bit younger at thirty-four. People attending Presbyterian denominations (as an example) had a median age in 2014 of fifty-nine, about two decades older. See Michael Lipka, "Which U.S. Religious Groups Are Oldest and Youngest?" Pew Research Center, published July 11, 2016, https://tinyurl.com/2ztu9ja8.

2 Barry Reisberg et al, "Evidence and Mechanisms of Retrogenesis in Alzheimer's and Other Dementias: Management and Treatment Import," *American Journal of Alzheimer's Disease and Other Dementias*, 17, no.4 (July–August 2002): 202–212. https://doi.org/10.1177/153331750201700411. [*Note*: follow this link to access full article and table: https://tinyurl.com/mu9ccyz7.]

3 Olivier Pierre Tible, Florian Reise, Egemen Savaskan, and Armin von Gunten, "Best Practice in the Management of Behavioural and Psychological Symptoms of Dementia," *Therapeutic Advances in Neurological Disorders* 10, no. 8 (August 2017): 297–301, https://doi.org/10.1177/1756285617712979.

4 This is an example of when we, as those on the outside looking in, need to refrain from judgment. Dementia can be hard to manage, and sometimes loved ones and caregivers resort to whatever works, within the limits of safety and overall kindness: It was kind of this woman to be taking her grandfather out and spending time with him.

5 Allan Pease and Barbara Pease, "Understanding the Basics," *New York Times*, September 24, 2006, https://tinyurl.com/5n933mtr.

6 Cail, *Alzheimer's: A Crash Course for Friends and Relatives*, 157.

7   Alzheimer's Weekly, "Experience 12 Minutes in Alzheimer's Dementia." *YouTube* video, 8:03, produced by ABC News, August 21, 2012, https://alzheimersweekly.com/2014/05/experience-12-minutes-in-alzheimers-on/.

8   GBD 2019 Dementia Forecasting Collaborators, "Estimation of the Global Prevalence of Demenita in 2019 and Forecasted Prevalence in 2050: An analysis for the Global Burden of Disease Study 2019," *The Lancet* 7 no. 2 (February 2022): E105–125, https://tinyurl.com/3ecnpupn.

9   Although the Alzheimer's Association website lists three main stages of dementia, and we use a three-stage model for these activities, the disease is often described in seven stages. You can see the early, middle, and late stages we use listed as subheadings directly under stages four through seven of the handout.

10  Marina Katz, "Virtual Dementia Tour Leaves Participants Frustrated but Sympathetic." *ABC* News, June 29, 2009, https://tinyurl.com/2zp5uxe2.

11  I cannot find research or anecdotal evidence confirming that many people with dementia experience *incessant* auditory disturbances. It does appear, however, that these headsets effectively create the level of confusion felt on a continual basis and thus seem to provide an accurate experience. The problem with balance, simulated by the shoe inserts, is common.

12  For a sad, disturbing depiction of the family, see Cynthia McFadden, Robbie Gordon, and Rashida Johnson, "Ultimate Love Triangle: Mother-in-Law's Alzheimer's Disease Strains Marriage." *ABC News*, June26, 2009, https://tinyurl.com/8xdp5e7a.

13  "No temptation has overtaken you but such as is common to man; and God is faithful, who will not allow you to be tempted beyond what you are able, but with the temptation will provide the way of escape also, so that you will be able to endure it" (1 Corinthians 10:13, NASB).

14  Cail, *Alzheimer's: A Crash Course for Friends and Relatives*, 99.

15  Josh Bascom, "An Honest Day," sermon delivered at Christ Episcopal Church, November 7, 2021, https://tinyurl.com/38v8pfvw.

16  John 11:1–43.

17  These interviews are part of a series National Public Radio did with Debaggio over a ten-year period. For links to the complete series, see: Melissa Block, "Alzheimer's Research Advocate Tom Debaggio Dies," *NPR*, February 22, 2011, https://www.npr.org/2011/02/22/133971224/Alzheimers-Advocate-Thomas-DeBaggio-Dies.

18  This webpage has a "print page" link at the bottom. As of this writing, the website does not contain a *Terms of Use* policy or (unlike the handout suggested for lesson one of this chapter). For information on fair use of copyrighted material: https://tinyurl.com/mrsw4b37. The late-stage characteristics listed on the page are shared across many websites and other sources.

19  Adriane Higgins, "Thomas Debaggio, Va. Gardener Who Wrote Poignantly about Alzheimer's, Dies at 69," *Washington Post*, February 23, 2011, https://www.washingtonpost.com/local/va-gardener-brought-alzheimers-to-light/2012/02/23/ABX4FkI_story.html.

20  BBC World News America, "Alzheimer's: The Long Goodbye, Pt 5," from a newscast televised by BBC World News America in 2008.

21  "Remain in me, and I will remain in you. . . . I am the vine; you are the branches. If a man remains in me and I in him, he will bear much fruit; apart from me, you can do nothing" (John 15:4–5, NIV).

# CHAPTER 7

1 Maja Lopez-Hartmann, et al. "The Effect of Caregiver Support Interventions for Informal Caregivers of Community Dwelling Frail Elderly: A Systematic Review," *Journal of Integrated Care* 12 (July–September, 2012), https://doi.org/10.5334/ijic.845, https://www.ncbi.nlm.nih.gov/pmc/articles/PMC3601532/. [*Note:* The authors concede that caregiver support groups may increase caregiver burden if the caregiver must secure alternative care in order to attend the group.]

2 Proverbs 4:6–7.

3 Juan Riboldi, "The Seven Keys to Successful Strategic Planning," *Forbes*, June 27, 2019. https://tinyurl.com/24vff2as.

4 Merlin, Stam, and Van Knippenberg, "Visions of Change as Visions of Continuity."

5 Daphne Johnson, interview with the author, February 28, 2022.

6 Daphne Johnston, *Reclaiming Joy Together* (Montgomery, AL: Respite for All Foundation, 2020): 205.

7 At one point in her husband's dementia, Karen Garner (see chapter 2) was transporting him back and forth on an almost daily basis to a church respite program located more than an hour from her home.

8 Johnson, interview with the author, February 28, 2022.

9 Johnston tells the story of a caregiver whose wife died of frontotemporal lobe dementia at fifty-one, after participating in the respite program at FUMC for three years. After her death, he sold the antique car they had enjoyed together and presented Johnston with a check for $50,000, telling her quietly, "We will have this respite program all over the world."

10 Winnie Chi, et al, "Community-Dwelling Older Adults with Dementia and Their Caregivers: Key Indicators from the National Health and Aging Trends Study," Washington, DC: US Department of Health and Human Services, January 29, 2019, https://tinyurl.com/yckrkfh6.

11 Churches often have large rooms available during the week, when a respite program runs, which can quickly be set up to accommodate its activities. This is one of the main advantages of housing respite programs in religious settings, where the main congregational events occur during weekends and evenings.

12 https://www.respiteforall.org, at present click *Respite Roadmap* to obtain information about the training videos.

13 Daphne Johnston, *Reclaiming Joy Together*, 75.

14 Marsha Mercer, "Finding a Caregiver Support Group That's Right for You," AARP, August 31, 2021, https://tinyurl.com/43xb3fbu. *Note:* This article contains an inset by psychologist Barry J. Jacobs listing three reasons caregiver groups fail, among them the problem caregivers have securing care for a loved one in order to attend.

15 Mark 4:35–39.

16 Elsie Greto, "The Value of Community Psychiatric Services for the Elderly's Dementia Caregiver Support Group: Exploring the Perspectives of Participants," *Patient Experience Journal* 8, no. 1 (2021), https://tinyurl.com/ywrpucbb.

17 I would discourage any round-robin or group praying, as it makes some people feel awkward. I am one of them. I hate feeling pressured to pray aloud in front of people, and the purpose of a caregiver group is to alleviate stress, not cause it.

18 Attorney Kenneth Schwartz, for whom the Schwartz Center for Compassionate Healthcare is named, died at age forty from lung cancer. Before his death, he affirmed the impact of kind acts, made in a moment's time, on a life and death situation—true

of both cancer and dementia: "It has been a harrowing experience for me and my family. . . . [Acts] of kindness . . . have made the unbearable bearable." Kenneth B. Schwartz, "A Patient's Story," *The Boston Globe Magazine*, July 16, 1995.

19   Dale S. Ryan, (undated), "The Promises and Pitfalls of Congregation Support Groups."

20   Linda A. LeBlanc and Melissa R. Nosik, "Planning and Leading Effective Meetings," *Behavior Analysis in Practice* 12, no. 3 (September, 2019): 696–708, https://doi.org/10.1007/s40617-019-00330-z, https://tinyurl.com/2r7v7fua.

21   Robin Dunbar, "Breaking Bread: The Functions of Social Eating," *Adaptive Human Behavior and Physiology* 3 (March 2017): 198–211, https://link.springer.com/article/10.1007/s40750-017-0061-4.

22   It can be understandably tempting for caregivers to lament the challenges of their lives when surrounded by people in the same circumstance. But this is only appropriate if there is no comprehension by the people requiring this care of what is being said about them. It's unlikely this would be true of everyone in a group that can still sit quietly in a restaurant and eat with minimal assistance.

23   Check out this Pinterest page for many suggestions: https://tinyurl.com/473e76th.

24   Screening for aggressiveness could be wise from a legal standpoint. See chapter 3, footnotes 10–12.

25   If the budget allows, provide each caregiver with a blank book or binder. Look at this article and accompanying links for memory book ideas: Powell, Kimberly. "Make a Memory Book for Your Family." ThoughtCo. https://tinyurl.com/3epub72f.

26   I've often wished elderly people could be surrounded by visible images of what they did before their lives became so fully dictated by the breakdowns of age. A part of respect, I believe, is consciously keeping track of the good, brave, admirable, kind, interesting things that came before the losses and indignities, and a memory book can help with this.

27   Lynda Everman and Don Wendorf, interview with author, April 20, 2022.

28   Reaction to eye contact does vary by culture. In Asian societies, for example, eye contact may be associated with anger or aggressiveness, a point to keep in mind. See Hiranori, Akechi, et al, "Attention to Eye Contact in West and East: Autonomic Responses and Evaluative Ratings," [Abstract] *PLoS One* 8, no. 3 (March, 2013), https://doi.org/10.1371/journal.pone.0059312.

29   Currier was killed in 2014, at age fifty-seven, in a bicycling accident. His sample worship service, however, is a timeless, practical template to use as a starting point in developing a dementia-friendly service: Currier, Jonathan, "Sample Worship Services," (undated): https://tinyurl.com/35wmyf39.

30   Richard Morgan (Presbyterian Church, USA) and David Fetterman (United Methodist), in the essay "That All May Worship," tell the cautionary tale of a guest minister who preached for too long in a service held at a dementia care facility. At the end, he expressed his happiness at having been invited to speak. "I would love to come back," he exclaimed, and a woman cried out in dismay, "I sure hope not!" This essay, in *Dementia Friendly Worship*, includes many practical ways to make services more meaningful to people with advanced dementia. (Everman and Wendorf, 152).

31   Sam Hodges, "Retired Bishop Serves Memory Care Unit as Chaplain," UM News, June 30, 2016, https://tinyurl.com/bdenefsz.

32   Hodges, "Retired Bishop Serves Memory Care Unit as Chaplain."

33 It cannot be a space shared with screaming infants and fretting toddlers or, even if not in use as such, a space outfitted for babies or regarded as the church nursery.

34 Volunteers who have received respite training will be prepared to serve in a comfort room.

35 There are many soft, lifelike dolls available. For one example, see JC Toys 20-inch Large Soft Body Baby Doll: https://tinyurl.com/xt2mahar.

36 These books are by Sunny Street Books, which publishes materials that are calming and interactive for people with dementia: see sunnystreetbooks.com.

37 See Shadowbox Press: https://tinyurl.com/2ra3muwf.

38 The ideas, except for the last one, are from the website DailyCaring, created by Connie Chow and Brian Yu. This website contains a wealth of information on senior caregiving, as well as a robust list of engaging, comforting objects for people with dementia: https://tinyurl.com/bdaxuf2d.

39 A rummage bag is a large pocketbook or toiletry bag filled with common objects that would be interested to inspect and handle. Avoid sharp items and objects that can be swallowed or taken apart. This idea is from an excellent article: Linda Conti, "Managing Difficult Behaviors in Dementia," *Today's Geriatric Medicine* 9, no. 2 (March/April 2016), p. 16: https://tinyurl.com/5bnbcdbj.

40 See item 4 of "Hosting at the Church," page 147, for how to set up a dementia-friendly restroom.

41 It could read simply "In use by a caregiver. Please wait a moment."

42 Mary McDaniel Cail, "Op Ed: How to Care for Caregivers," *Los Angeles Times*, November 20, 2014, A-15, https://tinyurl.com/mr3xrv7y.

43 Gordon Hardy, "Why Give? Religious Roots of Charity," *Harvard Divinity School News Archive*, November 26, 2018, https://tinyurl.com/yd7sd75v.

44 Yasmin Anwar, "Highly Religious People Are Less Motivated by Religion Than Are Non-believers," *Berkeley News*, April 30, 2012, https://tinyurl.com/4s4mha63.

45 Emma Seppala, "The Compassionate Mind," *Association for Psychological Science*, May/June, 2013, https://tinyurl.com/mv5hvhsf.

46 Tara Parker-Pope, "The Science of Helping Out," *The New York Times*, April 9, 2020, https://tinyurl.com/4tfur8jn.

47 Elizabeth Berstein, "The Science of Prayer," *The Wall Street Journal*, May 17, 2020, https://tinyurl.com/3d44sen8.

48 In a book, I think, by Catherine Marshall, although I'm not sure which one.

49 James 5:16.

50 I Corinthians 12:27.

51 Gregory A. Smith, "About Three-in-Ten U.S. Adults Are Now Religiously Unaffiliated," *Pew Research Center*, December 14, 2021, https://tinyurl.com/yk5779ht.

52 Gabe Bullard, "The World's Newest Major Religion: No Religion," *National Geographic*, April 22, 2016, https://www.nationalgeographic.com/culture/article/160422-atheism-agnostic-secular-nones-rising-religion.

53 "Kimberly Bowman Newlen," *Greenville Online*, February 11, 2014, https://tinyurl.com/yc6rpjrt.

54 Matthew 13:31–33.

55 Hebrews 4:13.

56 Romans 8:28.

## APPENDIX 1

1 "Do you not know that your body is a temple of the Holy Spirit, who is in you, whom you have received from God? You are not your own; you were bought at a price. Therefore honor God with your body." First Corinthians 6: 16–17, NIV.

2 *Publisher's Weekly*, "Making Loss Matter: Creating Meaning in Difficult Times," https://tinyurl.com/mrp97r8a.

## APPENDIX 2

1 "What is Alzheimer's Disease? Questions and Answers," Texas Department of State Health Services (2021): https://dshs.texas.gov/alzheimers/qanda.shtm.

2 Alzheimer's Disease International, "New Study Predicts the Number of People Living with Alzheimer's to Triple by 2050," London: Alzheimer's Disease International, January 7, 2022, https://tinyurl.com/2p8pnsud.

3 George Szasz, "Dr Alzheimer and My Wish for a Time Machine," *British Columbia Medical Journal* (March 18, 2018), https://tinyurl.com/bdecnhab.

4 Alzheimer's Association, "Cause and Risk Factors for Alzheimer's Disease," Chicago: Alzheimer's Association, Accessed May 14, 2021, https://tinyurl.com/4h864e9y.

5 William L. Herring et al., "Predicted Lifetime Health Outcomes for Aducanumab in Patients with Early Alzheimer's Disease," *Neurology and Therapy* 10 (August 2021): 919–940, https://doi.org/10.1007/s40120-021-00273-0.

6 Rudimar L. Frozza, Mychael V. Lourenco, and Fernanda G. De Felice, "Challenges for Alzheimer's Disease Therapy: Insights for Novel Mechanisms Beyond Memory Defects," *Frontiers in Neuroscience* 12, no. 37 (February 6, 2018), https://doi.org/10.3389/fnins.2018.00037.

7 Centers for Disease and Control Prevention, "Fatal Degenerative Neurologic Disease in Patients Who Received Pituitary-Derived Human Growth Hormone," Atlanta, Georgia: Centers for Disease and Control Prevention, *Morbidity and Mortality Weekly Report* 34, no. 24 (June 21, 1985): 359–360, 365–366, https://www.cdc.gov/mmwr/preview/mmwrhtml/00000563.htm.

8 Silvia A. Purro et al., "Transmission of Amyloid B Protein Pathology from Cadaveric Pituitary Growth Hormone." Research Letter. *Nature* 564 (December 2018): 415–419. https://doi.org/10.1038/s41586-018-0790-y.

9 Alison Abbot, "Transmissible Alzheimer's Theory Gains Traction," *Nature*, December 13, 2018. https://tinyurl.com/mr47ndnj.

10 Carey Mulligan, *Carey Mulligan Discusses Her Gran's Dementia* (Plymouth, United Kingdom: Alzheimer's Society, 2012), 3:53 minutes. https://tinyurl.com/2p9ct3mt.

## APPENDIX 3

1 Be careful not to let things lapse into too much humor. The idea is to simulate a caregiver support group in terms of seriousness, so emphasize this intention if the discussion is getting carried away.

# Bibliography

**Abbot**, Alison. "Transmissible Alzheimer's Theory Gains Traction." *Nature*, December 13, 2018. https://tinyurl.com/mr47ndnj.

**Adams**, Jill U. "Do Microbes Trigger Alzheimer's?" *The Scientist*, September 1, 2017. https://tinyurl.com/3967urbn.

**Algoe**, Sara B., Patrick C. Dwyer, Ayana Younge, and Christopher Oveis. "A New Perspective on the Social Functions of Emotions: Gratitude and the Witnessing Effect." *Journal of Personality and Social Psychology* 119, no. 1 (July 2020): 40–72. https://tinyurl.com/p2bvnh62.

**Alzheimer's Association**. "2022 Alzheimer's Disease Facts and Figures." Chicago: Alzheimer's Association, 2022. https://tinyurl.com/2p9ex25d.

———. "Cause and Risk Factors for Alzheimer's Disease." Chicago: Alzheimer's Association, Accessed May 14, 2021. https://tinyurl.com/4h864e9y.

**Alzheimer's Disease International**. "New Study Predicts the Number of People Living with Alzheimer's Will Triple by 2050." London: Alzheimer's Disease International, January 7, 2022. https://www.alzint.org/news-events/news/new-data-predicts-the-number-of-people-living-with-alzheimers-disease-to-triple-by-2050/.

———. "World Alzheimer's Report." London: Alzheimer's Disease International, September 2019. https://tinyurl.com/2p82f7vy.

**Alzheimer's Society**. "*Carey Mulligan Discusses Her Gran's Dementia*." *YouTube* video, 3:54. May 22, 2012. https://tinyurl.com/4x29tdtn.

**Alzheimer's Weekly**. "Experience 12 Minutes in Alzheimer's Dementia." YouTube video, 8:03, produced by ABC News, August 21, 2012. https://tinyurl.com/3ekv3msp.

**American Bar Association Commission on Aging**. "Types of Abuse Defined in Adult Protective Services Statutes." Washington, DC: American Bar Association, June 2021. https://tinyurl.com/2jj5f3dn.

**American Council on Aging**. "2021 Nursing Home Costs by State and Region." Arlington, Virginia: American Council on Aging, March 4, 2022. https://tinyurl.com/4nsynb59.

**Andrade**, Andreia, Omonigho M. Bubu, Andrew W. Varga, and Ricarco S. Osorio. "The Relationship Between Obstructive Sleep Apnea and Alzheimer's Disease." *Journal of Alzheimer's Disease* 64, Suppl 1 (May 2019): S255–270. https://doi.org/10.3233/JAD-179936.

**Anwar**, Yasmin. "Highly Religious People Are Less Motivated by Religion Than Are Non-believers." *Berkeley News*, April 30, 2012. https://tinyurl.com/4s4mha63.

**Armstrong**, Melissa, Slande Alliance, Angela Taylor, Pamela Corsentino, and James E. Galvin. "End of Life Experience in Dementia with Lewy Bodies: Qualitative Interviews with Former Caregivers." *PloS One* 14, 15 (May 2019): e0217039. https://doi.org/10.1371/journal.pone.0217039.

**Arterberry**, Brooke, Matthew P. Martens, Jennifer M. Cadigan, and David Rohrer. "Application of Generalizability Theory to the Big Five Inventory," *Personality and Individual Differences* 69 (October 2015): 98–103. https://doi.org/10.1016/j.paid.2014.05.015.

**Austin**, Daryl. "What You're Saying When You Give Someone the Silent Treatment." *The Atlantic*, March 26, 2021. https://www.theatlantic.com/family/archive/2021/03/psychology-of-silent-treatment-abuse/618411/.

**Bakowski**, Kris. "Thanksgiving: Dealing with Alzheimer's." *Creating Memories* (blog). November 18, 2004. https://tinyurl.com/5fexjdma.

———. "Loneliness." *Creating Memories* (blog). June 13, 2004. https://creatingmemories.blogspot.com/search?q=loneliness.

**Baumeister**, Roy F., Ellen Bratslavsky, and Catrin Finkenhaur. "Bad is Stronger than Good." *Review of General Psychology* 5, no. 4 (2001): 323–370. https://assets.csom.umn.edu/assets/71516.pdf.

**BBC World News America**. "Alzheimer's: The Long Goodbye, Pt 5." YouTube video, 8:16, from a newscast televised by BBC World News America posted August 6, 2008.

**Bennett**, D. A., J. A. Schneider, MD; Z. Arvanitakis, J. F. Kelly, N. T. Aggarwal, R. C. Shah, and R. S. Wilson. "Neuropathology of Older Persons Without Cognitive Impairment from Two Community Based Studies." *Neurology* 66 (June 2006): 1842. https://tinyurl.com/4c3h2bmf.

**Berstein**, Elizabeth. "The Science of Prayer." *The Wall Street Journal*, May 17, 2020. https://tinyurl.com/3d44sen8.

**Blandin**, Kesstan and Renee Pepin. "Dementia Grief: A Theoretical Model of a Unique Grief Experience." *Dementia (London)* 16, no.1 (January 2017): 67–78. https://doi.org/10.1177/1471301215581081.

**Block**, Melissa. "Alzheimer's Research Advocate Tom Debaggio Dies." *NPR*. February 22, 2011. https://tinyurl.com/27x6sf3p.

**Bowing**, Ann. "Mode of Questionnaire Administration Can Have Serious Effects on Data Quality." *Journal of Public Health* 27, no. 3 (September 2005): 281–291. https://doi.org/10.1093/pubmed/fdi031.

**Breel**, Kevin. "Confessions of a Depressed Comic." *TED Ideas Worth Spreading*, presented to a local audience at TEDxKids@Ambleside, May 2013. https://tinyurl.com/4uhfr3d9.

**Brookmeyer**, R., E. Johnson, K. Ziegler-Graham, and H. M. Arrighi, cited in GBD Dementia Forecasting Collaborators. "Estimation of the Global Prevalence of Dementia in 2019 and Forecasted Prevalence in 2050: An Analysis for the Global Burden of Disease Study." *The Lancet* 7 (February 2022): e112. https://tinyurl.com/25fcee7k.

**Brown**, Tyler. "Exegesis of Matthew 25:31–46 with an Emphasis on the Identity of 'All the Nations' and 'The Least of These.' " Academia. Accessed July 19, 2022. https://tinyurl.com/bdhw2aps.

**Buechner**, Frederick. "Theodicy." *Sermon Illustrations* (blog). November 19, 2018. https://tinyurl.com/ye27f6f9.

**Bullard**, Gabe. "The World's Newest Major Religion: No Religion," *National Geographic*, April 22, 2016.

**Cail**, Mary McDaniel. "How to Care for Caregivers." *Los Angeles Times* (online), November 19, 2014. *Los Angeles Times* (print), November 20, 2014. A-15. https://tinyurl.com/mr3xrv7y.

——. "How to Handle a Friend's Tears." *The All-Weather Friend* (blog). April 27, 2016. https://tinyurl.com/3hxy3new.

**Carder**, Kenneth L. *Ministry with the Forgotten: Dementia through a Spiritual Lens*. Nashville: Abington Press, 2019.

——. Interview by the author. September 24, 2021.

**Cary**, Benedict. "The Muddled Tracks of All Those Tears." *New York Times*, February 2, 2009. https://tinyurl.com/5yvmshsu.

**Centers for Disease Control and Prevention**. "Fatal Degenerative Neurologic Disease in Patients Who Received Pituitary-Derived Human Growth Hormone." Atlanta, Georgia: Centers for Disease and Control Prevention, *Morbidity and Mortality Weekly Report* 34, no. 24 (June 21, 1985): 359–60, 365–6. https://tinyurl.com/sv7z89aa.

**Chandler**, Sam. "In the Name of God: Father, Son, and Holy Spirit." Sermon for The Cathedral of St. Philip in Atlanta, Georgia, May 18, 2008. https://tinyurl.com/28zrt7er.

**Chi,** Winnie, Emily Graf, Landon Hughes, Jean Hastie, Galina Khatutsky, Sari B. Shuman, E. Andrew Jessup, Sarita Karon, and Helen Lamont. "Community-Dwelling Older Adults with Dementia and Their Caregivers: Key Indicators from the National Health and Aging Trends Study." Washington, DC: US Department of Health and Human Services, January 29, 2019. https://tinyurl.com/yckrkfh6.

**Cho,** Sarah. "How to Analyze Open-Ended Responses." SurveyMonkey, Accessed July 14, 2022. https://tinyurl.com/2p9ajkyu.

**Chudoba,** Brent. "How Much Time Are Respondents Willing to Spend on Your Survey?" SurveyMonkey. Accessed July 17, 2021. https://tinyurl.com/2ptyn5ex.

**Columbia University Irving Medical Center**. "Study Shows Where Alzheimer's Starts and How It Spreads." December 22, 2013. https://tinyurl.com/52vrk42z.

**Conners,** Michael H., Lena Quinto, Ian McKeith, Henry Brodaty, Louise Allan, Claire Bamford, Alan Thomas, John-Paul Taylor, and John T. O'Brian. "Non-pharmacological Interventions for Lewy Body Dementia: A Systematic Review." *Psychological Medicine* 48 no. 11 (August 2017): 1749–1758. https://doi.org/10.1017/S0033291717003257.

**Conti,** Linda. "Managing Difficult Behaviors in Dementia." *Today's Geriatric Medicine* 9, no. 2 (March/April 2016): 16. https://tinyurl.com/5bnbcdbj. 5/02)

**Cooper,** Avraham Z. and Jeremy B. Richards, "Lectures for Adult Learners: Breaking Old Habits in Medical Education." *The American Journal of Medicine* 130, no 3 (March 2017): 376–381. http://dx.doi.org/10.1016/j.amjmed.2016.11.009.

**Cox,** Daniel. "Churches Face Challenges in Upgrading to Religion 2.0." PPRI, August 6, 2012. https://tinyurl.com/2p9crzsj.

**Culebras,** Antonia and Sanam Anwar. "Sleep Apnea Is a Risk Factor for Stroke and Vascular Dementia." Abstract. *Current Neurology and Neuroscience Reports* 18, no. 53 (June 2018): https://tinyurl.com/2pfmyt5r.

**Cunningham,** E. L., B. McGuinness, B. Herron, and A. P. Passmore. "Dementia." *The Ulster Medical Journal* 84, no. 2 (May, 2015): 79–87. https://tinyurl.com/2y3du5fk.

**Currier,** Jonathan, "Sample Worship Services." accessed September 19, 2022. https://tinyurl.com/35wmyf39.

Curry, Michael. "The Power of Love," YouTube video, 13:36, from Bishop Michael Curry's Royal Wedding Sermon recorded by CBC News on May 19, 2018. https://tinyurl.com/mtdm4mdp.

DeLancey, John. "Ancient Mirrors," *Biblical Israel Ministries and Tours* (Blog). December 1, 2016. https://tinyurl.com/3bvwzxdr.

Deming, Adam Wang, Martin S. Hagger, and Nikos L. D. Chatzisarantis. "Ironic Effects of Thought Suppression: A Meta-Analysis." Abstract. *Perspectives on Psychological Science* 15, no. 3 (May, 2020): https://journals.sagepub.com/doi/10.1177/1745691619898795.

Dickens, Charles. *Great Expectations: A Norton Critical Edition*, edited by Edgar Rosenberg. New York: Norton and Company, 1999.

Dilip, V. Jeste, Brent Mausbach, and Ellen E. Lee. "Caring for Caregivers / Care Partners of Persons with Dementia." *International Psychogeriatrics* 33, no. 4 (April 2021): 307–310. https://doi.org/10.1017/S1041610221000557.

Drahl, Carmen. "John O'Keefe, May-Britt Moser, and Edvard Moser win 2014 Nobel Prize in Physiology or Medicine." *Chemical and Engineering News*, October 6, 2014. https://tinyurl.com/yytp3522.

Duff, Karen E. "Research." Colombia University Department of Pathology and Cell Biology, 2022. https://tinyurl.com/2fjcdp5k.

Dunaetz, David R. and Julie Bocock. "Ministry Involvement of Church Staff and Volunteers: The Role of Organizational Commitment and Work Engagement." *Theology of Leadership* 3, no. 1 (Fall 2020): 52–67. https://tinyurl.com/3scm6ve7.

Dunbar, Robin. "Breaking Bread: The Functions of Social Eating," *Adaptive Human Behavior and Physiology* 3 (March 2017): 198–211. https://doi.org/10.1007/s40750-017-0061-4.

Efran, Jay. "What to Do if Your Client Cries: If It's Not Broken, Don't Fix It." *Why We Cry* (blog). *Psychotherapy Networker*, May/June 2012, https://tinyurl.com/484kc6hu.

Emerson, Ralph Waldo. "*Terminus.*" https://tinyurl.com/2tvzaham.

Ernst, J., A. Mehnert, A. Dietz, B. Hornemann, and P. Esser. "Perceived Stigmatization and Its Impact on Quality of Life—Results from a Large Register-Based Study Including Breast, Colon, Prostate, and Lung Cancer Patients." *BMC Cancer* (November 9, 2017): https://tinyurl.com/4vdnjvuh.

Everman, Lynda. Interview by the author. April 20, 2022.

**Everman**, Lynda, Don Wendorf, Kathy Fogg Berry, Robin Dill, Stephen M. Glazer, Richard L. Morgan and William B. Randolf, eds. *Dementia Friendly Worship: A Multifaith Handbook for Chaplains, Clergy, and Faith Communities.* London: Jessica Kingsley Publishers, 2019.

**Everyone Matters**. "This is Love! Lady Touches Soul of Alzheimer's Sufferer with Christian Hymns." YouTube Video, 5:43. February 14, 2015. https://tinyurl.com/ycktew9p.

**Fain**, Constance Frisby. "Minimizing Liability for Church-Related Counseling Services: Clergy Malpractice and First Amendment Religion Clauses." *Akron Law Review* (July 2015): 221–258. https://tinyurl.com/6jchsrus.

**Feil**, Naomi. *The Validation Breakthrough: Simple Techniques for Communicating with People with Alzheimer's and Other Dementias*, 3rd ed. Baltimore: Health Professions Press, 2012.

**Feldman**, Howard, Magali Haas, Sam Gandy, Darryle D. Schoepp, Alan J. Cross, Richard Mayeux, Reisa A. Sperling, Howard Fillet, Diana L. van de Hoef, and Sonja Dougal. "Alzheimer's Disease Research and Development: A Call for a New Research Roadmap." *Annals of the New York Academy of Sciences* (April 22, 2014): https://tinyurl.com/2c3e3bky.

**Finney**, John R. and H. Newton Maloney Jr. "Empirical Studies of Christian Prayer: A Review of the Literature." *Journal of Psychology and Theology* 13, no. 2 (1985): 104–115. https://journals.sagepub.com/doi/10.1177/009164718501300203.

**Fleck**, Carole. "Coping with Cognitive Declines at Work." *HR Magazine*, September 3, 2015. https://tinyurl.com/36h2b4ke.

**Francis**. "Why Does It Seem Like God Doesn't Answer Our Prayers Sometimes?" *America, the Jesuit Review* (weekly Wednesday audience, delivered May 26, 2021 at the feast of St. Philip Neri): https://tinyurl.com/524ecb6b.

**Frozza**, Rudimar L., Mychael V. Lourenco, and Fernanda G. De Felice, "Challenges for Alzheimer's Disease Therapy: Insights for Novel Mechanisms Beyond Memory Defects." *Frontiers in Neuroscience* 12, no. 37 (February 6, 2018): https://doi.org/10.3389/fnins.2018.00037.

**Garner**, Karen. Interview by the author. April 8, 2021.

**General Council of Finance and Administration of the United Methodist Church**. "HIPPA Privacy Rule and Local Churches." February 2004. http://s3.amazonaws.com/Website_GCFA/HIPAA_Privacy_Rule_and_Local_Churches.pdf.

Gentleman, Amelia. "The Raw Horror of Alzheimer's." *The Guardian*, June 1, 2010. https://tinyurl.com/2ccjw5vb.

Ghesquiere, Angela. "I Was Just Trying to Stick it Out Until I Realized I Couldn't: A Phenomenological Investigation of Support Seeking Among Older Adults with Complicated Grief." *Omega (Westport)* 68, no. 1 (May 2013):1–22. https://doi.org/10.2190/om.68.1.a.

Girard, Jeffery M., Jeffrey F. Cohn, Mohammad H. Mahoor, S. Mohammad Mavadati, Zakia Hammal, and Dean P. Rosenwald. "Nonverbal Social Withdrawal in Depression: Evidence from Manual and Automatic Analysis." *Image and Vision Computing* 32, no. 10 (October 2014): 641–647. https://doi.org/10.1016/j.imavis.2013.12.007.

Gomperts, Stephen N. "Lewy Body Dementia: Dementia with Lewy Bodies and Parkinson Disease Dementia." *Continuum* 22, no. 2 (April 2016): 435–463. https://doi.org/10.1212/CON.0000000000000309.

Grant, Adam M. and Francesca Gino. "A Little Thanks Goes a Long Way: Explaining Why Gratitude Expressions Motivate Prosocial Behavior." *Journal of Personality and Social Psychology* 98, no. 6 (2010): 946–955. https://doi.org/10.1037/a0017935.

Greto, Elsie. "The Value of Community Psychiatric Services for the Elderly's Dementia Caregiver Support Group: Exploring the Perspectives of Participants." *Patient Experience Journal* 8, no. 1 (2021): 166–173. https://tinyurl.com/ywrpucbb.

Griffith, Ezra E. H. and John L. Young. "Clergy Counselors and Confidentiality: A Case for Scrutiny." *The Journal of the American Academy of Psychiatry and Law* 32, no. 1 (2004): 43–50. https://tinyurl.com/5n6krsnr.

Griffiths, Alys Wyn. "Relational Counselling as a Psychosocial Intervention for Dementia: Qualitative Evidence from People Living with Dementia and Family Members." *Dementia (London)* 20, no. 6 (August 2021): 2091–2018. https://doi.org/10.1177/1471301220984912.

Hamdy, R. C., A. Kinser, J. V. Lewis, R. Copeland, A Depelteau, T. Kendall-Wilson, and K. Whalen. "Hallucinations Are Real to Patients with Dementia." *Gerontology and Geriatric Medicine* 3 (January–December 2017): https://doi.org/10.1177/2333721417721108.

Hammar, Richard. "Understanding Pastoral Liability." *Christianity Today*, the Church Law & Tax Store, 2017. https://tinyurl.com/3tjswxer.

Hardy, Gordon. "Why Give? Religious Roots of Charity." *Harvard Divinity School News Archive*, November 26, 2018. https://tinyurl.com/yd7sd75v.

**Harper**, Lori, Bonnie M. Dobbs, Shana D. Stites, Martha Sajatovic, Kathleen C. Buckwalter, and Sandy C. Burgener. "Stigma in Dementia: It's Time to Talk About It." *Current Psychiatry* 18, no.7 (July 2019): 16–23. https://tinyurl.com/yckzuhcd.

**Henry**, Maya L. and Maria Luisa Gorno-Tempeni, "The Logopenic Variant of Primary Progressive Aphasia," *Current Opinion in Neurology* 23, no. 6 (December 2010): 633–637. https://journals.lww.com/co-neurology/Abstract/2010/12000/The_logopenic_variant_of_primary_progressive.14.aspx.

**Herring**, William L., Ian Gopal Gould, Howard Fillit, Peter Lindgren, Fiona Forrestal, Robin Thompson, and Peter Pemberton-Ross. "Predicted Lifetime Health Outcomes for Aducanumab in Patients with Early Alzheimer's Disease." *Neurology and Therapy* 10 (August, 2021): 919–940. https://doi.org/10.1007/s40120-021-00273-0.

**Herrmann**, Lynn K., Elisabeth Welter, James Levernz, Alan J. Lerner, Nancy Udelson, Cheryl Kanetsky, and Martha Sajatovic. "A Systematic Review of Dementia-related Stigma Research: Can We Move the Stigma Dial?" *The American Journal of Geriatric Psychiatry* 26, no. 3 (March 2018): 316–331. https://doi.org/10.1016/j.jagp.2017.09.006.

**Hide**, Kerrie. "Symbol Ritual and Dementia." *Journal of Religious Gerontology* 13 no. 3–4 (2002): 77–90. https://tinyurl.com/munfhczu.

**Higgins**, Adriane. "Thomas Debaggio, Va. Gardener Who Wrote Poignantly About Alzheimer's, Dies at 69." *Washington Post*. February 23, 2011. https://tinyurl.com/3m248tbp.

**Hillman**, Alexandra and Joanna Latimer. "Cultural Representations of Dementia." *PLOS Medicine* 14, no. 3 (March 2017): https://journals.plos.org/plosmedicine/article?id=10.1371/journal.pmed.1002274.

**Hodges**, Sam. "Retired Bishop Serves Memory Care Unit as Chaplain." *UM News*, June 30, 2016. https://tinyurl.com/bdenefsz.

**Hogan**, David B., Nathalie Jette, Kirsten M. Fiest, Jodie I. Roberts, Dawn Pearson, Eric E. Smith, Pamela Roach, Andrew Kirk, Tamara Pringsheim, and Colleen J. Maxwell. "The Prevalence and Incidence of Frontotemporal Lobe Dementia." *The Canadian Journal of Neurological Sciences* 43 Suppl 1(June 2016): S96–S109. https://doi.org/10.1017/cjn.2016.25.

**Howden**, William D. " 'Good Sermon, Preacher': The Effects of Age, Sex, and Education on Hearer Response to Preaching." *Review of Religious Research* 31, no. 2 (December 1989): 196–207. https://www.jstor.org/stable/3511190.

**Jawabri**, Khalid H. and Sandeep Sharma. "Physiology, Cerebral Cortex Functions." National Library of Medicine, April 22, 2022: https://tinyurl.com/ym968u6v

**Joaquin**, Anna Dina L. and Andrea W. Mates. "'I don't know what to do. Pray I guess.': Faith and coping with Frontotemporal Dementia." *Journal of Religion, Spirituality & Aging* 30 no. 3 (April, 2018): 251–267. https://tinyurl.com/3xyjevp9.

**Johnston**, Daphne. Interview by the author. February 28, 2022.

———. "Begin a Chapter." Respiteforall.org. Respite for All Foundation. Accessed March 19, 2022. https://www.respiteforall.org/begin-a-chapter.

———. *Reclaiming Joy Together: Building a Volunteer Community of Real Hope for Those with Dementia*. Montgomery, AL: Respite for All Foundation, 2020.

**Kapasi**, Alifiya, Charles DeCarli, and Julie A. Schneider. "Impact of Multiple Pathologies on the Threshold for Clinically Overt Dementia." *Acta Neuropathologica* 134, no.2 (May 2017): 171–186. https://link.springer.com/article/10.1007/s00401-017-1717-7.

**Katz**, Marina. "Virtual Dementia Tour Leaves Participants Frustrated but Sympathetic." *ABC News*, June 29, 2009. https://tinyurl.com/2zp5uxe2.

**Keller**, Timothy. "Four Models of Counseling in Pastoral Ministry," *Redeemer City to City*, 2010. https://tinyurl.com/9excjux4.

**Khosravi**, Mohsen. "Lewy Body Dementia: Ursodeoxycholic Acid as a Putative Treatment for Gastrointestinal Dysfunction." *European Journal of Translational Myology* 31, no. 2 (July 2021): 9876. https://doi.org/10.4081/ejtm.2021.9876.

**Kim**, Sun Kyung and Myonghwa Park. "Effectiveness of Person-Centered Care on People with Dementia: A Systematic Review and Meta-analysis." *Clinical Interventions in Aging* 12 (February 2017): 381–397. https://doi.org/10.2147/CIA.S117637.

"Kimberly Bowman Newlen," *Greenville Online*, February 11, 2014. https://tinyurl.com/4uf4fsmn.

**Kliever**, James. "Cool Flyer Design Ideas: 50 Examples You Can Learn From." Canva.com, Accessed March 28, 2022. https://tinyurl.com/mr3whby2.

**KPBS Public Media**. "Extended Interview with Alzheimer's Patient Don Hayden." YouTube video, 6:37. February 22, 2008. https://www.youtube.com/watch?v=uAlkCMfTASQ.

**Krammer**, Roderick M. "Rethinking Trust," *Harvard Business Review*, June 2009. https://hbr.org/2009/06/rethinking-trust.

**LeBlanc**, Linda A. and Melissa R. Nosik. "Planning and Leading Effective Meetings." *Behavior Analysis in Practice* 12, no. 3 (September, 2019): 696–708. https://doi.org/10.1007/s40617-019-00330-z.

**Lewis**, C. S., *The Problem of Pain*. New York: Touchstone, 1996.

**Lifeway Research (staff)**. "Pastors' Long Work Hours Come at the Expense of Ministry, People." *Lifeway Research*, January 5, 2010. https://research.lifeway.com/2010/01/05/pastors-long-work-hours-come-at-expense-of-people-ministry/.

**Liljegren**, Madeline, Georges Naasan, Julia Temlett, David C. Perry, Katherine P. Rankin, Jennifer Merrilees, Lea T. Grinberg, William W. Seeley, Elisabet Englund, and Bruce L. Miller. "Criminal Behavior in Frontotemporal Dementia and Alzheimer Disease." *Jama Neurology* 72 no. 3 (March 2015): p. 295–300. https://jamanetwork.com/journals/jamaneurology/fullarticle/2088872.

**Lipka**, Michael. "Which U.S. Religious Groups Are Oldest and Youngest?" Pew Research Center, July 11, 2016. https://tinyurl.com/2ztu9ja8.

**Lopez-Hartmann**, Maja, Johna Wens, Veronique Verhoeven, and Roy Remmen. "The Effect of Caregiver Support Interventions for Informal Caregivers of Community Dwelling Frail Elderly: A Systematic Review." *Journal of Integrated Care* 12 (July–September, 2012): https://ijic.org/articles/10.5334/ijic.845.

**Low**, Lee-Fay Low and Farah Purwaningrum. "Negative Stereotypes, Fear and Social Distance: A Systematic Review of Depictions of Dementia in Popular Culture in the Context of Stigma." *BMC Geriatrics* 20, no. 477 (November 2020): https://bmcgeriatr.biomedcentral.com/articles/10.1186/s12877-020-01754-x.

**Lumley**, Mark A., Jay L. Cohen, George S. Borszcz, Annmarie Cano, Alison M. Radcliffe, Laura S. Porter, Howard Schubiner, and Francis J. Keefe. "Pain and Emotion: A Biopsychosocial Review of the Recent Research." *Journal of Clinical Psychology* 67, no. 9 (September 2011): 942–968. https://doi.org/10.1002/jclp.20816

**MacMillan**, Malcolm. "Phineas Gage: Unravelling the Myth." *The Psychologist* 21 (September 2008): 828–831. https://tinyurl.com/mr38mfsd.

**Mahoney**, Colin J., Jonathan D. Rohrer, Rohani Omar, Martin N. Rossor, and Jason D. Warren. "Neuroanatomical Profiles of Personality Change in Frontotemporal Lobar Degeneration." *The British Journal of Psychiatry* 198 no. 5 (January 2018): https://tinyurl.com/2p8wk8hh.

**Marsh**, Samuel E. and Matthew Blurton-Jones. "Examining the Mechanisms of B-amyloid and A-synuclein Pathologies." *Alzheimer's Research Theory* 4 no. 2 (April 2012): https://doi.org/10.1186/alzrt109.

**Marshall**, Catherine. *Something More*. New York: McGraw Hill Book Company, 1974.

**Maurer**, Konrad, Stephen Wolk, and Hector Gerbaldo. "Auguste D and Alzheimer's Disease." *The Lancet* 349, no. 9064 (May 1997): 1546–1549.

**McCall**, Rebecca Carlson, Kristy Padron, and Carl Andrews, "Evidence Based Instructional Strategies for Adult Learners: A Review of the Literature." *CUNY Academic Works, Bronx Community College* (2018), 39–40.

**Mercer**, Martha. "Finding a Caregiver Support Group That's Right for You." *AARP*, August 31, 2021. https://tinyurl.com/43xb3fbu.

**Merlin**, Venus, Daan Stam, and Daan van Knippenberg. "Visions of Change as Visions of Continuity." Abstract. *Academy of Management Journal* 62 (June 14, 2019): https://doi.org/10.5465/amj.2015.1196.

**Mesulam**, Marsel. Alissa Wicklund, Nancy Johnson, Emily Rogalski, Gabriel C. Leger, Alfred Rademaker, Sandra Weintraub, and Eileen H. Bigio. "Alzheimer's and Frontotemporal Pathology in Subsets of Primary Progressive Aphasia." *Annals of Neurology* 63, no. 6 (June 2008): 709–719. https://doi.org/10.1002/ana.21388.

**Middlebrook**, David O. "Pastor Confidentiality: An Ethical and Legal Responsibility." *Assemblies of God*, February 2, 2010. https://news.ag.org/en/Features/Pastoral-Confidentiality-An-Ethical-and-Legal-Responsibility.

**Morelli**, Sylvia A., Jared B. Torre, and Naomi I Eisenberger. "The Neural Bases of Feeling Understood and Not Understood." *Social Cognitive and Affective Neuroscience* 9, no. 12 (December 2014):1890–1896. https://doi.org/10.1093/scan/nst191.

**Morgan**, Richard and David Fetterman. "That All May Worship," In Everman, Lynda, Don Wendorf, Kathy Fogg Berry, Robin Dill, Stephen M. Glazer, Richard L. Morgan and William B. Randolf, eds. *Dementia Friendly Worship: A Multifaith Handbook for Chaplains, Clergy, and Faith Communities*. London: Jessica Kingsley Publishers, 2019.

**Muhammad**, Imran and Saquib Mahmood. "An Overview of Human Prion Diseases." *Virology Journal* 8, no. 559 (December 2011): https://virologyj.biomedcentral.com/articles/10.1186/1743-422X-8-559.

**Nacht,** Jacob. "The Symbolism of the Shoe with Special Reference to Jewish Sources." *The Jewish Quarterly Review* 6, no. 1 (July 1915): 1–22. https://doi.org/10.2307/1451461.

**Naquin**, Charles E., Terri R. Kurtzberg, and Liuba Y. Belkin. "The Finer Points of Lying Online: Email Versus Pen and Paper." *Journal of Applied Psychology* 95, no. 2 (March 2010): 387–394.

**National Institute of Neurological Disorders and Stroke**. "Brain Basics: Know Your Brain." July 25, 2022. https://tinyurl.com/45fnmfwn.

**Nelson**, Peter T., Dennis W. Dickson, John Q. Trojanowski, Clifford R. Jack, Patricia A. Boyle, Constantinos Arfanakis, Rosa Rademakers, Irina Alafuzoff, Johannes Attems, and Carol Brayne, et al. "Limbic Predominate Age-Related TDP-43 Encephalopathy (LATE): Consensus Working Report." *Brain* 142, no. 6 (June 2019): 1503–1527. https://academic.oup.com/brain/article/142/6/1503/5481202.

**Ngu**, Dilys and Antonia Phillip. "A Possible Case of Limbic-Predominate Age-Related TDP-43 Encephalopathy (LATE) in Black Female with Caregiver Burden and Limited Resources: A Novel Presentation with Symptoms Similar to Alzheimer's Disease [Poster Number: LB-5]." *The American Journal of Geriatric Psychiatry* 30, no.4 (April 2022): S118–119. https://doi.org/10.1016/j.jagp.2022.01.023.

**Nouwen**, Henri. *Adam: God's Beloved.* Anniversary Edition (Ossining, New York: Orbis Books, 2012): 16–17.

**O'Brien**, Claire. "Auguste D. and Alzheimer's Disease." Abstract. *Science* 273, no. 5271 (July 5, 1996): https://tinyurl.com/2nmd35uv.

**Orloff**, Judith. "The Health Benefits of Tears." *Psychology Today*, July 27, 2010. https://tinyurl.com/3uct9xr6.

**Parker-Pope**, Tara. "The Science of Helping Out." *The New York Times*, April 9, 2020. https://tinyurl.com/4tfur8jn.

**Patterson**, C. H. "A Current View of Client-Centered or Relationship Therapy." *Sage Social Science Collections* (Summer, 1969): https://tinyurl.com/2p8ukhxt.

**Patterson**, C. H. "Some Misconceptions of and Questions About Client-Centered Therapy." *The Therapeutic Relationship.* Monterey, California: Brooks Cole Publishing Company, 1985.

**Paul**, Ian. "What Did Jesus Have Against Goats?" *Psephizo* (blog), September 13, 2018. https://tinyurl.com/25724fs7.

**Pazzaglia**, Angela M., Erin T. Stafford, and Sheila M. Rodriquez. "Survey Methods for Educators: Selecting Samples and Administering

Surveys." Washington, DC: US Department of Education, Institute of Education Sciences, National Center for Education Evaluation and Regional Assistance, Regional Educational Laboratory Northeast and Islands, August 2016. https://eric.ed.gov/?id=ED567752.

**Pease**, Allen and Barbara Pease. "The Definitive Book of Body Language." *New York Times*, September 24, 2006. https://www.nytimes.com/2006/09/24/books/chapters/0924-1st-peas.html.

**Pew Research Center**. "Why Americans Do (and Don't) Go to Religious Services." Washington, DC: Pew Research Center, August 1, 2018. https://tinyurl.com/ycks367x.

**Pfeiffer**, Sacha and Jonaki Mehta. "This Experimental Drug Could Change the Field of Cancer Research." *NPR Radio IQ*, June 7, 2022. https://tinyurl.com/8876ztes.

**Powell**, Kimberly. "Make a Memory Book for Your Family." *ThoughtCo*, September 3, 2021. https://tinyurl.com/3epub72f.

"Prayer Lists: How to Protect Privacy." Adapted from The Deacon's Bench Newsletter 16, no. 3. ChurchAdminPro.com, 2005. https://www.churchadminpro.com/Articles/HIPAA/HIPAA%20-%20Prayer%20Lists%20-%20How%20To%20Protect%20Privacy.pdf.

**Prentice**, D. A., and K. M. Carlsmith. "Opinions and Personality: On the Psychological Functions of Attitudes and Other Valued Possessions." In *Why We Evaluate: Functions of Attitudes and Other Valued Possessions*, edited by G. R. Maio and J. M. Olson. 223–248. New Jersey: Lawrence Erlbaum Associates Publishers, 2000.

**Purro**, Sylvia A., Mark A. Farrow, Jacquiline Linehan, Tamsin Nazari, David X. Thomas, Zhicheng Chen, David Mengel, Takashi Saito, Takaomi Saido, Peter Rudge, and Sebastian Brandner. "Transmission of Amyloid B Protein Pathology from Cadaveric Pituitary Growth Hormone." *Nature* 564 (December 2018): 415–419. https://doi.org/10.1038/s41586-018-0790-y.

**Reinhard**, Susan C., Lynn Friss Feinberg, Ari Houser, Rita Choula, and Molly Evans. "Valuing the Invaluable: 2019 Update, Charting A Path Forward." AARP Public Policy Institute, November 2019. https://tinyurl.com/mr3y259j.

**Reisberg**, Barry, Emile H. Franssen, Liduin E. M. Souren, Stefanie R. Auer, Imran Akram, and Sunnie Kenowsky. "Evidence and Mechanisms of Retrogenesis in Alzheimer's and Other Dementias: Management and Treatment Import." *American Journal of Alzheimer's Disease and Other*

*Dementias* 17, no. 4 (July–August 2002): 202–212. https://journals. sagepub.com/doi/10.1177/153331750201700411.

**Riboldi**, Juan. "The Seven Keys to Successful Strategic Planning." *Forbes*, June 27, 2019. https://tinyurl.com/24vff2as.

**Rogers**, Carl R. "Significant Aspects of Client Centered Therapy." *American Psychologist 1*, no. 10 (1946): 415–422. posted online by Christopher D. Green, York University, Toronto, Ontario. https://psychclassics. yorku.ca/Rogers/therapy.htm#f1.

**Rosato**, Michael, Gerard Leavey, Janine Cooper, Paul De Cock, and Paula Devine. "Factors Associated with Public Knowledge of and Attitudes to Dementia: A Cross-Sectional Study." *PLoS One* 14, no. 2 (February 2019). https://journals.plos.org/plosone/article?id=10.1371/journal. pone.0210543.

**Rutledge**, Fleming. *The Crucifixion: Understanding the Death of Jesus Christ*. Grand Rapids, MI: William B. Eerdmans Publishing Company, 2015.

**Ryan**, Dale S. "The Promises and Pitfalls of Congregation Support Groups," *The National Association for Christian Recovery*, accessed March 28, 2022. https://tinyurl.com/2p8vbwmv.

**Saybrook University**. "A Conversation with Carl Rogers: The Job of a Therapist." June 26, 2012. YouTube video, 28:14. https://tinyurl. com/34fab8w3.

**Schwartz**, Kenneth M. "A Patient's Story." *The Boston Globe Magazine*, July 16, 1995. https://tinyurl.com/ympyrx3d.

**Seppala**, Emma. "The Compassionate Mind." *Association for Psychological Science*, April 30, 2013. https://tinyurl.com/mv5hvhsf.

**Smietana**, Bob. "Most Churches Offer WiFi but Skip Twitter." Lifeway Research, January 8, 2018. https://tinyurl.com/mr2rxucm.

**Smith**, Angela. "The Stages of Caregiving: The Spiritual Connection for the Journey with Alzheimer's." *American Journal of Pastoral Counseling* 4, no. 3 (July 2010): https://doi.org/10.1300/J062v04n03_03.

**Smith**, Gregory A. "About Three-in-Ten U.S. Adults Are Now Religiously Unaffiliated," *Pew Research Center*. December 14, 2021. https://tinyurl. com/yk5779ht.

**Solomon**, Cindy. "Free Resource Helps Congregations Care for People with Dementia Diseases and Their Loved Ones." Encore Ministry, accessed September 21, 2022. https://tinyurl.com/yavkevhd.

**Spector,** Diane. "What Sand Grains Look Like Through a Microscope." BusinessInsider.com, January 27, 2014. https://tinyurl.com/3hk8jz94.

**Stein,** Rob. "Legal System Struggles with Dementia Patients." *Washington Post,* July 28, 2003. https://tinyurl.com/mr3a9x7t.

**Stoorvogel,** Henk. "Moving Sermons: Studies into the Persuasive Effects of Preaching." PhD diss. University of Twente, 2019. https://research.utwente.nl/en/publications/moving-sermons-studies-into-the-persuasive-effects-of-preaching.

**Szasz,** George. "Dr Alzheimer and My Wish for a Time Machine." *British Columbia Medical Journal* (March 18, 2018): https://bcmj.org/blog/dr-alzheimer-and-my-wish-time-machine.

**Taylor,** Richard. Dementia Alliance International. "Alzheimer's from the Inside Out." *YouTube* video, 23:48. April 6, 2016. https://tinyurl.com/5x93mmer.

**Texas Department of State Health Services.** "What is Alzheimer's Disease? Questions and Answers." 2021. https://dshs.texas.gov/alzheimers/qanda.shtm.

**Tible,** Olivier Pierre, Florian Reise, Egemen Savaskan, and Armin von Gunten. "Best Practice in the Management of Behavioral and Psychological Symptoms of Dementia." *Therapeutic Advances in Neurological Disorders* 10, no. 8 (August 2017): https://journals.sagepub.com/doi/10.1177/1756285617712979.

**Truscott,** Marilyn. 2004. "Looks Can Be Deceiving: Dementia, the Invisible Disease." Paper presented at the A.I.D Conference, Kyoto, Japan, October 15, 2004. https://tinyurl.com/fhkwd2z.

**UCLA Alzheimer and Dementia Care Program.** "Caregiver Training Part 1: Aggressive Language and Behavior." Accessed January 12, 2022. https://tinyurl.com/4mhu482h.

**The United States Department of Justice.** "State Elder Abuse Statutes." https://tinyurl.com/5ekmr5en.

**United States Department of Housing and Urban Development.** "Notice PDR-2121-01, Estimated Median Family Incomes for Fiscal Year (FY) 2021." huduser.gov., 2021. https://tinyurl.com/y4kbauru.

**Vingerhoets,** Ad J. J. M. and Lauren M. Blysma. "The Riddle of Human Emotional Crying: A Challenge for Emotion Researchers." *Emotion Review* 8, no. 3 (July 2016): 207–217. https://journals.sagepub.com/doi/10.1177/1754073915586226.

**Vingerhoets**, Ad J. J. M., Lauren M. Blysma, and Jonathan Rottenberg. "Crying: A Biopsychosocial Phenomenon." In *Tears in the Graeco-Roman World*, edited by Thorsten Fogen. Berlin: Gruyter, 2009. https://pure.uvt.nl/ws/portalfiles/portal/1109829/KlinPsy_Vingerhoets_Crying_2009.pdf.

**Weissbourd**, Richard, Melina Batanova, Virginia Lovison, and Eric Torres. "Loneliness in America: How the Pandemic Has Deepened an Epidemic of Loneliness and What We Can Do About It." Harvard University School of Education, Accessed December 16, 2021. 1–15. https://mcc.gse.harvard.edu/reports/loneliness-in-america.

**Wendorf**, Don. Interview by the author, April 20, 2022.

**Wharton**, Tracey and Bryan K. Ford. "What is Known about Dementia Recipient Violence and Aggression Against Caregivers?" *Journal of Gerontology Social Work* 57 no. 5 (June 2014): 460–477. https://www.tandfonline.com/doi/abs/10.1080/01634372.2014.882466.

**Whitlatch**, Carol J., and Silvia Orsulic-Jeras. "Meeting the Informational, Educational, and Psychosocial Needs of Persons Living with Dementia and Their Family Caregivers." *The Gerontologist* 58, no. 1 (February 2018): S58–73. https://tinyurl.com/s4xz2d5h.

**Wijngaarden** Els Van, Hugo Van Der Wedden, Zerline Henning, Rikke Koman, and Anne-Mei The. "Entangled in Uncertainty: The Experience of Living with Dementia from the Perspective of Family Caregivers." *Plos One* (June 13, 2018): https://doi.org/10.1371/journal.pone.0198034.

**Williams**, Susan Schneider. "The Terrorist Inside My Husband's Brain." *Neurology* 87 no.13 (September 2016): 1308–1311. https://n.neurology.org/content/87/13/1308.

**Wooden**, Cindy. "Public Mass Ban in Italy Leads to New Focus on 'Spiritual Communion.'" *National Catholic Reporter*, March 16, 2020. https://tinyurl.com/43b95jdw.

**Young**, Juan Joseph, Mallika Lavakumar, Deena Tampi, Silpa Balachandran, and Rajesh R. Tampi. "Frontotemporal Lobe Dementia: Latest Evidence and Clinical Implications." *Therapeutic Advances in Psychopharmacology* 8, no. 1(January 2018): 33–48. https://journals.sagepub.com/doi/10.1177/2045125317739818.

**Zou**, Yong-Ming, Li-ping Liu, Hui-hong Zhang, and Yu-ying Zhou. "Olfactory Dysfunction in Alzheimer's Disease." *Neuropsychiatric Disease and Treatment* 12 (April 2016): https://doi.org/10.2147/NDT.S104886.